CHESAPEAKE REFLECTIONS

A Journey on a Boat and a Bike

By Ken Carter

AMANTHA PUBLISHING COMPANY
Marathon, Florida

CHESAPEAKE REFLECTIONS

A Journey on a Boat and a Bike

By Ken Carter

Published by:
Amantha Publishing Company
Post Office Box 473
Marathon, FL 33050
(305) 743-9020

ISBN 0-9628793-4-7: $19.95 Softcover

All photographs copyright © 1991 by Ken Carter
Back cover photograph of author by Joan Pellegrino
Map of Chesapeake Bay by Joan Pellegrino
Design assistance and typesetting by Keys Graphics,
    Marathon, Florida

ACKNOWLEDGEMENTS

I wish to thank all those wonderful people of Chesapeake Bay country who befriended us throughout our journey and let us know the true meaning of hospitality. They are the inspiration behind this book. Lisa Bell provided me with information about the Poe grave and the legends surrounding it. Kathy Magruder filled me in on some important facts about Talbot County and the Eastern Shore. Mrs. Dorothy C. Watson gave me insight into a part of St. Michaels that I am particularly fond of. Victoria Blacksin supplied me with material about Solomons. And Ellsworth Shank helped me fill in a few blanks about Havre de Grace.

To my friends who suffered through reading rough drafts and told me to keep on writing, I owe a very special debt of gratitude. They are: Mary Gladys Pieper, Jim and Clay White, Don and Vera White, Dori Bradley, Gloria Goodman, and Ray and Sue DiMarco.

There's a very special place in my heart for Susie Walters, whose expertise helped to make this book a reality.

And without Joan Pellegrino's brilliant editing, saintly patience, and phenomenal faith, none of this would have happened. I hope she knows how I feel.

TABLE OF CONTENTS

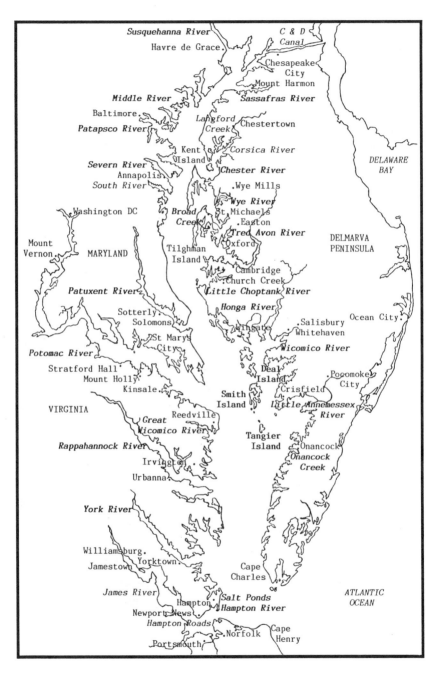

Chesapeake Bay

Schooner Delphina

DEDICATION

to

Jeryl Keane, Ph.D.

She gave me a glimpse of the summit.

Then she turned around and told me
to get my head out of the clouds.

Her admonition forced me to think.

CHAPTER ONE

Hampton River

The Atlantic Fleet, moored at the piers of the Norfolk Naval Base, came into view as we started down Norfolk Reach. After the aggravation of being delayed that morning by a broken bridge, an engine-room fire, and a terrifying squall, I thought those mighty warships looked rather peaceful.

As we sailed our schooner, *Delphina*, past the Navy's piers, I was finally starting to unwind. Of course, I didn't know at the time that in two days I would be on those same piers and in trouble with the Navy. Or that the trouble would create more anxiety than the morning's traumas had.

Joan and I have sailed many voyages on *Delphina*, including two Atlantic crossings, and things have usually gone the way we planned or expected. We had no reason to believe a cruise on Chesapeake Bay would be any different. But lots of things happened that summer that we couldn't have anticipated.

Chesapeake Bay! Even now, so far from its spell, I get excited thinking of what that name brings to mind: the beauty of its shores, the tranquility of its anchorages, the bounty of its waters, the generosity of its lands, the depth of its history, and the strength of character forged into its people over many years of hardship. For years, we were told by other sailors about the magnificence of the Bay's cruising grounds, but we had to be content with vicarious journeys through the words and pictures of other travelers.

We had a taste of the Bay in the fall of 1982, when we sailed down its full length on our way to Florida, but that's all we had—a taste. We wanted a feast. We wanted to explore all of the Bay, sail into rivers and creeks, and visit waterfront communities by boat and inland communities by bicycle. We wanted to experience Chesapeake Bay. We wanted to *absorb* it.

Leaving Norfolk behind us, we sailed across Hampton Roads, the world's largest natural harbor, and entered the channel leading to the Hampton River. For the next three nights, we would be anchored in the Hampton harbor, and we could relax after the voyage from our home port in the Florida Keys.

As we entered the harbor, we passed by several seafood plants. Many colorful workboats, some with their crews unloading the catches or hosing down the decks, lined the wharfs. The smell of fish and salt filled the air as the water from the hoses exploded off the boats in great bursts of spray. The last time I had smelled this combination of fish and salt was years ago in a small New England village, and I was glad to find this smell still evoked images of friendly harbors.

The river was full of boats that were either going back and forth or were tied to piers at marinas. I could see why Hampton civic boosters brag that their city is the boating capital of the southern Bay. We continued up the channel until we were opposite the Visitor Center in the heart of downtown Hampton. We maneuvered into a spot off the channel and dropped our anchors.

We could have tied up at the nearby city docks, which Hampton provides to visiting boaters for a modest fee, but in the summer we like to anchor and catch a cooling breeze. And since there is no charge to anchor, we save money. The only worry we have is that our boat will be gone when we return from a visit ashore. But *Delphina* hasn't run away yet, and I almost don't worry about her anymore.

Despite Hampton's having been founded in 1610, we didn't see any sign of colonial antiquity from where we had anchored. The buildings on the eastern shore of the river belong to Hampton Institute, a university founded in the last century. The western shore is filled with seafood plants and marinas, and the downtown area near the Visitor Center has modern hotel and office buildings. The city looks eager to move into the next century. We were eager to go ashore to see what remains of its colonial heritage.

After ensuring everything was secure on deck, I heard a man's cheery voice.

"Welcome to Hampton!"

Looking aft, I saw a bearded man in his thirties rowing a dinghy toward *Delphina*.

"Hi! I was watching you come up the river," he said. "I'm working on my sailboat over there on the end of the pier next to the yacht club. This sure is a nice-looking boat. Pinky schooner, isn't she?"

"She sure is," I replied. "Are you familiar with the design?"

"Not really. Only from the little I've read about them. I've never seen one before. Did you build her?"

"No, we didn't. We had her built of steel for us in the Florida Panhandle from a design by Merritt Walter. In fact, she has the same designer and builder as *American Rover*. You've heard of that boat, haven't you?"

American Rover, a replica of a nineteenth-century coastal trading schooner, charters from Norfolk's Waterside.

"Oh, sure."

"Would you like to come aboard and have a drink?" I asked him.

We had bought a set of deck chairs in Florida, and I wanted to put them to use in entertaining newfound friends.

"Thanks. I'd really like to, but I left my dog on my boat, and she'll start howling pretty soon. I've got to get back. Enjoy your stay!"

Joan joined me on deck and helped me put the outboard motor on our dinghy, *Flipper*. We went ashore.

Hampton's hospitality toward its guests includes a floating dinghy dock, an amenity much appreciated by those who anchor. One of our guidebooks advised that the dinghy should be locked to the float, and the outboard locked to the dinghy. Being a victim of a previous dinghy theft, I followed this advice by using a stainless steel cable and a single lock. It's no fun to have to swim to the boat in the middle of the night.

We walked over to the Visitor Center to get brochures on things to do in the area. We picked up so many that reading them would take us a few hours. We decided to read them later, and I went to a pay phone to call Freed Lowrey.

Freed Lowrey was one reason we had made Hampton our first stop in the Chesapeake area, although I had never met the man and didn't know much about him. I did know that he is the Class Scribe of the class of 1967 for the West Point Alumni Association magazine, *Assembly*, and he is a recently retired Army officer who has lived in Hampton for a number of years. I have subscribed to *Assembly* for many years and have enjoyed the humorous quality of Freed's writing. After reading his many anecdotes about his family and learning of his irreverence for stuffed-shirt institutions and those who promulgate them, I wanted to meet this person. Besides, he might give us some information about the Bay.

My first contact with Freed was in May, after Joan and I had confirmed our vacation plans. I called him from Florida and told him we would be coming to the Bay and would like to take him and his family sailing. He was flabbergasted.

"But you don't even know us! We know nothing about sailing! You don't know what you're letting yourself in for!" he protested.

"Well, you get to know people pretty fast sailing with them," I informed him. "We really want to meet you."

"Hey, Ken, don't get me wrong. We'd like to meet you, too, but you don't have to take us sailing."

After a while he admitted that he really would like to go sailing and so would his family. I told him I would call with an exact date when we got to North Carolina.

On July 8, I called from North Carolina and told him we'd be in Hampton on July 14.

We were in Hampton, and it was July 14. Freed's wife, Suzi, answered the phone.

"Freed's not here right now, Ken. Where are you?"

I told her.

"Well, then you're going to have dinner here tonight. You guys can shower here, too. In fact, you're welcome to stay in our spare bedroom. And you can do any laundry you have. Freed and I once took a sixty-day motor-home trip, and I know what you people need!"

All this, and she hadn't met us yet! I explained we didn't like to leave *Delphina* alone overnight, but we would be happy to accept everything else, especially the showers. We arranged for Freed to meet us at five in front of the Visitor Center. She saw only one problem.

"How's Freed going to recognize you?" she asked.

Looking around our rendezvous area, I saw few other people. Recognizing us wouldn't be a problem. I thought I'd have a little fun.

"Tell Freed I have long, curly, black hair, and I'm wearing granny glasses, a Grateful Dead tee shirt, plaid Bermuda shorts, and purple tennis shoes." To ensure he wouldn't miss us, I added, "We'll be standing there with a laundry bag."

Silence at the other end for about five seconds, then a chuckle followed by a full-throated laugh. I liked her sense of humor.

Back on *Delphina*, we got ready to meet Freed. Because we planned to tour the historic area of Hampton the next morning, we decided to take our bikes ashore and leave them locked overnight to a lamppost near the dinghy float.

I don't know how we'd manage without our bikes. Cabs are expensive, and most places we visit have no public transit system. Our bikes take us anywhere within a radius of thirty miles, the limit of our physical capabilities. We use our bikes as our main land transportation when we're home; we don't need a car, so we don't own one. We can carry the bikes on *Delphina*'s deck even while we're sailing. By attaching a pair of plastic pipes to *Flipper*, we can tie the bikes upright in the dinghy and carry them ashore.

As I expected, Freed had no problem finding us, even though I didn't look as weird as I had told Suzi I would; Joan and I were the only persons in the area.

Freed was not at all as I had pictured him. He was six feet tall and weighed about two hundred pounds. The weight was evenly distributed over his large frame, and he looked solid and muscular. He was dressed in a sport shirt and a pair of shorts, but on him this clothing seemed more like a uniform than informal attire. As we introduced ourselves, just a trace of a smile came to his tempered face. Much to my surprise, he appeared to be every bit a combat-hardened, career infantry officer. Although this is what he was, I had never associated this visage with someone who writes so humorously in *Assembly.* This man looked *serious.*

As he put Vivaldi's *Four Seasons* on his car's stereo, he said, "Ken, I've got to tell you I'm glad you don't look the way Suzi said you'd look. That is some description you gave her!"

He broke into laughter, and the car plunged forward.

After a fifteen-minute ride through Hampton, we arrived at the Lowrey home. Suzi greeted us in the kitchen as if we were long-lost family members. People who are associated with military life tend to act that way.

"We got some steaks for dinner tonight," she happily told us.

Then a look of worried concern crossed her face.

"My, gosh! You're not vegetarians, are you?"

Joan assured her we weren't. I assured her that, after eating canned chicken and tuna fish for the past two weeks, I could eat a whole cow.

The evening passed quickly. Our conversations were carried on amid the merry mayhem of their three young boys and the boys' friends popping in and out of the house.

After we made plans to meet at the city docks the following afternoon for a sail on *Delphina,* Freed gave us a ride back to the riverfront.

Flipper was where we had left her. I unlocked the cable, and we went to *Delphina.* Although we were in the heart of a city, the night was strangely quiet.

We went ashore early in the morning for our sightseeing trip to the historic Hampton district.

The old buildings in the heart of the city have been restored, and the area has been converted to a pedestrian mall. In the center of the mall is a kiosk with a store directory and photographs of the way the original area has appeared through the years.

In this same area is St. John's Church, built in 1728.

It serves as the house of worship for Elizabeth City Parish, a parish which has been in continuous existence since 1610 and is the oldest English-speaking parish in the country. After seeing the historic district, we returned to *Delphina* to get ready for the afternoon sail.

Delphina is not the ideal boat on which to introduce a family of five to sailing. With a length of thirty-eight feet on deck and a beam of eleven feet, she is big enough, but there isn't sufficient comfortable seating for that many people.

We had chosen *Delphina*'s design because we wanted a strong boat that could carry us safely across an ocean. Her cockpit is small; only two people can sit there. In front of her cockpit is a small cabin top. Forward of her cabin top is a broad expanse of deck with three ventilators and two hatches. *Delphina*'s layout allows boarding seas to run off the boat quickly. Her heavy displacement and full keel provide stability and comfort in a seaway.

Delphina has two masts, four working sails, and a stern that looks almost like her bow. Her classic lines are accented by a black sheer stripe on her white hull. And she is a fun boat to sail. Under full sail in a good breeze, she really comes alive.

The weather forecast for that Sunday afternoon was southwest winds at twenty knots and a chance of showers and thunderstorms. We couldn't feel much wind in the shelter of our anchorage, and the high, thin overcast indicated we would probably not get a thunderstorm. If the wind forecast came true, and it didn't rain, we would have ideal conditions for an invigorating sail.

The Lowreys arrived at noon, and I ferried them to *Delphina* in *Flipper*. Soon *Delphina* was in the channel, and while Joan steered, I got Freed and the boys busy hoisting the sails. Suzi preferred to sit and watch.

The mainsail, staysail, and jib on *Delphina* are not

difficult to hoist, but the foresail, heavy because of its gaff, can be hard to raise, especially in a strong breeze. Because *Delphina* has no winches to coax the sails up the final foot, muscle power is needed to get the luffs truly taut.

Under my direction, Freed and the boys soon had all the sails up. Kyle, the oldest boy, managed to hoist the foresail with a little help from his dad.

For the final few hundred yards of the Hampton River channel, *Delphina* was headed into the strong southwesterly wind, and the sails, flogging violently, created an enormous racket. As soon as we passed the entrance buoy, Joan steered off the wind, and *Delphina* charged into Hampton Roads with all sails pulling. I turned off the engine.

The seas were about three feet high, and *Delphina* was heeled over fifteen to twenty degrees. The ride was exhilarating as we raced along at seven knots, *Delphina*'s top speed. The boys had a great time for about ten minutes. Ranging in age from eight to twelve, they got bored quickly despite all the action. All three descended into the main cabin and began feasting on the candy and soft drinks they had brought.

Freed took the helm, and Suzi continued to be content watching. We sailed past Old Point Comfort at the entrance to Hampton Roads and saw Fort Monroe and the Chamberlin Hotel. Built in the 1920s, this hotel dominates the shoreline along Old Point Comfort.

One of the boys noticed his father steering; he alerted his brothers, and the three boys came back on deck. Freed continued doing well, despite the boys' advice and encouragement.

Taking us past the island bastion of Fort Wool, Freed told us the fort has a history, dating to the Civil War, of defending Hampton Roads. The Army continued to use the fort until 1967. Today it is open to the public but is accessible only by boat.

Brendan, the middle son and namesake of the sixth-century Irish sailor-saint, surrendered to the urge to steer and relieved Freed. With only a minimum of instruction, he took command of the helm. Serious about his responsibility, he concentrated on the course and ignored his brothers' teasing. Even with a freighter heading our way and a tug passing us, Brendan calmly went about his business. The Navigator would have been proud.

After we had sailed into Chesapeake Bay as far as the Thimble Shoal light, a principal light near the ship channel leading to Hampton Roads, I relieved Brendan at the helm and turned *Delphina* around. As we reentered Hampton Roads, Freed reminded us that we were at the site of the battle between the *Monitor* and the *Merrimac*. The boys were excited as they saw the ships lined up at the Norfolk Naval Base. Ahead of us, near the mouth of the James River, the retired S.S. *United States*, reflecting her former glory, lay at her berth.

The wind, strong all afternoon, had been ideal for showing someone how exciting sailing can be. The boys and Freed agreed they had found the afternoon to be an adventure. Suzi, who had never abandoned her perch on the cabin top, refused to let her enthusiasm for sailing surface.

After we entered the Hampton River channel, Joan helped the boys drop and furl the sails, and I discussed with Freed our plans for the next day. Freed didn't give me much information about the Bay, but he told me about many things to do in the Hampton area. When I told him we wanted to visit Fort Monroe, he insisted that he be our guide. After all, he had been stationed there.

"I'll drive you there tomorrow morning. We can go to the Casemate Museum and anywhere else you want."

"But, Freed, don't you have to work tomorrow?" I

The Lowrey Family aboard Delphina

asked.

"No. I'll just put in an appearance."

Since retiring from the Army in June, Freed has directed a high school ROTC program. He explained that, because there isn't much work in the summer, taking a day off then isn't a problem.

Monday morning arrived with clear skies and a crispness in the air. The weather was perfect for sightseeing. Freed picked us up at ten, and we went to Fort Monroe.

Constructed in 1819, this fort is the largest stone fort in the United States and is the only active United States military installation with a moat. Named after President Monroe, the post was an early assignment for Robert E. Lee as a second lieutenant in the Corps of Engineers. The quarters that served as his home in 1831 are still in active service as a residence for an officer assigned to the post.

Another famous person who was stationed at the fort

Robert E. Lee's quarters at Fort Monroe

was Edgar Allen Poe, who served as a sergeant major of artillery from 1828 to 1829. After tiring of Army life and selling his enlistment for $75.00 in 1829, Poe secured an appointment to the Military Academy at West Point as a member of the class of 1834. His lack of military discipline kept him from graduating, however. In later years, Poe returned to the Fort Monroe area and entertained audiences with his poetry readings at a nearby hotel.

Jefferson Davis was imprisoned at Fort Monroe after the Civil War in conditions not at all befitting a person of his stature. Locked in a cell in a casemate within the confines of the fort, Davis complained that he was treated like a wild beast on exhibition.

Fort Monroe's active military status was evident as we entered the post. An armed military policeman saluted Freed as we passed the gate, and uniformed people carrying briefcases were entering and leaving various buildings. Now serving as the headquarters for the Army's Training and Doctrine Command, Fort Monroe was formerly the headquarters for the Continental Army Command.

Freed drove us past the mansion-like residences that face the Bay and serve as generals' quarters. The oldest home, appropriately designated Quarters Number One, has had many famous visitors, including Abraham Lincoln and the Marquis de Lafayette.

As we drove past other houses, Freed said, "A lot of these places are haunted. Really! People are always seeing ghosts. See that house over there? They don't let anyone live in it anymore, there are so many stories of ghosts being there. The Army just uses it for storage now."

Entrance to the part of the fort that is inside the moat is through a one-lane sally port. The Casemate Museum, located there, features Jefferson Davis's cell, shows a sample of the living quarters that were in the casemate until the beginning of World War II, and contains many interesting artifacts relating to the fort.

After we toured the museum, Freed offered to take us to see the fleet at the Norfolk Naval Base. I couldn't turn down this offer; big ships fascinate me.

Freed's last military assignment had been at the Norfolk Naval Base, and he was familiar with the layout of the waterfront.

When we got to the piers, I asked Freed, "Is it okay for me to take pictures of the ships?"

"Oh, sure, it's okay," he assured me. "Go ahead. We'll stop whenever you want."

Several times, Freed stopped the car, and I got out to take pictures. Then we came to the submarine pens.

"How does the Navy feel about my taking pictures of the subs?" I asked Freed.

"Oh, they don't care," he replied.

I thought his reply was rather glib, but I wanted to

The Casemate Museum at Fort Monroe

capture the mood of the starkly sinister submarines. I readily accepted his words as assurance that photographing the submarines is permissible, and I didn't think about it further.

I had taken four pictures when two men approached me. One of them looked angry; the other, sullen.

"Did you take pictures of that ship?" the angry one asked me.

He was wearing a dungaree uniform, and his collar bore the insignia of a chief petty officer.

"Yes, I did," I replied.

"Both of you come with me," he ordered.

His tone did not invite argument.

The other person he had addressed was the man accompanying him. This man was in his twenties, was dressed in civilian clothing, and had a camera hanging from his neck.

Suddenly I was in a distinctly uncomfortable position. The Navy is sensitive to possible espionage attempts, and I wondered if I would have to prove I wasn't a spy. As we left the spot where I had been taking the pictures, I realized I had no identification with me; I had left my wallet on *Delphina*.

Hurriedly, I looked toward where I had left the car and said sheepishly to Freed, "I'm in trouble!"

Freed didn't have time to reply. The Navy man was hustling us to the guarded gangway area of a huge submarine tender. On the way, I saw a sign warning that photographing from the pier is prohibited.

Addressing two sailors at the guard shack, the chief petty officer said, "I caught these two guys taking pictures over there. Keep an eye on them while I check in with the OD on the fantail."

He showed the identification card attached to his shirt and went up the gangway.

The two sailors were dressed in whites and carried

guns. They were as surprised to be guarding us as we were to be under guard.

The taller guard tried to reassure us.

"I don't know what he's talking about," he said. "They lifted the picture restriction a couple of months ago. Don't sweat it. As soon as he checks with the OD, he'll get the word."

"Man, I don't believe this!" cried the other man who was being detained. "I'm always taking pictures of the ship. Hell, I work on the damn reactor! Nobody ever said anything to me before!"

At this point, Freed joined our group and showed the guards his Army identification card.

"This idiot's with me," he confidently stated as he smiled and put his hand on my shoulder.

In Freed's mind, this simple statement would be sufficient to forestall my imminent execution as a spy. After reading Freed's articles for years and knowing him for two days, I was well versed in his lexicon. But I knew my guards weren't tuned in to the nuances of Freed's sense of humor. In my mind, he wasn't helping my case one bit. The image of a jail cell loomed larger.

"Do you think I'll be able to keep my film?" I asked the taller guard.

I had to get my mind off that jail cell. Besides, some of the pictures on the roll in the camera had nothing to do with the Navy.

"Sir, believe me, you have nothing to worry about," he assured me.

The phone in the guard shack rang. I hoped the caller was the chief petty officer. The taller guard answered and listened with bored detachment.

"Aye, aye," he said finally and hung up. "Like I said, no problem. You are free to leave now, both of you. You can take your film and cameras, but it might be a good idea if you didn't take any more pictures."

As we walked back to the car, Freed was chuckling. "I guess some old chief just got a hair and wanted to score a few points," he said. "Let's go get some lunch." I was too relieved to discuss the incident further.

Over lunch, Freed suggested we visit the Yorktown battlefield and go for a ride on the Colonial Parkway, which begins at Yorktown, goes past Williamsburg, and ends at Jamestown. I told him it was a great idea, and Joan agreed.

We stopped at the battlefield and visited the museum at the Visitor Center. Later, as we were driving along the Colonial Parkway, I reflected on how Joan and I usually tour an area. If we can walk, we walk. If any distance is involved, we ride our bikes. But whatever method we use, it is slow. We like to get a *sense* of the place.

We whizzed past the beautiful scenery at fifty miles per hour. Glimpses of Yorktown, Williamsburg, and the Colonial Parkway convinced Joan and me that we should return to this area and tour it on our bicycles.

After reaching Jamestown, the original English settlement in the Chesapeake Bay area, we returned to the Hampton waterfront.

We already had told Suzi and Freed that we would see them on our return trip, so saying good-bye to Freed was not so prolonged as it might have been.

The next morning we would weigh anchor for Onancock, on the Bay's Eastern Shore. After the fifty-mile passage, we would be deep into Chesapeake country and in an entirely different setting from downtown Hampton.

We would also be a lot farther away from the United States Navy.

CHAPTER TWO

Onancock Creek

The strong southwesterly breeze that had been blowing the past two days was still blowing when we left for Onancock that Tuesday morning. Having this wind to push us rapidly northward was an unexpected gift from heaven. With all sails up, *Delphina* was breezing up the Bay at seven knots. The early morning sky was hazy, but the haze wasn't heavy enough to hide the many blue patches of sky among the clouds.

By the time we arrived in Onancock, we would have traversed the Bay's width and almost a quarter of its length. Chesapeake Bay extends two hundred miles from the mouth of the Susquehanna River in the north, to the Atlantic Ocean between Cape Charles and Cape Henry in the south. It's as wide as twenty-five miles in Virginia, south of the Potomac River, and as narrow as four miles in Maryland, north of the Potomac.

Prior to the last ice age there was no Chesapeake Bay, only the Susquehanna River winding its way to the Atlantic Ocean. As the last ice age ended, the melt water from the enormous glaciers ran into the oceans and caused the flooding of vast areas of land. Some of that flooded land was the valley through which the Susquehanna River flowed; thus Chesapeake Bay was formed.

The silt that has been deposited in the Bay over the years makes its water shallow; the average depth of the Bay is just twenty-one feet. The deepest water is along the original Susquehanna riverbed, where the Bay reaches a depth of one hundred forty feet near Kent Island. This old riverbed provides a natural channel for large ships plying their way up the Bay.

Early in the afternoon, the trees on the low banks of the Eastern Shore became visible through the haze. We couldn't sail any closer to the shore because of the shoals that extend into the Bay, so the scenery remained a hazy blur. Around four o'clock, the entrance markers for Onancock Creek appeared over the horizon. As Joan steered toward them, I remembered a conversation I had had with a friend shortly before we left Florida.

"What are you going to do about the sea nettles up there?" he asked. "I hear they've gotten so bad that raw-water intakes on boats are always getting clogged. Can't keep their engines from overheating."

Knowing that there is little wind on the Bay during July and August, we planned to use our engine often. To keep nettles from being sucked up with our cooling water, I epoxied a plastic screen over the thru-hull opening. The screen is flush with the hull and allows the pests to slip by. That's the theory anyway.

A mile into the creek, my confidence in our defensive measure weakened. There were *billions* of sea nettles around *Delphina*. Massive gelatinous globs, comprised of thousands of nettles, whirled down the creek with the strong ebb current. Never had I seen anything to compare with such a proliferation of life. Not even the hordes of mosquitoes that we have encountered in the Everglades matched what I was seeing.

Nervously watching the water-temperature gauge, Joan continued steering up the creek. The creek narrowed, and I was relieved to see that the globs were dissipating. Beautiful homes, nestled among the trees on shore, appeared frequently. The late afternoon sun was strong through the light haze and highlighted the most impressive houses.

Early that spring, I had listed Onancock as a must-see town, not because of its beauty or its remoteness, but because, according to a guidebook, the town calls itself the Cobia Capital of the World, and its waterfront has a sign proclaiming this distinction. Cobia is my favorite fish to eat. In the Keys in the winter, they are caught in large numbers, but I never get enough. By the early spring, the cobia return to northern waters, and I have to do without. I was excited about getting this fish in the summer at the Cobia Capital of the World.

We anchored at the head of the creek, in front of a large estate with a sweeping lawn that came to the water's edge. A nanny was pushing a toddler on a swing, a scene typical of life in the last century. No other cruising boats were there; we had this charming spot to ourselves.

After dinner, I rowed the dinghy to the town's modern marina. I didn't see the "Cobia Capital of the World" sign. Maybe it had been removed when the waterfront was renovated.

The area was deserted except for three elderly men having an animated discussion at the far end of the parking lot. Not wanting to intrude, I stayed in *Flipper* and rowed back to *Delphina*, just as the sun was setting.

Early the next morning, we were greeted by a smiling harbormaster as we approached the marina's bulkhead.

"Just tie up your dinghy here," he said. "I guess that's your boat out there. Where're you folks from?"

Joan told him, and after we had secured *Flipper*, the harbormaster gave us a tour of the marina.

"Yessir, we finished redoing the waterfront a couple of years ago, and we're proud of what we have here."

He noticed that we had brought our bikes.

"We have a bicycle rack over there behind my office. Feel free to use it."

"What happened to the 'Cobia Capital of the World' sign?" I asked him.

The harbormaster looked at me with a puzzled expression.

"You know, I remember that sign, but I don't rightly know what happened to it. It hasn't been here for years."

"Do you know where we could get some cobia?" I asked.

Again, the harbormaster looked puzzled.

"We haven't had a cobia run here for years now," he replied. "The boys catch some over on the ocean but not here. But, you know, I did hear that this spring a fella caught one out in the Bay. Maybe they're coming back."

We wished him a good day and walked over to Hopkins & Brother General Store at the other end of the waterfront. Established in 1842, it is one of the oldest stores on the East Coast.

Entering the building, I thought I was entering another century. Much of the merchandise that was on the shelves was what the store sold in the 1800s. Even the cash registers were antiques. The only modern appurtenance that I noticed was the electric lighting, and that was unobtrusive. The atmosphere was undeniably that of an old-fashioned general store. Since it was break-fast time, the staff of the store was busy serving in the adjoining restaurant. We decided to go into town and return to this fascinating place later.

Onancock, one of three principal towns on Virginia's Eastern Shore, is over three hundred years old and has many beautiful, old homes. People are friendly and happy to see visitors. The residential neighborhoods, with a melange of housing styles, have a *neighborliness* to them. As we rode our bicycles through the streets, people

Hopkins & Brother General Store at Onancock

coming the opposite way in their cars waved to us. We listened to the birds, heard the wind through the trees, smelled the freshly mown lawns and the perfume of the flowers, and saw the people working in their gardens or on other projects around their houses.

On Market Street, we passed Kerr Place, a Federal mansion built in 1799 by a Scottish merchant. Well preserved, it serves as the headquarters for the Eastern Shore of Virginia Historical Society and is open to the public.

We reached the outskirts of town and decided to ride to a seafood market on U.S. Highway 13, the principal north-south artery on the Delmarva Peninsula. Not giving up on my quest to get fresh cobia, I had asked someone else in town where I could buy some. Again, I received the same puzzled look as I had from the harbormaster. Had everyone forgotten that Onancock is the Cobia Capital of the *World*?

"Well, if anybody's got any, that place will," I was told.

We rode on a state road through farmland on our way to Highway 13. This stretch taught us that riding bikes on Virginia's rural roads is a frightening experience. The lack of a paved shoulder meant we had to share a lane with cars and trucks. Some vehicles did get into the left lane when they passed us, but it was hard for us to relax when they sped by at over fifty miles per hour.

Although the traffic increased tremendously on Highway 13, we were more comfortable riding the two miles south to the seafood market because the highway has a paved shoulder. We entered the building and went to the clerk. She was apologetic when I asked for cobia.

"Why, I can't remember the last time we had cobia. I've got plenty of fresh drum and flounder, though."

A sign advertising fresh soft crabs for $5.00 per dozen was hanging on the wall.

"Well, how about a dozen soft crabs then?" I asked.

She went to a freezer and returned with a small box.

"That'll be $7.00," she said.

"But I thought they were $5.00," I protested and pointed to the sign.

"Oh, that's for *fresh* ones. You don't want *them*. They have to be cleaned. These frozen ones are already cleaned and wrapped individually. And besides, they're a little bigger."

She pulled a frozen crab from the box to make her point. It looked pretty small to me, but I reasoned that twelve of them would make a filling and tasty dinner.

"Okay, we'll take them," I said.

Returning to town, I kept thinking how great it would be to have some hard crabs to eat with the soft. We could catch those ourselves. I had heard all that is needed is some string, a few lead sinkers, and chicken necks. When we returned to *Delphina*, we could sip cocktails and catch all the crabs we wanted.

The supermarket was our first stop in town. I didn't see chicken necks displayed with the packages of chicken parts in the meat case, so I rang the butcher's bell.

The glass partition behind the case opened, and a man behind the partition asked, "Yes?"

"I'd like to get some chicken necks, please."

Again, I received the same look that I had gotten whenever I had asked for cobia. That look was starting to frustrate me.

"I don't have any chicken necks. What do you want 'em for, crab bait?"

"That's right."

"Well, then you want back portions," the man informed me. "I got packages of 'em in the case here. Good luck!"

I thanked him and picked up a package.

Earlier that morning, we had noticed a large discount store in town near the marina. A sign in its window advertised the lowest prices on hardware, fishing tackle, and assorted merchandise, including fresh fish.

Our second stop in town was that store. A young clerk approached us as we entered.

"Anything I can help you find?" he asked.

I was glad he offered to assist us because the store had numerous displays of every item imaginable. We could spend an hour finding string and sinkers.

"We need some string and sinkers for catching crabs," I said.

He knew exactly where they were.

I was curious that a discount store like this one sold fresh fish. Did *this* store have cobia?

"What kind of fish do you have?" I asked.

There was no way I was going to ask for *cobia*. I had learned something that day.

"Right now we have some nice fresh drum, red and black, some flounder, and some soft crabs. What are you interested in?"

"Oh, nothing. I was just curious."

As he rang up our purchase, the clerk asked, "Do you have a dip net?"

After I told him we didn't, he led me through an opening at the rear of the display area. We came into a hangar-like room that contained large items including rugs, furniture, appliances, lawn tractors, and garden implements. In the center of this vast space sat a heavy, middle-aged man smoking a cigar, talking on the phone, and looking like a hustling Big Daddy. He gave me the impression he was trying to obtain consignments of commodities from brokers all over the world so he could fill the empty spaces in this enormous room.

The clerk took me to a table where different types of dip nets were displayed. I chose the cheapest one. As we left the store with our purchases, I hoped that someday I could come back to this store and look at everything in it.

Before going back to *Delphina*, we stopped again at Hopkins & Brother General Store. The store, deeded to the Association for the Preservation of Virginia Antiquities, serves also as the ticket agent for the tour ship *Capt. Eulice*. The sale of tickets from the store's ticket window continues a service provided when steamboat tickets were sold there over a century ago. *Capt. Eulice* leaves from the store's pier daily on its run to Tangier Island, a Virginia fishing community located in the Bay about ten miles from Onancock.

If it was possible, Joan and I wanted to sail to Tangier the next day. Our cruising guides, all published in different years, gave conflicting accounts about the ease of a keel boat's getting into the harbor. I hoped the captain of *Capt. Eulice* would give me some navigational information about the waters around Tangier Island. Unfortunately for us, however, the ship and her captain had left at ten o'clock.

I found the store manager in his large office. A handsome, bearded man in his thirties, he looked as if he belonged on the water. When he saw me standing by the doorway, he interrupted a meeting he was having with his employees.

"What can I do for you?" he asked.

"We'd like to sail to Tangier tomorrow, and I need to know the water depths in the entrance channels."

"Is that your pinky schooner out there on the hook?" he asked. "I've been admiring her all day."

"Yes, she is."

True to my initial impression of him, he told me of the many classic boats he had sailed on. At last, he got to the subject of Tangier Island.

"Oh, you should have no problem going in either channel," he said. "What do you draw?"

"Five four," I told him. "Will we be able to use the Sound channel?"

The island has two approaches: one from the west, or Bay side, and the other from the east, or Tangier Sound side. We would save a lot of time if we could use the Sound channel.

"They just dredged the Sound channel last year, and it's at least six feet. You'll have no problem."

The six-foot depth would give us an eight-inch clearance at low tide. To a non-boater, that doesn't seem like much of a margin, but it was plenty to satisfy us.

The manager's remark about the depth of the channel was a cue for the gathered employees. Three people spoke up at once and told me what *they* knew about the channel. Apparently, everyone in the room was related to Tangier watermen, and water depth is a frequent topic of conversation among watermen. All the gathered employees had a say, and the consensus was we could negotiate the channel with no problem.

Feeling confident with this information, I asked the

manager about Smith Island, ten miles north of Tangier. Smith Island is also a fishing community, but with one very important difference: it is located in Maryland.

The manager didn't hesitate to answer.

"No one ever goes to Smith Island," he said.

There were some muted chuckles and snorts in the room.

"Really, no one ever does."

He smiled when he repeated his answer.

I guessed I would have to wait until we got to Crisfield, Maryland, before I'd get any local knowledge on Smith Island.

Back on *Delphina*, we cut lengths of string and attached a sinker and bait to each one. Soon we had ten strings at staggered locations on the boat. We were serious about getting some crabs.

After tying the last line, I went below to mix drinks.

Suddenly Joan yelled out, "Ken, we got one!"

Dashing onto the deck, I looked toward where she was pointing. A string was moving away from the boat and quivering; a crab had taken the bait. Joan grabbed the dip net, and slowly I retrieved the line. Soon the crab was visible through the murky water.

"Here, you get it," Joan pleaded as she handed me the net.

It was my first time catching a crab, but I knew that the proper technique is to place the net under the crab while the crab is still in the water. When the crab is lifted out of the water, it will drop off the line and fall into the net. This crab was big, but I managed to stay calm and catch it. After I took its picture, I placed it in the cockpit. Soon we had caught a dozen, and I judged they would fit nicely into our large pressure cooker.

While Joan was in the galley preparing a feast of crabs, I was sitting in one of our deck chairs, drinking a gin and tonic, and thinking about impressions that

Our first Chesapeake Bay crab

people make, especially when they go cruising on a boat.

Before meeting us and learning differently, Suzi Lowrey had the impression that Joan and I are wealthy because we can go sailing on our boat for three-month periods. What she didn't realize is that we work seven days every week from December through May, and our three-month cruise is simply combining our weekends, holidays, and a modest vacation.

While we are cruising, we don't spend much money on a daily basis. We anchor whenever possible. Owning a sailboat, we don't spend much on fuel. Our food costs are kept to a minimum by buying in bulk when items are on sale and by canning our own meat. For example, for this trip we bought three hundred pounds of chicken at 49¢ per pound, parboiled it, skinned it, boned it, and preserved it in canning jars. With a sauce, the canned chicken served with noodles, rice, or spaghetti is a sumptuous entree for only $2.00.

The major expense of cruising is the cost of a properly equipped boat. We can afford *Delphina* because she's our home. Of course, living on a boat isn't the way everyone wants to live, but for us it's ideal, as long as we don't develop materialistic cravings.

The following morning we would be going to Tangier Island, a centuries-old community of Chesapeake Bay watermen. From reading about these men in William Warner's book *Beautiful Swimmers*, I had developed a respect for them that bordered on awe, and I looked forward to observing firsthand what I had read.

As I drained my drink and went below for dinner, I realized I wanted to make a good impression on the watermen of Tangier Island.

CHAPTER THREE

Tangier Island

Going out Onancock Creek the following morning was slow as we motored against the strong flood tide, but from the way the tops of the trees on the shore were bending over, we knew a strong breeze would carry us across Tangier Sound. We wasted no time getting the sails hoisted after we cleared the last channel marker at the entrance to the creek. As the jib filled with the fresh wind, *Delphina* responded eagerly by leaping into Tangier Sound, a body of water that figured prominently in the early history of our country.

Captain John Smith, who issued glowing reports to England after discovering Chesapeake Bay, was not so enthusiastic about his discovery of Tangier Sound. He named the islands he found there the Isles of Limbo, an altogether unflattering appellation. Maybe he gave these islands that name because of their low-lying, treeless expanses of land and marsh which were not suitable for the agriculture he envisioned. Nonetheless, shortly after its discovery in 1608, the area experienced an influx of settlers.

Some of these early settlers had no desire for agrarian pursuits; they wanted to be left alone to harvest the bounty of nature from the surrounding waters. These settlers became known as watermen, a term indigenous to Chesapeake Bay but sometimes heard around the Sounds of North Carolina.

During the Revolutionary War, the watermen were staunchly loyal to the Crown. Taking advantage of the watermen's knowledge of the local waterways, the British enlisted their support in attacking the shipping and naval forces assembled by the rebelling colonists. Using shoal-draft sailing barges, the watermen were effective in disrupting the patriots' commerce. These privateers were called picaroons, perhaps because their viciousness reminded their victims of fierce Caribbean pirates.

The final battle of the Revolutionary War, fought at Yorktown in 1781, did not bring an end to the picaroons' depredations. Naval forces from Virginia and Maryland continued to engage the picaroons to end their marauding. In 1782, a major battle took place in Kedges Straits, just north of Smith Island, where a patriot fleet of five barges and one ship met a comparable picaroon fleet. The picaroons won this hard-fought encounter after a series of unfortunate events on the patriots' vessels. After this battle, little is known of further engagements between the opposing forces. With the signing of the Treaty of Paris in 1783, all picaroon activity ceased, and the picaroons returned to the quieter lives they had known before the Revolutionary War.

As we approached Tangier Island after a short, brisk sail from the mouth of Onancock Creek, we saw that the island is flat, low, and nearly treeless. We entered the channel leading to the harbor. This channel was sharply defined, not only by numerous markers placed by the Coast Guard, but also by the abrupt sides created by the dredger. Ahead of us, on both sides of the channel as far as we could see, were numerous crab shanties and piers built on flimsy pilings that resembled stilts.

I saw a modern house being built and thought it

strange that someone was building on Tangier because the island's population is declining. In 1940, the population was approximately thirteen hundred, and by 1975, this number dropped to an estimated nine hundred; the 1990 population was roughly eight hundred. The style of that house didn't look like one a Tangier waterman would choose; it looked like one a wealthy urbanite would want for a vacation home.

The channel widened as we neared the center of activity. Crab pounds were everywhere, as were picturesque crab shanties adorned with buoys, flags, and signs with religious sayings such as "Jesus Never Fails." Nearly all the pounds had someone, usually a woman with a dip net, tending them.

Since the late 1800s, watermen have been impounding crabs that are ready to molt. These crabs, called peelers, are separated within pounds according to their state of molting. Twenty-four hours each day, attendants, working in shifts, watch these crabs and look for those that are molting. Just as a crab wriggles free of its old shell, the attendant separates it from the others. Crabs that have molted are called soft crabs and are packed for market differently from their hard cousins. After being sorted by size, they are placed on trays. Three trays, separated by ice, eelgrass, and paper, are placed in a standard-sized, waxed, cardboard box. Shipped to market in this manner, the soft crabs live four or five days.

Over the years, the shedding pound operation has been improved, and floating pounds have largely been replaced by above-water tanks. Pumps constantly provide fresh Bay water to the pounds, and light bulbs overhead provide illumination for working at night. Covers built over the pounds keep the hot sun from overheating the crabs in the shallow water of the tanks. Most piers have a crab shanty that provides shelter for the attendant and contains amenities such as an old couch, a refrigerator, and a radio or television to help the attendant pass the long hours.

We entered a turning basin and looked for a place to anchor or tie up. Two long piers were in front of us, but they were reserved for tour boats. Another pier had two fuel pumps, but the space there was to be used by boats getting fuel. The current was strong and whipped us past this area and down the channel. We saw fewer crab pounds and more slips.

It was noon, and the crabbers would be returning soon with their catches, so I was reluctant to dock *Delphina* in a slip that might be a workboat's space. At the end of this stretch, near where the channel leads into the Bay, we did see some other pleasure boats tied to finger piers.

I yelled out to one sailor who was working with a line on his boat, "Is it okay for us to tie up in the empty slip next to you?"

Crab shanty and shedding pounds at Tangier Island

"I guess so. We came in last night, and there hasn't been anyone in that slip since then," he shouted back.

Delphina, with her twenty-horsepower diesel engine and thirteen-ton displacement, is not easy to maneuver. The strong current on our beam would make entering the narrow slip difficult. As I tried to come into the slip with the maximum throttle I felt safe using, the current pushed against *Delphina's* keel and swung her stern forcefully toward the bow of a workboat docked nearby. There was no way we could get into that slip, and I quit trying after the first attempt.

We went back to the basin and anchored. Some of the people working the crab pounds watched us indifferently. While I set a second anchor, a large boat entered the basin, made a turn, and tied up to a crab-pound pier near us. In getting to the pier, the boat had come uncomfortably close to *Delphina.*

"Joan, I'm going to take *Flipper* over to the fuel dock and find out where else we can anchor or tie up," I said.

As I approached the dock, a man standing there said, "That's a bad place to anchor, what with the tour boats coming in here."

"I'd appreciate your telling me a safe place to anchor or somewhere to tie up," I told him.

The man replied, but I couldn't understand what he said. It sounded like gibberish. Not wanting to look like a fool, I didn't pursue his answer further. I thanked him and returned to *Delphina.* I raised the anchors, and we started back to the scene of our earlier attempt to tie up. Joan remembered reading in a brochure that there is a Parks Marina in Tangier, but our guidebooks didn't give any information about it. Maybe we had missed seeing the sign for the marina, and we would see it the second time around. Getting the boat secured was becoming an obsession with me.

About three hundred yards down the channel on our

port side was a wharf that was vacant. If I turned *Delphina* around and headed her into the current, I wouldn't have a problem bringing her alongside the wharf. I hoped the wharf wasn't a waterman's dock. Joan pointed out a stall labeled "Hers" on the pier and an unlabeled stall next to it. This wharf could be Tangier's version of a marina. We moored and decided to wait for the watermen to return before going ashore. I wanted to be sure *Delphina* was in no one's way.

We didn't have to wait long. Workboats in large numbers began to come in around one thirty. Most boats had two crewmen, the owner and a culler. All the boats were loaded with baskets of crabs, the fruits of the day's labor. While the men aboard the boats docked the boats and unloaded the catches, they shouted back and forth to each other in a good-natured banter. I tried to hear what they were saying, but the loud exhaust noises that filled the air stifled most of the words before I could hear them.

Sitting on Delphina and waiting for an opportunity to talk to one of these men, I noticed that, with only one or two exceptions, their workboats were the best-maintained work vessels I had ever seen. With gleaming, varnished mahogany transoms and brilliant white topsides, they would make any wooden-boat admirer take notice. Each vessel bore a two-word feminine name on the sides of the bow and also on the transom, where the home port of Tangier was identified. These people were proud of their boats.

A workboat pulled into a slip that was perpendicular to the wharf we were on. The lone occupant skillfully handled the dock lines and then walked past *Delphina* without looking at us.

Seeing my chance, I quickly asked, "Is it okay for us to tie up here?"

Continuing to look straight ahead, and not stopping, he replied, "Yup."

Knowing that watermen have a reputation for being taciturn, I wasn't surprised by his curtness. I had hoped, though, that I'd be able to talk with a waterman about his way of life. This particular waterman was preoccupied with other matters. I'd have to wait until I found a waterman who wasn't working. From what I had seen so far, I thought I'd have a long wait.

The waterman's terse reply at least gave us the confidence to go ashore and visit without worrying that *Delphina* was in somebody's way. We unloaded our bikes and began riding along the narrow main street.

For over two hundred years, the residents of Tangier Island were isolated from the progress on the mainland. They were happy keeping to themselves, harvesting the Bay's bounty, and living in harmony with each other. Occasionally, the outside world encroached, as when twelve thousand British soldiers landed during the War of 1812 and used the island as a staging area for an assault on Baltimore.

When the Chesapeake Bay Bridge from Annapolis to Kent Island opened for traffic in 1952, the changes the bridge brought to the Eastern Shore did not, for the most part, affect Tangier. But in the late 1950s, several Tangier residents appeared on a national television show, and viewers wanted to see more of these people and to tour Tangier Island.

Although crabbing is the main industry on Tangier, tourism is becoming increasingly important. Visitors are eager to see an authentic, unspoiled Chesapeake watermen's community where the residents still speak Elizabethan English. Every day in the tourist season, hordes of people come to the island on tour boats from several ports on the mainland. Others arrive by plane. And a few, like us, arrive on their own boats.

The residents have responded to this invasion by providing guided tours of the island on golf carts, opening gift shops, and—an idea that could be attributed to a mind educated at the Harvard Business School—setting out about a hundred boxes, each containing mimeographed copies of an island recipe or a bit of lore. Hanging on a fence near the tour-boat docks, each box has its own money receptacle into which a buyer can deposit the 25¢ that each copy costs. While the tourists are waiting to get back on the tour boats, they look over the contents of these boxes and drop in one quarter after another as they find items of interest.

As we rode along, we didn't see any cars on the narrow streets. The houses had small yards enclosed by chain-link fences. Some of them had tombstones in the front yard.

About halfway down the main street, we came to a white, two-story clapboard house with red shutters and an enclosed porch. A neat, well-trimmed yard surrounded the house. A small sign, attached to the front of the house, had a colorful painting of the island and read:

Hilda Crockett's
CHESAPEAKE HOUSE
Family Style Meals Only

We had met some sailors in North Carolina who told us that if we could get to Tangier, we had to eat at Mrs. Crockett's house.

"She makes the best crab cakes in the world!" they told us. "Serves them family style, too."

These words gave me an image of a sweet, grandmotherly matron bringing steaming dishes out of her kitchen and setting them before a dozen guests seated at a large table in her dining room—a scene from *The Waltons*. Joan and I agreed, if we did get to Tangier, we would eat with Mrs. Crockett.

We leaned our bikes against the fence, walked onto

the large, screened-in porch, and knocked on the front door. A middle-aged woman answered the door.

"Good afternoon, ma'am," I said to her. "We'd like to find out about having dinner with you tonight."

"Our last seating is at five o'clock."

She was very businesslike. I found her tone unsettling.

"Well, we'd like to make reservations, if we can," I said.

"You don't need reservations for that seating. All the boat people have left by then."

This reply was puzzling. What did boat people have to do with her family-style dinners?

"Great!" I said. "We'll see you at five!"

From the end of the main street, we saw two other areas on the island that had clusters of houses. Riding on dirt roads, we visited both and occasionally met residents on bicycles or mopeds. Golf carts, full of sweating tourists dressed in colorful clothing, bounced along these same roads. Each cart was driven by a resident guide, who was giving a running commentary over a loudspeaker system mounted on the cart.

As we toured the island, we saw derelict boats sunk in the mud at low tide, creeks meandering through the marsh grass, old weather-beaten houses ready to fall down, and beautiful cranes and egrets stalking their prey.

We returned to the waterfront, left our bikes at the end of the street, and walked past a man doing repairs on a boat docked near *Delphina*.

"Do you know who we're supposed to pay for tying up here?" I asked him.

"Yeah, a lady'll come out right about dusk," he replied, without stopping his work.

The stalls that Joan had seen on the pier were showers, something that we certainly needed after our

Derelict house and family plot on Tangier Island

ride. There was plenty of hot water and lots of pressure, and I could feel the grime coming off my body.

Delphina has no shower; we had chosen to use the space for storage because it's difficult and messy to take a shower in a seaway. When we can't get a shower ashore, we use a garden hose on deck; an electric pump provides the necessary pressure. This system works well, but we have no water heater, and using only cold water straight from our tanks is often an unpleasant experience.

Shortly before five, we left for dinner. Because going out to dinner is a special occasion for us, we were all duded up for a night on the town: Joan was wearing a lovely dress and white shoes, and I was wearing slacks, a dress shirt, and loafers.

At the Chesapeake House, the same woman from that afternoon greeted us.

"Come right on in and go through that door," she told

us. "Just have a seat at the first table."

I was shocked when I saw the inside of the house; it was not what I had expected. To my left was a room full of tables, the kind that belong in a refectory. On the walls of the entrance hall hung framed reviews raving about the food. As we entered the spacious room that we had been directed to, we saw that it was full of tables and chairs. The Chesapeake House looked more like a mess hall than somebody's home; a lot of people could eat there at one time.

We sat down. We were alone.

Another couple soon joined us. They were from Washington, D.C. and had come on a tour boat from Reedville, Virginia. They were spending the night in one of the guest houses on the island. They also had heard of Hilda Crockett's fame, but had heard more than we had.

"In the height of the season, they feed about six to eight hundred people a day," the man told us. "When the tour boats are in port, this place is packed. There's one seating after another. They really have a big business here. They even added a mobile home to have room for more tables."

I was amazed at what he said. My preconceptions couldn't have been further from reality.

Questions raced through my mind. Did Mrs. Crockett add each table as the need arose? Was the phenomenal success something that had happened overnight? Was the Chesapeake House listed on the New York Stock Exchange? Was Mrs. Crockett still the sweet old grandmother I imagined her to be, or was she a hard-driving business executive with a doctorate from Wharton? But most importantly, did she still serve the *best* crab cakes in the world?

True to family-style dining, our waitress started bringing out plates heaping with food. She informed us that we four were the only guests for dinner that night.

But she continued to bring out the food: baked ham, fried clams, corn pudding, string beans, beets, potato salad, cole slaw, applesauce, home-baked rolls, and finally, the crab cakes. She placed two huge crab cakes on each of our plates.

"It's all you can eat except for crab cakes. Don't forget to save room for dessert!" our waitress said and scurried back to the kitchen.

If those crab cakes were not the best in the world, I don't know what could have made them better. The spice was evident, but delicate. There wasn't one bit of shell in the crab cakes to interrupt our pleasure. The texture was perfect: each crab cake had a crisp outer coating and a firm, moist center that was not at all mushy. These crab cakes were made of ingredients in perfect harmony. I relished each bite.

The bill for both of us was less than $25.00, which included a generous tip.

As we went to pay in the entrance hall, our waitress came to us and said, "I'll be right back."

She left the house and returned a few minutes later with the woman who had originally greeted us.

"Are you Mrs. Crockett?" I asked the woman as she pulled out a key and unlocked the cash register.

"No, I'm not. She died a while back. I'm her granddaughter. And this is her great-granddaughter," she said and nodded toward our waitress.

As we went back to *Delphina*, I found myself wondering if Mrs. Crockett had died before the business had grown to be so large. If she had, what would she think of it now?

As promised by the man we had seen earlier working on the boat, a woman appeared to collect the dockage fee soon after we returned to *Delphina*. I had seen her leave the same house the taciturn waterman had entered after telling me "Yup." This woman was probably the waterman's wife.

"It's $10.00," she said, when I asked the cost.

Those were the only words she said, and she left as soon as I paid her.

I mixed a drink and went on deck to reflect on our visit to Tangier Island.

I sat down and looked at an unspoiled, authentic fishing village that looked as if it were far removed from the outside world. Ironically, the tourists never see this image: they shatter the atmosphere as soon as they come ashore.

I saw no crowds and heard no golf-cart loudspeakers. No gift shops were open, and the restaurants were closed. The waterfront activity had stopped, but the workboats bobbed at their moorings and silently reminded me the activity would soon start anew. I heard two people loudly conversing in the distance, but I couldn't understand their heavy brogue. The scene was what I had imagined Tangier Island to be at night.

I sat silently under a black, star-filled sky and heard the muffled gurgle of a water pump on a nearby shedding pound, the subtle sounds of the denizens of the marsh settling down for the night, and an occasional noise from a house. In a short while, before the sun rose, the area would come resoundingly awake with the exuberant noises of workboats and their crews going out for another day on the water. And the setting of an authentic, unspoiled fishing village would last until the arrival of the first tour boat.

The Tangier residents have accepted the tour boats with equanimity, but to say that they *tolerate* hundreds of strangers on their small island would not be accurate. Unless directly involved in tourist-related businesses, the islanders *ignore* the visitors. Residents walking or riding their bikes passed by tourists walking the opposite direction without acknowledging them with a smile or a greeting; generally they continued looking straight ahead. A few disinterested people had watched us anchor in the turning basin, and a few watermen had waved to us from their boats, but otherwise no one had noticed us. How often does a schooner from Florida visit there? Could it be, I wondered, that the people of Tangier have become *world-weary*?

We planned to arise with the watermen in the morning and to sail on a fair tide to Crisfield, Maryland, on the mainland of the Eastern Shore. Finishing my nightcap, I went below.

CHAPTER FOUR

Little Annemessex River

The strong southwesterly breeze was still blowing as we left the channel and entered Tangier Sound. Crisfield is only eleven miles northeast of Tangier Island, and the wind would get *Delphina* to Crisfield's Somers Cove before noon.

As we went up the Little Annemessex River, the approach to Crisfield, we couldn't see the entrance to Somers Cove. Joan slowed our speed to bare steerageway, and I tried to reconcile our chart with what I was seeing. Adding to my confusion was a profusion of powerboats coming and going. Soon we noticed that most of these boats were coming from an area to the rear of a large tour boat moored to a pier ahead of us. Joan increased the throttle, and with slightly more confidence, we surged forward. As we went past the large tour boat, we saw Somers Cove in front of us. Somers Cove is a land-locked harbor that contains the largest marina in Maryland. Owned by the State, this marina has three hundred twenty-five slips and can accommodate vessels up to one hundred fifty feet long.

Choosing to be where we could catch some of that wonderfully cooling breeze, we anchored opposite the Coast Guard station. Looking around the waterfront area of Somers Cove, I was eager to get ashore and see what delights awaited us in town.

When we had planned our cruise on the Bay, we tried unsuccessfully to schedule our visit to Crisfield for Labor Day weekend. Every Labor Day weekend since 1947, the town has celebrated the bounty of its local waters with the Crisfield Labor Day Festival. There are crab-picking contests, boat-docking contests, boat races, cooking contests, a beauty pageant, a parade, an arts-and-crafts show, and the most famous event, the crab race. In this race, the hardy blue crabs of the Chesapeake are pitted against crabs from anywhere in the world, with only one proviso—the challengers must be *edible*. Of course, the Crisfield Labor Day Festival is a wonderful opportunity for the outsider to see the hard-working watermen hard at play.

Our first stop ashore was the J. Millard Tawes Museum that serves also as the Visitor Center. Named after a native of Crisfield who was governor of Maryland from 1959 to 1967, it is conveniently located on the waterfront of Somers Cove. The Visitor Center receptionist gave us tour maps of Somerset County that showed the back roads in the country and a walking-tour map of Crisfield.

We started the walking tour at the town dock that, when we arrived at two o'clock, was a scene of frenetic activity. Workboats from all over Tangier Sound were coming in to unload their baskets of crabs. Ferries, mail boats, freight boats, party-fishing boats, pleasure boats, and tour boats were moving in and out of the area in controlled confusion. People were happy, yelling back and forth, teasing one another about the day's catch, and asking about plans for the weekend. Under the pavilion at the end of the pier, old-timers were having a wonderful time jawing at the celebrated Liar's Bench. The lively atmosphere of the area was contagious, but we reluctantly left and started walking toward the alleyways that lead to the area where the Crisfield seafood industry began in 1866.

Although Crisfield dates its origin to the early seventeenth century when it was the village of Annemessex, it didn't achieve prominence until after 1866, the year John W. Crisfield succeeded in having a branch of the Eastern Shore Railroad terminate in Crisfield. Then, oysters were the principal catch from the local waters. Oysters, in fact, were so prolific that much of the town is built on their discarded shells. With the establishment of oyster processing plants, Crisfield quickly became the Seafood Capital of the World. In its heyday, Crisfield shipped more than one hundred railcars of seafood each week.

During the early years of the seafood boom, the rowdy crews that brought the seafood to town participated in bouts of drinking and fighting at local saloons. This activity quickly got out of hand, or so the town fathers

Crisfield waterfront

thought, and in 1875, they passed a law banning alcohol in Crisfield. The principal effect of this ordinance was the creation of speakeasies and booming bootlegging operations which lasted until 1939, when the prohibition of alcohol consumption in Crisfield was repealed. By this time, however, the town had achieved a notoriously high crime rate.

No physical evidence of the speakeasies remains today, but walking along the narrow alleyways on the waterfront, we sensed how life had been. Nestled snugly among the buildings along a back alley, one legal remnant of the old days, a blacksmith shop, is still in business making implements for watermen. Not believing what I was seeing, I stood there for a few minutes and watched two blacksmiths working inside. With a little concentration, I imagined I was in the last century.

Continuing our walk up West Main Street, we came to a boatyard and saw a skipjack in the yard. Skipjacks that dredge oysters during the winter months in the Maryland waters of Chesapeake Bay are the only sailboats in the United States that continue to work under sail alone. Because of the declining fortunes of the oyster industry and the hardships involved in working on these boats, the fleet of working skipjacks gets smaller each year. At the turn of the century, there were hundreds of these boats on the Bay; today there are just over thirty that continue to dredge. Twenty-two skipjacks are listed on the National Register of Historic Places.

Someone had started to restore this skipjack, but a lot of work remained. As we walked around to her stern, we saw her name was *Anna McGarvey,* and her home port was Annapolis, Maryland. The name seemed familiar to me, and going through some of the literature we had, I read that she had been the skipjack on exhibit, in the water, at the Tawes Museum. I hoped she would be restored to her original condition. In the foreseeable future, museums may be the only places where these magnificent vessels can be seen in all their beauty.

We chose Sunday for a bike ride in the country because the weather was forecast to continue fair through the weekend, and on Saturday the Watermen's Folklife Festival, an event we didn't want to miss, was scheduled at the Tawes Museum.

Saturday morning, before the Festival began, we went on a short bike ride. Not far from town, we noticed a number of abandoned houses that were in decent shape. These houses had peeling paint and overgrown yards, but they looked fit for someone to live in. Many of the places didn't have "For Sale" signs, but they all had prominent "No Trespassing" signs. Maybe the owners had abandoned these homes because of hard times or had passed away with no heirs.

We passed by the former home and workshop of the late Ward brothers, Lem and Steve, known internation-

Skipjack Anna McGarvey *undergoing restoration*

ally for their exquisite waterfowl carvings. A sign in front of the place read "Wildfowl Counterfeiters in Wood." We later learned that their carvings, and those of other artists, can be seen in Salisbury, Maryland, at the Ward Museum of Waterfowl Art.

Coming to an old brick house, I stopped to admire its lines. A man in his sixties was placing steel reinforcing mesh into forms for a concrete porch. He looked up and smiled at me.

I smiled back.

"Just admiring your house," I said. "It's quite nice!"

Joan pulled up alongside me and stopped.

"Why, thank you!" he said. "Would you like to take a look inside?" Seeing my hesitation, he added, "Really! I think you'd find it interesting, too."

We crossed the road, and he led us inside the house. The lower level was only a gutted-out shell, but it had a smooth concrete floor.

"The first thing I had to do to restore this place was get everything out of here," he said. "The original wood flooring had all rotted out, and some big blacksnakes had started living in here. I was mighty careful, believe me! And then I pulled off all the plaster and laths on the walls. After that I put in the floor, reinforced concrete, just like I'm doing out there on the porch. But I'll tell you, sometimes I think I just took on too much."

He hadn't done any renovation work upstairs other than to replace some window panes. The rooms were all furnished as they would have been before the turn of the century and contained beds, dressers, washstands, and a couple of trunks.

"These rooms are just the way they were when we bought the place," the man told us. "Except, of course, my wife washed the curtains and the bedspreads."

We went outside to look at the rear of the house.

"How old is the house?" I asked.

"As near as I can figure it, the front portion was built around the 1870s," he answered. Pointing to different colors on the bricks, he added, "Some later additions were made, but I don't know when."

We returned to the front yard, and I thanked him for his time.

"Please come back when I'm finished with it, if I ever am."

As I pedaled away, I hoped that *Anna McGarvey* had someone like this man to rebuild her.

At Somers Cove, the show was getting under way. People were busy setting up their exhibits or otherwise getting ready for a busy day.

At one end of the exhibit area, a group of men and boys was sawing planks and hammering nails. We wandered over to them to see what they were making. It was a flat-bottom skiff, twelve feet long. Building without any written plans or blueprints, the group was working in silent harmony—a perfect orchestration of woodworking skills. As one plank was sawn, a man quickly applied caulking to its edges and placed it on the side or bottom of the boat's frame. While he held it, a boy started pounding evenly spaced nails to secure the plank to the frame. Next, two men worked on the plank; one planed it fair, and the other filled the nail holes with putty.

The unison with which these boat builders worked was a joy to watch. How did they do it? Did they rehearse for weeks? Were they professional builders who did this every day? Probably not, because the young boys worked as effortlessly and silently as the men. I was tempted to ask them their secret, but I didn't want to interrupt. The finished boat would be the top prize in a raffle later that day, and someone was going to win a well-built boat. I'd be happy to win a videotape of the building process.

Several wood carvers were displaying their work at the Festival. I saw something out of the corner of my eye, and I thought somebody had brought a pet duck to the exhibit. But as I approached the duck, I saw it was a carving.

Besides the wildfowl carvings, ship models were on display. As we approached a man and woman sitting next to a lovely two-foot model of a fishing schooner, the woman suddenly sat up.

"Why, you're the people we saw riding bikes past our house this morning!" she exclaimed.

Her excitement caught us off guard, but Joan quickly recovered.

"We were riding this morning," she said. "I remember seeing you loading things into a car."

The fact that we had ridden past their house was all the woman needed to introduce herself and her husband.

"I'm Anita Lord, and this is my husband, Rainbow. He's the one who builds the models."

We introduced ourselves, and I shook Rainbow's hand,

A fine example of the wildfowl-carvers' art

a very large hand. I couldn't picture hands as large as his working on the small details of a model ship.

Joan and Anita got into a lively conversation about Crisfield. Anita, a Crisfield native, talked about the services, schools, hospital, and economy of Crisfield. Anita also spoke of Salisbury, the largest city on the Eastern Shore.

"There are some wonderful stores there," she said. "And the kids love it, of course, with the movies, the park, and the zoo."

I wanted to learn more about how Rainbow had built the schooner I was admiring.

"Did you build this model the same way a boat builder would build the full-size boat?" I asked.

Boat builders make frames and put planks over the frames to construct the hull. Some model makers carve the hull instead of following that technique.

"Yes, I did. I make all my models that way. Are you familiar with wooden-boat construction?"

"Only the basics," I told him. "Did you build this schooner from a set of blueprints?"

"Naw, it's a Chappelle design that I saw in a book. Let me show you some of the other models I've made."

He opened a photo album in front of him and showed me pictures of his work. Started as a hobby in his youth, model making became his profession after he had worked a few years as a waterman. His creations are collected internationally, and he has been commissioned to make models of famous vessels, including the *Constellation* and the *Pride of Baltimore*.

At last, I found someone who could tell me about his life as a waterman. But Joan and I weren't the only ones attracted to this outgoing couple. Other people were looking at Rainbow's models and obviously had questions for him. Although we could have talked for hours with the Lords, we had to move on and let them conduct their business.

We quickly walked past the rest of the booths. It was hot. If I was going to broil in the sun, I'd rather do it while I was catching some crabs. We went back to *Delphina,* loaded our crabbing gear and some lemonade in *Flipper,* and went over to Janes Island State Park. In little over an hour, we had caught a dozen and returned to *Delphina.*

After dinner, we listened to the forecast for Sunday—settled weather with the temperature in the mid-nineties. Hoping to avoid the extreme heat, we started our bike ride at dawn.

In semi-darkness, we pedaled from the marina and passed the area of subsidized housing that Crisfield is justifiably proud of. These buildings are not the typical projects found in big-city ghettos, but are attractive, well-kept homes that the inhabitants also take pride in.

We left town on Route 413. This is the major road into Crisfield, but the traffic was light. We planned to ride on back roads that would take us to Pocomoke City. The first back road we took was to Marion.

As we entered this farming village, the dominant sight was a huge, decrepit silo complex. Soon after, we came to a few ramshackle buildings and an unusual sight for seven thirty in the morning: about twenty men were barbecuing hundreds of pieces of chicken over a brick grill that was five feet wide and at least thirty feet long. They were cooking in the same methodical manner as the men and boys on the preceding day had built the skiff, but these men were laughing and joking and having a merry time. I stopped.

"Why are you cooking all these chickens?" I asked the first man who noticed me.

"We're all with the Marion Volunteer Fire Department, and we're having a barbecue this afternoon to raise funds," the man replied.

He looked at my camera and asked where I was from. "Way down in the Florida Keys," I told him. "You know, this has to be the largest barbecue grill I've ever seen. How often do you do this?"

"Oh, we use it only about twice a year. The grill's community property, and different groups use it at different times. It gets a lot of use!"

After taking a picture, I mounted my bike to continue riding down the road.

"Now you be sure to come back this afternoon and have some chicken!" the man yelled after me.

The road wound through rich farmland. The principal crops we could recognize were corn and soybeans. An aroma, one I couldn't recognize, was in the air. It wasn't fertilizer, but it added an element to what we were seeing and hearing that left no doubt that we were in the country.

We were also seeing roadside litter and numerous "Adopt-A-Highway" signs stating that some family, business, or organization from the locality was responsible for picking up the litter. Much of the litter looked as if it had been in place for a long time. Where were the highway adopters? A commitment proclaimed should be a commitment kept.

As we came to Hudsons Corner, we noticed antique farm implements placed in the corner of a yard and a gaily painted farm wagon that was falling apart. We were at the Burgess Early Americana Museum, begun by Lawrence Burgess in 1975 when he converted his chicken house to storage for his collection of antiques. Over the years, this man has amassed a remarkable collection of old farm implements and antique household items. The collection is displayed on two stories of the old chicken house and in several outbuildings.

We turned onto another road and rode a couple of miles to the village of Rehobeth. During the colonial period, Rehobeth was an important center for the import and export of tobacco, but now it's a quiet residential village.

At Rehobeth, we had our first glimpse of the Pocomoke River, known for overhanging cypress trees that give the river a wild, scenic splendor. The Indians named the river Pocomoke, meaning "tan waters," because tannic acid seeping from the roots of the cypress trees makes the water dark brown. Since the river is navigable all the way to Pocomoke City and beyond to Snow Hill, we had considered going up it on *Delphina*. To reach the mouth of the river, however, a vessel must cross the wide, shallow Pocomoke Sound. Although a marked channel crosses the Sound, it's subject to shoaling. Also, taking *Delphina* on a round-trip up the Pocomoke River to Pocomoke City would involve four days of motoring. We decided, therefore, that it would be better for us to see Pocomoke City by land.

We stopped at the Coventry Parish Ruins, on the edge of Rehobeth. The brick walls, of Flemish bond construction, are all that remain of the Anglican church that was built there in 1784.

The back road ended at U.S. Highway 13, and we had to take this busy, noisy road the remaining two miles to Pocomoke City. This picturesque town, on the banks of the Pocomoke River, bills itself as the Friendliest Town on the Eastern Shore. We could see its charm as we crossed the drawbridge that spans the river and leads onto the main street. The riverbank is lined with a bulkhead that visiting boats can moor to. The town has a beautiful municipal park, spotlessly clean, and a downtown area that has not been ruined by the uniform appearance of franchise stores. Not only were the streets litter-free, but they were empty of cars since it was Sunday morning. We had an unobstructed view of the stores, which had prosperous-looking businesses inside.

Coventry Parish Ruins at Rehobeth, Maryland

In many towns we have visited, the main streets have succumbed to the tinsel and plastic of strip shopping centers on a highway outside town and have become blighted areas. But not in Pocomoke City. The town was a finalist in the All-America City competition a few years ago.

Pocomoke City was the halfway point on our trip, and we were hungry and thirsty. Riding through the town, we couldn't find an open restaurant or cafe, so we went out to Highway 13 to find someplace to eat. We found a fast-food place and had a tasteless meal washed down by a tasteless soft drink.

On the ride back to Crisfield, we were able to take different roads from those we had taken to Pocomoke City. We saw many chicken farms, and I noticed that the aroma that was in the air was stronger near the chicken houses. I realized the odor was chicken excrement; surprisingly, I found it was not an unpleasant odor. Maybe

I'm just a country boy at heart.

Many of the chicken farms are affiliated with major chicken processors, and we saw identical, small signs near the farms' entrances that showed the affiliations. I recalled that Salisbury is the home of Perdue Chickens, and the Eastern Shore is renowned for chickens almost as much as it is for seafood.

We got onto Route 413 just north of Marion. On the side of the highway was a large sign for the Marion Volunteer Fire Department Chicken Barbecue. The traffic was heavy, so I guessed the barbecue would be successful. However, it would have to be successful without us—we were still full of that fast-food stuff. I couldn't see where the food was being served, but I did see the grill. It looked strange, almost forlorn, now that it was clean and had no fire, no smoke, and no army of chefs hovering over it.

The distance from Marion to Crisfield is only six miles, but we seemed to pedal forever. We were tired, the hazy sun was hot, and the scenery was boring, especially since we were seeing it for the second time. We stopped at the supermarket on the outskirts of Crisfield and bought an ice-cold six-pack of beer to take back to *Delphina*. We had earned it.

I sat in *Delphina*'s cockpit and tried to shake the feeling I had that I had missed something in Crisfield. Despite its bawdy and colorful past, the town seemed tame to me. Maybe Crisfield really comes alive only for the Labor Day Festival. Maybe it's so wild and crazy then that it takes the residents a year of quiet living to recuperate from the last Festival and to prepare for the next one.

I tried to figure out a way to get back to Crisfield for Labor Day. In a week, we would be picking up my nephew for a one-week trip on the Bay, and after that our schedule was full until the middle of September; we couldn't attend the Labor Day Festival.

As I thought about the rest of our trip, I realized I hadn't spoken to anyone about the Tangier Sound entrance channel to Smith Island. I read over our three guidebooks again, but I couldn't find anything definite about the depth. One book warned that the strong currents that flow perpendicular to the narrow channel can easily push a boat onto a shoal. To be on the safe side, we decided to go around the north side of Smith Island and enter from the Bay side.

I went to sleep that night hoping the wonderfully persistent southwest wind would last a few more days.

CHAPTER FIVE

Smith Island

The weather pattern of fair skies and a strong south-westerly breeze that we had been blessed with since our arrival in the Bay continued for our passage to Smith Island. The prolonged periods of calms that are normal for the Bay in the summer had yet to become a reality, and we were being spoiled by the ideal sailing we were enjoying.

We timed our arrival at the entrance light for the western, or Bay, channel to coincide with high tide. Our guidebooks warned that, although the channel was dredged within the past three years, rapid shoaling occurs at the entrance. They advised that keel boats should enter at high tide. This advice is good, provided *the depth is known.* If a vessel runs aground at high tide, it's in trouble because the situation will worsen as the tide ebbs.

We didn't know the depth in the channel. We were gambling that, at low tide, the depth was at least four feet. At high tide, the depth would be six feet, enough for *Delphina* to get over any shoal in the channel entrance. I hoped any shoal we might encounter would not be large in area, and we could bounce over it. The only damage to *Delphina* if we did bounce over a shoal would be the loss of some paint from the bottom of her keel.

Before we entered the channel, Joan furled the sails, and I started the engine. Arriving at the entrance light, I increased the throttle, and *Delphina,* doing six knots, entered the channel. The depth sounder registered a small shoal immediately past the entrance light, but we didn't touch bottom. Thereafter, the depth sounder indicated the channel was deep the rest of the way into Ewell, the largest of Smith Island's three communities.

According to what I had read, I thought we'd have no problem securing *Delphina* at Ewell. We had a choice of two docks: the town dock or the dock at Evans General Store. The town dock was the first one we came to, and we tied up there. A sign on a piling stated "No Free Dockage—Pay at Ruke's." I felt relieved that finding a space for *Delphina* had been so easy. Then I saw another sign, smaller than the first, on a different piling. It read "No Docking 10-2, Reserved for Tour Boat." The time was ten thirty; the tour boat would be there any minute. We quickly slipped *Delphina*'s lines and left the pier.

We began an earnest search for the Evans Dock. Passing one pier after another, we failed to see any sign for Evans General Store. We came to the end of the piers and the beginning of a creek. I turned *Delphina* around and headed back.

We had passed a fuel dock that one of our guidebooks indicated was a source of information about anchoring or docking. I decided to stop there to find help. Not wanting to take up the space where boats would tie up for fuel, I went fifty feet past the fuel pump and secured *Delphina* to a bulkhead.

Before I had a chance to step ashore, a woman came out of the fuel-dock office and shouted to me, "You can't stay there! That's private property!"

I knew that. A sign on a piling said it was. *Delphina,* with Joan aboard, was only going to be there for a couple of minutes while I got some information. This situation was uncannily similar to our experience with the man on the fuel dock at Tangier, and I had to struggle to overcome my feeling of utter frustration.

"For God's sake," I wanted to shout back to this woman, "I'm only a simple sailor who wants to visit your lovely island for a little while and meet its friendly people! Won't you please, *please,* just tell me where to go?"

But, of course, I kept calm.

Smiling at her, I said, "Yes, ma'am, I know. I'm only here to ask you a question. I have a guidebook that says to stop at the friendly fuel dock in Ewell to find out where to anchor or tie up. Will you please tell me where we might?"

She smiled back. I had won her over with my charm.

"Oh, sure!" she said. "Just go to the general store back that way."

She pointed toward where we had just come from.

"Can't miss it; it's the biggest dock."

I thanked her profusely, and Joan let go the lines. I turned *Delphina* around. Once more, we intently sought the general-store dock, but soon we were at the head of the small creek again.

"Joan, I'm going to sound my way in here, and drop the hook as soon as I can," I said. "We'll just stay here until two and go back to the town dock."

Joan agreed.

At one thirty, we weighed anchor and left the creek. The tide was going out, and the depth sounder was indicating that if we stayed in the creek any longer, we might not be able to leave. Also, if the tour boat had left, we could get *Delphina* secured before the workboat fleet returned.

Nearing the town dock, I saw that the tour boat, *Capt. Tyler,* had not left. The boat was large and had more than a hundred passengers. We spent about fifteen minutes waiting alongside the boat while *Delphina* rode easily into the current at low speed.

Promptly at two, *Capt. Tyler* pulled out, and we were able to take its place. Not wanting to have any problem with that "No Free Dockage" sign, I immediately went to Ruke's and paid the modest $10.00 fee.

We were located in the center of town, and we were anxious to get on our bikes to see the rest of the island.

As we walked our bikes off the pier, a pickup truck drove down the pier. We hadn't seen a pickup on Tangier Island, and we were surprised to see one on Smith. Then we saw buses parked in a lot at the end of the pier. Later, reading the tour-boat's brochure, we learned that the buses are used by the tour-boat personnel to carry their passengers on a tour of the island. Both Smith and Tangier Islands are small enough that a visitor, with a little effort, can stroll and see most of the sights. On Tangier, the golf carts that carried the less adventuresome tourists looked quaint, almost amusing. On Smith, the buses looked ridiculous, almost obscene.

Reaching the main street, we saw a car approaching us. I had to look twice because at first glance it appeared no one was driving the car. Then I saw a boy driving. He was barely tall enough to see over the steering wheel. A girl, looking bored, was sitting next to him. Both were chubby and looked about fourteen years old. They drove by us and went down the street to a residential area. We walked our bikes across the street to the large Methodist church.

Although the population of Smith Island is about seven hundred fifty, there are three churches, all Methodist. Each community has its own church. Methodism is prominent on the Eastern Shore because of the zeal of Joshua Thomas, a waterman and Tangier resident in the early nineteenth century. Converted to the faith by

Methodist preachers visiting Tangier Island, he became a parson himself and spread the Word to the people of Smith Island. In time, he became known as the Parson of the Islands and began taking his message to the mainland on his sailing vessel, *Methodist.*

We got on our bikes to tour the neighborhood where the car had headed. As soon as I mounted my bike, I heard a roar behind me. Looking back, I saw a boy on a dirt bike coming down the road. Apparently, he had removed the muffler to make the machine louder than it normally would be. He raced past us and went toward the houses.

The street that ran through the neighborhood was heavily tree-lined. In the shade, the temperature was pleasantly cool. We had not seen any neighborhood on Tangier that had this many trees.

On the same street is Evans General Store. The store had a dock behind it, but the dock was fully occupied by boats. If we had found this dock from the water, we couldn't have moored *Delphina* to it.

We left the neighborhood and turned left past the church onto the road that goes to the village of Rhodes Point. The tarred road was sticky in the hot sun, and our bike tires made a squishy sound as we pedaled along.

We passed the elementary and middle schools on our way out of Ewell. There is no high school on Smith Island; high school students are educated in Crisfield. They used to stay on the mainland during the week and return home for the weekend. In 1974, however, a daily ferry service began for these students, and thus Smith Island has the nation's only daily school boat.

The road cut across open marsh. Coming at us from the opposite direction was the same car with the same boy and girl. Following closely behind the car was the boy on his dirt bike. They were not racing, just cruising. Throughout the remainder of the afternoon, we continued

Methodist Church on Smith Island

to see these young people, riding back and forth, around and around. No wonder the poor girl looked bored.

Halfway to Rhodes Point from Ewell, on the side of the road, is the modern sewage treatment plant, looking incongruous in the middle of a pristine marsh. An area for the disposal of white goods was adjacent to the plant. I had read in a guidebook that residents of Smith Island dump their trash and old cars anywhere they want, but the only evidence we had seen of this practice was near the waterfront.

As we entered Rhodes Point, I thought the village exhibited more of the flavor and atmosphere of a fishing village than any other Chesapeake Bay community we had yet visited. Stark houses faced a creek that was full of piers and crab pounds. Derelict skiffs, in various stages of submersion, lay around the shoreline. A pair of old trawlers, weeping rust from their galvanized fastenings, were rafted together near a dilapidated wharf. Crab pots and their colorful buoys were stacked or strewn about. Workboats, in different states of repair, were tied to piers or pilings.

From the end of the street, we could see the houses and church steeple of Tylerton across the marsh. This would be our only view of Tylerton since no road connects Tylerton to either Ewell or Rhodes Point.

We were standing in a small boatyard that had five workboats on land. Two men were re-caulking the bottom of one of the boats. They were conversing, and we were close enough to hear their words, but because of their heavy accents, we couldn't understand what they were saying.

Returning to Ewell, we saw that the tide was rising: the water in the marsh covered the sides of the road. The rising tide was normal and was not rising because of a storm.

Seeing this slight flooding reminded me of what I had

Weathered house on Smith Island

read about Chesapeake Bay storms and their effects on the land around the Bay. High storm tides, combined with strong winds and powerful waves, have caused some islands to disappear. Sharps Island, at the mouth of the Choptank River, had over seventy acres of land in 1900. Today there is no land left; only a shoal, marked by a leaning light tower, remains. On Tangier Island, water now covers an area where houses used to be. Watts Island, east of Tangier, is rapidly disappearing. And the list goes on.

Some of the residents of Smith Island believe that the island's level topography, combined with the labyrinth of creeks and sloughs, allows storm waters to wash over the island without doing any harm. William Warner's opinion, stated in his book *Beautiful Swimmers,* is that Smith Island may be getting larger because of the Bay's depositing on the island what it has picked up in the north.

Although no scientific study has been done to prove this theory, William Warner's opinion is reasonable. Five thousand acres of marsh, the Glenn L. Martin National Wildlife Refuge, protects Smith Island to the north and east and provides a repository for silt and sediment that is washed into the marsh by storms. This building process is the same one performed by mangrove trees in the Florida Keys.

When we returned to Ewell, we noticed two restaurants in the center of town, Ruke's and the Bayside Inn. Until recently, Mrs. Frances Kitching had served meals family-style to the public. She had begun in much the same manner as Mrs. Crockett on Tangier Island. In 1987, Mrs. Kitching retired and closed her establishment, to the dismay of cruising boaters who regarded it as somewhat of a culinary mecca because of its seafood specialties.

Although it was late in the day when we returned to *Delphina,* a few watermen, performing various chores, were still on the water. They were engaged in the same easy-going banter that we had heard in Tangier.

From watching the watermen at work on both Smith and Tangier, I'd never have guessed that there are differences on their islands. An often-heard anecdote about the islanders is the one that has a resident of Tangier telling an outsider that people from Smith Island "are a little funny up there." When the outsider visits Smith Island, a resident there tells him that the Tangier Islanders "are a little funny down there."

Whatever the truth may be, the inhabitants of both islands are hard-working people living in a sometimes harsh natural environment. Daily, hundreds of outsiders, gawking at them and their way of life, swarm over their small islands. Marine diseases and pollution in the Bay threaten the livelihood the islanders have known since their forefathers settled the islands. The lure of the mainland takes their children away from the islands to pursue an entirely different way of life from the one their families have followed for generations. The resultant stresses of these changes would overwhelm a lesser people, but to all outward appearances, the hardy islanders take them in stride. I knew I would be leaving Smith Island without knowing for certain the source of their strength. Whatever the source may be, we could all benefit from partaking of it.

We planned to leave early the next morning for the Potomac River across the Bay. We'd have a rising tide as we went out the channel, and I wondered if we would get stuck on the shoal I had noticed that morning.

CHAPTER SIX

Potomac River Virginia

We awoke to the roar of workboats heading out to the Bay. It was dark, but by the time we were ready to get under way, there was enough light to see our way out the channel. Remembering the shoal near the entrance, I had the engine at full throttle as we neared it. And we hit it, hard, but *Delphina* bounced ahead and kept going forward. I lowered the speed, and we entered the Bay without touching bottom again.

Smith Island quickly fell below the hazy horizon as we sailed for the Potomac. We were returning to Virginia for a change of scenery and culture. From Smith Island we could easily have gone to Deal Island, another watermen's community to the north, but we thought a change of environment would sharpen our senses. Too much of a good thing can lead to taking it for granted.

The Potomac is most often associated with Washington, D.C. and Mount Vernon, but among cruising boaters it is well known for having some of the most beautiful creeks and anchorages on the Bay. A boater can choose to cruise on the river for the distance of ninety-five miles to the nation's capital or poke around the numerous creeks that are within twenty miles of the mouth. We chose the latter. In six days we would be picking up my nephew at

St. Mary's City, Maryland, and we didn't want to be more than a two-day sail from there.

The mouth of the Potomac, from Point Lookout in Maryland to Smith Point in Virginia, is nearly ten miles wide. On a typically hazy day in the summer, one shore can't be seen from the other. The size of the river and its easy navigability led to the early settlement of its shores. Plantations were started in the seventeenth century by the English rulers' granting large tracts of land to select individuals. Tobacco was the major crop, and ships from England tied up to wharfs on the banks of the Potomac to exchange goods from the home country for hogsheads of tobacco.

As we entered the river, we saw more sailboats than we had seen anywhere else on our trip other than the Hampton area. The sailors were having a magnificent time with the persistent southwesterly wind, and so were we, sailing close-hauled as we neared the entrance light for the Yeocomico River on the Virginia shore. It was still morning; the strong wind had enabled us to have a fast passage from Smith Island.

We rounded Horn Point and entered the West Yeocomico River. The sound of bulldozers clearing trees on the point destroyed the serenity of the scene; another subdivision was being built. As we went farther into the river, the banks became higher. When we anchored at our intended spot, we were amid high bluffs with large, lovely homes. The landscape was altogether different from the low-lying vistas of the Eastern Shore.

The dockmaster at the nearby Kinsale Harbour Marina was friendly and let us leave *Flipper* at the end of one of their piers. We generally have found marina personnel to be friendly and open to our tying up our dinghy at their facility. Sometimes a marina has charged a modest fee for this privilege and let us use their showers and laundromat.

I was looking forward to getting more chicken backs at Kinsale. Not having eaten crabs since Crisfield, I was anxious to catch some. Maybe it's the hot, spicy seasoning that makes my salivary glands active when I think of eating steamed crabs. Oysters on the half shell with a hot seafood sauce are the only other food that has this effect on me. Regardless, the urge to please my palate was strong. I *had* to find some chicken for bait.

At the top of the nearby hill was the grocery store that one of our guidebooks indicated we would find. When we reached the store, it was closed and out of business. Some of the fixtures were still inside; otherwise, it was empty. I was surprised. While the town appeared to be quiet, it looked large enough to support a small grocery.

Kinsale, one of the earliest settlements on the Potomac, owes its early and long-lasting success to the stable depth of the West Yeocomico River. A stop for steamboats in its early years, the town has a wharf and other facilities for shipping grain. Grain barges continue to come there, but the town appears more interested in maintaining its residential flavor than pursuing any commerce. Other than the closed store, the only indication of a business in town was a mini-storage building where equipment could be rented, but that also looked closed.

If we were going to get any chicken, we would have to buy it in a store located somewhere other than in Kinsale. Our state highway map showed we were in rural Virginia, the Northern Neck, home of Northern Neckers, as the residents proudly call themselves. The town of Callao was six miles south; the town of Hague was four miles north. We were in the middle of cornfields, in the middle of a hot afternoon. A bike ride wasn't an inviting prospect, but we rode out of town anyway.

As we stood at the junction with Route 202 pondering where to go next, cars and trucks roared past us in excess of fifty miles per hour. Where were all these vehicles coming from or going to? We were in the *sticks,* weren't we? Was Interstate 95 ever this busy? Looking at Route 202, I saw no paved shoulder. That cinched it; I had no desire to risk my life for chicken. We turned around and returned to *Delphina.*

One reason we wanted to cruise the Virginia shore of the Potomac was to visit Stratford Hall, the birthplace of Robert E. Lee. The closest secure anchorage we could find was in Nomini Creek. Currioman Bay, a possible anchorage, was closer to Stratford than Nomini Creek, but the depths and protection were questionable.

The bike ride from Nomini Creek to Stratford would be a thirty-mile round-trip. We didn't know what the road conditions would be, but other travelers have suffered in their quest for historical knowledge, and a challenge always adds to the learning experience. First, however, we had to get to our anchorage.

After I studied the chart and our guidebooks the next morning, I knew the easiest part of the passage would be the sail to the mouth of Nomini Creek. Navigating in the creek, however, would not be a routine exercise. Nomini Creek has adequate depths all the way to Mount Holly, where we would anchor, but it also has some sharp turns. Fortunately, the creek is marked with aids to navigation, and if I followed them, I would avoid trouble.

The sail to Nomini Creek was routine, pleasant, and relaxing. I successfully negotiated the tricky entrance to the creek and continued to relax on our way to Mount Holly.

As we passed daybeacon "10," the depth sounder was reading twelve feet. Suddenly we stopped. We were hard aground. I was shocked.

"What the hell?" I asked no one in particular.

I looked back at the marker, then ahead at a pier with some workboats tied to it. Knowing exactly where we were, I looked at the chart. The depth was charted at one foot where we had stopped. What was I doing *there*? Trying in vain to get off the shoal by reversing with full throttle, I realized we would be there for a while. I was furious with myself. How could I be so *stupid?* Searching for an answer, I read the appropriate sections of our guidebooks again. I found the answer in *A Cruising Guide to the Chesapeake:*

> After passing this red [marker], pay no attention to the numerous oyster stakes that look like channel markers but are not. Give the lobster claw point a wide berth, as a shoal makes out. Then swing to starboard and follow the shore until you are past the 1-foot shoal with the pile on the opposite shore.

I had not swung to starboard; consequently, I was on the one-foot shoal.

"Why the hell didn't you tell me about this?" I yelled to Joan.

"I didn't know I had to," she calmly replied.

Joan has a way of keeping cool in a crisis.

"Well, damn it, something like that is important!" I continued to yell.

No way was I going to let her off the hook.

"I know. I'm surprised you didn't make a mental note of it when we read the guidebooks this morning," she said in her soft voice.

When I get myself in a jam, and she gets so logical about it, I really get frustrated.

"Well, at least the tide's coming in," I said. "We'll just sit here and wait to get lifted off."

I had quit yelling. Now I was using a petulant tone. Not wanting this grounding to spoil our day, I was trying to hint to Joan that I might forgive her oversight eventually.

I watched the current coming in and realized that, when it lifted us up, it might put us farther onto the shoal.

"Joan, we're going to have to get an anchor out and kedge off. That's the only way I see us getting out of here."

Using *Flipper,* I placed an anchor in deeper water astern of our position and brought the bitter end of the anchor line back to *Delphina.* Joan led the line through a stern hawse and along the deck to the windlass on the bow. After placing three wraps around the drum, I cranked as Joan took in the line. The work was strenuous; a boat displacing thirteen tons does not move readily when it's mired in mud.

Suddenly the bow swung. We were off! But I had to work quickly to keep *Delphina* from finding the shoal again while we had no control over her movement. Scurrying aft to the cockpit, I put the transmission in reverse and increased the throttle. As the boat moved quickly astern, I brought in the anchor line. We didn't need to get that wrapped around our propeller! Soon everything was under control, and we were once again going up the creek. We didn't discuss the grounding incident the rest of the day.

One problem with relying on guidebooks on a cruise is that they don't always reflect current conditions, and as they do elsewhere, changes occur rapidly on the waterfront. At the anchorage we had chosen, we were expecting to find a pier, fuel, ice, and a store. When we arrived, however, we found a decrepit building and a broken pier. Nevertheless, when we looked at the place through our binoculars, we saw that it was a good spot to leave the dinghy and unload our bikes. Actually, it was the *only* place we could go ashore. All other possible landing sites in the vicinity were private.

Our Virginia road map showed that the community of Mount Holly was near our anchorage. Surely this was the location of the store mentioned in the guidebook. Arriving there, however, we saw that Mount Holly has a historical church, an inn, and a few houses. We were on Route 202, and Hague was five miles south. My hunger for crabs had not been sated; we *needed* chicken backs. We made the bold decision to tackle Route 202. After all, we had to go north on it the next day to get to Stratford Hall.

The traffic was heavy, fast, and *loud*. I found that eighteen-wheelers, roaring past me at sixty miles per hour, made me feel unsettled. Occasionally these monsters, mindful of us, went into the left lane as they passed us, but seemingly they were unaware of the possibility of oncoming vehicles around curves.

We came to a crossroad. On our left was a large farm-equipment dealer. On our right was a group of run-down buildings. On the farthest building was a sign for a grocery store. We wouldn't have to go to Hague after all.

As I walked to the door under the sign, I noticed some posters of women's hairstyles and an advertisement for hair straightener. Odd things to have outside a grocery, I thought. I opened the door and saw a very large room, bereft of any furnishings other than an old couch, a chair, a flimsy coffee table, and two barber chairs. One of the barber chairs was occupied by a woman getting her hair cut by another woman standing behind her. Sitting on the couch were two other women. The scene didn't register in my mind; I was still thinking of the sign for a grocery store.

"Good afternoon, ma'am," I said to the lady who was standing. "Do you have any chicken backs?"

The hairdresser stopped mid-clip. The lady getting her hair done dropped her jaw, and the two on the couch started to giggle. The hairdresser closed her scissors and used them to point.

"You kin try nex' do'. It's a grocery sto'. Sometimes dey have chicken."

She giggled too. I thanked her and closed the door.

Without telling Joan what had happened, I went in search of the second door. I found it around the corner. No wonder I hadn't seen it. Opening the door, I looked in and saw a small, wiry man restocking a lower shelf with canned goods. He was alone in the store; it looked safe to ask my question.

"Do you have any chicken backs?"

The man stopped what he was doing and looked at me.

"No suh, Ah shua don't," he replied. "Ah don't carry any meat a'tall. Down de road aways dey's a gas station and sto'. She's likely ta have some."

After he told me that this place was another mile or so toward Hague, I thanked him and left the store. Joan agreed to continue our search for chicken.

The promised store, with two gas pumps, soon appeared on our left. Before I went in, I looked through the large plate-glass windows to make sure the business inside was a grocery and not a garage.

Joan and I entered the store.

"Excuse me, ma'am," I addressed the woman behind the counter. "Do you sell any chicken here?"

The store was a typical convenience store and probably didn't have fresh chicken for sale. No harm in asking, though.

"No, Ah don't. Down in Hague you kin git yo'self some. Dey's a supahmahket deyah. You folks ridin' dem bikes in dis heat?" she asked.

"Yes, ma'am, and it is a hot one, believe me," I answered.

Sweat was pouring off me.

"Well, God bless you!"

Her blessing was probably combined with a silent

prayer for our survival. I thanked her, and we continued our trip to Hague. The road became hillier; I hoped we didn't have much farther to go. At last the outskirts of town appeared, and soon we were inside a cool, air-conditioned supermarket. I didn't have to ask anyone any questions. Going directly to the poultry case, I selected two packages of chicken backs. On the way to the checkout counter, I got a six-pack of beer from the cooler; Joan got fixings for a salad. We were going to celebrate this success.

The bike ride back to *Delphina* seemed to be faster, but our experience on Route 202 hadn't filled us with eager anticipation for our long trip to Stratford Hall the next day.

Back on *Delphina,* I quickly got to work setting the crab lines. Despite having a dozen freshly baited lines in the water, in an hour we had caught only two crabs, both too small to keep.

We began the ride to Stratford at seven the following morning. Halfway to the town of Montross, we turned onto Route 3, a major artery on the Northern Neck, and the traffic was heavy. On the outskirts of Montross, we stopped at a convenience store and looked for a county map that would show us back roads to Stratford. We had no luck, and we didn't find any other stores open at that hour.

Eight hilly miles farther, we came to a sign for Stratford Hall. Finally, we turned off Route 3 onto a quiet country road. During our two-mile ride to the entrance gate for Stratford, only one car passed us. The gate at the entrance was closed, and a sign informed us that the plantation didn't open until ten. It wasn't nine yet, so we decided to go farther down Route 3 to Westmoreland State Park.

This forested park extends from Route 3 to the Potomac and has several campgrounds, numerous hiking trails, a swimming pool, a playground, and a picnic area. The riverfront consists of sandy beaches and high cliffs that are repositories for fossils of creatures that lived in the Miocene Sea. After hiking a few of the short trails, we rode our bikes to the highest cliff overlooking the river.

Joan spotted something strange under a large shade tree a few feet from the edge of the cliff. We rode closer and saw a tripod with binoculars. Nobody was present, but a pickup truck was approaching. The truck stopped under the tree, and the driver got out.

"Who are you spying on?" Joan asked.

The man looked like a private detective. He was probably looking in on a tryst on a boat below.

The man appeared surprised by the question, but smiled when he answered.

"Oh, I'm not spying, ma'am. I'm a range officer for the Navy. What you see in front of you is the world's longest firing range over water—other than the ocean, of course. The Navy's doing some firing from Dahlgren today, and I have to make sure there aren't any boats in the way."

He looked through the binoculars as he finished speaking. Something squawked on the portable two-way radio he was carrying. In reply to this noise, the man spoke into the radio.

"I have him in sight," he said. "He has turned away. It's all clear."

"What's the Navy firing today?" I asked him.

"They're testing a sixteen-inch gun as part of the *Iowa* investigation. They can't use the actual gun from the ship, so they use a gun that's the same age and has the same amount of wear," he replied.

"Any chance we could stay here and watch?" I asked.

A sixteen-inch gun can hurl a shell with the weight of a small car about twenty-six miles. The test would be interesting to watch.

"Fine with me, but about all you'll see is a big splash."

He further said that he didn't know how much longer it would be until the firing. We decided to return to Stratford rather than wait for a big splash. The range officer lit a large cigar and made himself comfortable in the shade of the tree. We rode away.

The gatekeeper at Stratford couldn't have been more enthusiastic in his welcome. As soon as we arrived at the gate, he bounded out of the gate house with an agility that belied his age and physique. His expression was dominated by his wide smile.

"Good morning, folks!" he said. "Welcome to Stratford Hall! We're so happy to have you here!"

Maybe he had been instructed to treat each visitor as the lord or lady of the manor, returning after a long absence, but he was so sincere in his unrestrained happiness at seeing us that I had to wonder if we actually were important people.

After collecting our money for the entrance fee and giving us tickets and a brochure, he briefly told us what we would be seeing.

"And you're just in time to have a plantation lunch at the dining room!" he concluded.

"What will they be serving?" Joan asked.

"Ma'am, I'm awful sorry, but I don't rightly know! You see, they just hired me last week, and I'm still learning."

Stratford Hall was built in the late 1730s by Thomas Lee, progenitor of one of America's most famous and historic families. Five of his six sons played direct roles in the forging of the United States. One of his grandsons, Robert E. Lee, commanded the Confederate forces in the Civil War. It seems character was as much a product of this plantation as was tobacco.

Today Stratford continues as a working farm on sixteen hundred of the original acres. After many years of neglect, the plantation was purchased by the Robert E. Lee Memorial Foundation in 1929 and restored to its former grandeur.

We had a delightful ride to the Visitor Center. We stopped at a small plot of ground that displays a sample of the different crops grown on the plantation. A little farther on, we rode along a fenced pasture where enormous Black Angus bulls were grazing. The farm buildings that we saw were modern and well maintained.

We arrived at the Visitor Center, locked our bikes, and entered. The man who was in attendance at the information desk had seen us park our bikes and asked where we had come from.

"We rode over from Mount Holly this morning. Our boat is anchored there in Nomini Creek," Joan told him.

"You don't say! When I went over the Mount Holly bridge this morning, I saw a sailboat anchored and wondered whose it was. Do you mean to say you rode your bikes all the way here?"

"Yes, we did," I said. "We took Routes 202 and 3. We tried to get a county map showing back roads, but we couldn't. Do you have any suggestions for going back?"

He gave us directions for returning on the same roads that he took commuting to work.

"It's hilly, but you won't run into as much traffic. You still have to get on Route 3 in Montross. The trip'll take you about the same time."

He then told us we had time to watch the video presentation before the next guided tour of the Great House.

"After you've gone on the guided tour, please feel free to spend the rest of the day here," he continued. "You can visit the mill house down on the beach. And don't miss the view from the cliffs! Today you'd be able to see the other shore. Also, there's a shady walk down to the spring house. Before you leave for the day, look over the exhibits we have here in our museum."

After seeing the videotape, we met our guide, a middle-aged woman dressed in colonial attire, in a reception room near the Great House. Our group comprised only seven people, and our guide had the time and knowledge to answer many questions. The tour concluded in the kitchen where we were treated to ginger snaps and apple cider. We said our farewells to our group members and guide and left the kitchen to walk around the grounds.

The large, brick carriage house has been restored and contains outstanding examples of the coach-makers' art. Each carriage room has a carriage and the necessary harnesses for horses to pull the carriage.

The formal garden had to be replanted when restoration of the plantation was undertaken. We strolled through this garden admiring its perfect symmetry. From the garden, we had a short hike down to the spring house in a shady glen. Although Robert E. Lee was only three years old when he moved from Stratford, he was able to remember this spring during his later years.

The Great House at Stratford Hall

We returned to the Visitor Center to see the exhibits. I went directly to the large portraits of the Lees. Standing in front of the images of these distinguished patriots, I wondered why such strength of character developed in these men. Although they were wealthy, they selflessly risked everything they owned to found a country based on principles they believed in. The agonizing decision made by Robert E. Lee to lead an army in a bitter war against the same government his father and uncles had helped create was a testament to his strength of character.

As I thought about these men, I realized how weak my knowledge of our forefathers is. All I know of George Washington's early life is that he chopped down a cherry tree and didn't lie about it. I'm certain that I could learn many lessons from a study of the lives of our founding fathers.

We got our bikes and rode along the lane that goes to the riverfront. On both sides of the road, we saw the rustic cabins where the directors of the Robert E. Lee Memorial Foundation, forty-three women from as many states, stay when they come for their biannual meetings.

Looking at the river from the cliffs, we had the same spectacular view that we had had from the park. Signs are posted warning people not to get close to the edge.

The dirt road to the beach and mill house begins at the cliffs. We saw that the road was too steep to ride our bikes down, so we left them at the cliffs and walked. It was almost too steep for that! But people were *driving* down the precipitous incline in defiance of every law of gravity I have ever learned.

At the bottom of the hill, we stopped to watch a group of noisy children gathered around a picnic table. They had been beachcombing and had gathered a nice assortment of prehistoric sharks' teeth. Their level of excitement was so high that at first I thought they had found gold doubloons instead of teeth.

I was disappointed that I couldn't see inside the mill house because it was locked and the windows were covered, but I was impressed with the size of the wheel, the largest I have ever seen. Around the rafters of the roof covering the mill was a large community of hornets' nests.

After a climb that would have challenged Hillary, we returned to our bikes. On the way out of the plantation, we stopped at the Visitor Center to get some candy and soft drinks. We needed some fuel for the ride back to *Delphina*.

Following the directions given us by the man at the information desk, we had a peaceful ride to the outskirts of Montross. The back roads had allowed us to avoid those treacherous highways for half the distance to Mount Holly.

Safely back on *Delphina,* we reread what information we had on St. Mary's City and decided to head directly there the next morning. I was disheartened by the fact that, after all the trouble we had gone to to get those chicken backs, we had not caught one decent crab. Perhaps the Maryland waters would treat us better.

CHAPTER SEVEN

Potomac River Maryland

After spending almost two weeks on Chesapeake Bay, we were getting some of the summer weather that the area is known for. The southwesterly wind was light, the haze had settled in, and it was hot and humid. We were sailing toward St. Clement's Island. In the haze we could see few details on the Maryland shore.

St. Clement's Island is across the Potomac River from, and almost due north of, the entrance to Nomini Creek. The original Catholic settlers to Maryland landed on the island in 1634 and celebrated the first Mass in the English Colonies. To commemorate this event, the State of Maryland erected a large cross on the site in 1934. We came close to the island to view this impressive cross, which provides a stark reminder of the religious persecution and other hardships faced by the early settlers.

The colonists were pleased with the area, and their governor, Lord Leonard Calvert, negotiated the purchase of a tract of land from the Piscataway Indians. Subsequently the settlers, aboard their two ships, the *Ark* and the *Dove,* sailed up the St. Mary's River and settled on this land. Named St. Maries Citty, the settlement became Maryland's original capital.

The passage from St. Clement's to the mouth of the

St. Mary's River was uneventful, almost boring. The heavy haze blotted out all details of the shoreline, and few other boats were on the river. With relief, we reached the entrance buoy to the St. Mary's River and headed *Delphina* north, up the river. The haze thinned after we left the Potomac, and we were able to see details on the shore.

The St. Mary's River is wide and over twenty feet deep for most of its length. The river is easy to navigate, and we were able to admire the scenery, which looked different from the scenery on the Virginia shore of the Potomac. There were more rolling, grassy hills and fewer high, wooded bluffs. Few houses were grouped together in subdivisions; most were spread out and looked like manor homes. As the river narrowed at Church Point, we saw the replica of the *Dove,* moored to its wharf. On top of a hill behind the wharf, the reproduction of Maryland's first State House, built by the State as part of its tricentennial celebration in 1934, majestically stood watch over the river.

Past Church Point is Horseshoe Bend, a large and deep bay. This bay provides an ideal gathering place for cruising or racing fleets. The hospitable St. Mary's College provides dock space to visiting racing fleets, and we had read that it's a remarkable sight to see over three hundred sailboats rafted to these piers or anchored nearby after the annual Governor's Cup Race in August. We weren't upset, however, to learn that we were a week early for this spectacular gathering.

The College allows visiting cruising boats to be tied to their pier for a maximum of two hours. This courtesy allows many visiting boaters a trip ashore without using a dinghy. We noticed two sailboats moored to the outside dock.

We anchored near the pier and used *Flipper* to take us and the bikes ashore. The College has a serious sailing program, and because of their large fleet of sailboats moored inside the dock area, we found no room to tie the dinghy on their dock. We put *Flipper* on the beach and tied her to a tree.

St. Mary's City is no longer the bustling metropolis it was three hundred fifty years ago. In fact, it's not even a town, as most people think of towns: there is no commercial district. St. Mary's College, the Trinity Episcopal Church, and an agency of the Maryland Department of Housing and Community Development, called Historic St. Mary's City, are located there and, along with some homes, compose the community of St. Mary's City.

Historic St. Mary's City brings alive the early colonial period through the talents of costumed performers and through authentic reproductions of the town's early buildings. The replica of the *Dove*, which we had seen earlier, is also part of this project. We would see the next day how realistic the living history is. But first we had to replenish our liquor supply and get some bread.

After we had unloaded our bikes, a distinguished-looking couple approached us.

"We were hoping you were the folks on the pinky schooner that left here three years ago," the man said.

Joan and I looked at each other. Three years ago we had been in Europe. We had never been to St. Mary's City before.

"No, it wasn't us," Joan said.

"The reason we came to see you is that a lovely pinky schooner, just like the one you came in on, was here then. The owners were the nicest people. They spent quite a while here, and we got to know them. Then one day they sailed away, saying they would return. We thought you were they when we saw you coming up the river."

"No, sorry to disappoint you," Joan said. "Do you live on the river here?"

"Yes, we live not too far from Chancellor's Point," the

woman replied.

We talked a little about *Delphina,* and then I asked about the nearest place to replenish our stores. They advised us a store that sold food, beer, and liquor was three miles north on Route 5. It would be an easy bike ride, they said, but if we chose, we could order what we wanted by phone, and the store would deliver. Delivery is a service the store provides for visiting boaters.

As they left to return home, I thought they seemed a little sadder than when they had greeted us. Apparently, our arrival had reminded them of some former good times and some people they missed very much. I like to think the other pinky, having completed an exciting trip around the world, will return to St. Mary's City, and its owners will have great tales for their old friends whom they left so long ago with only a promise. In the cruising life, things like that happen.

Joan and I did something we rarely do—we went our separate ways. Joan went to investigate the Visitor Center; I went to the store.

A pleasant surprise awaited me at the store: liquor prices were about a third less than what they had been in North Carolina and Virginia.

Arriving back at the dock before Joan, I went over to talk to the people on the two cruising boats. Two couples were together on the pier, midway between the two boats. One of the men was talking.

"Well, we'll just go anchor on the far side of the bay. That should be far enough away from the noise."

As I approached the little group, they looked at me with welcoming smiles. After we exchanged greetings, I asked the man what noise he was talking about. The place seemed very quiet.

"Around midnight tonight, a club from somewhere around Annapolis is finishing a race here. The College is expecting about eighty boats. You know what it's like

when those people get together—party city. I don't want
to be around!"

We exchanged a few generalities about noisy anchorages and how well sound travels over water. I thought
that, if the race ended after midnight, after having
started in Annapolis, the racers would be too tired to
party when they arrived at St. Mary's City. So *Delphina*
would stay where she was. I saw Joan returning, and I
left to join her at the dinghy. She was very excited.

"This place is great! Wait'll you see the Visitor Center!
I got all kinds of information!"

She seemed to be gloating.

"Well, I got all kinds of booze! Let's go home and
party!"

As it turned out, we were the only ones who even
came close to making party sounds that night. The fleet
did arrive that night, but did so silently.

Although we arose early Saturday morning, we didn't
go ashore until nearly ten. The exhibits at Historic St.
Mary's City didn't open until then, so we got *Delphina*
ready for Thackeray, my eight-year-old nephew, who was
scheduled to arrive at four on Sunday with his parents
and brother.

At a family reunion the previous summer, we took
Thackeray for a half-day sail on *Delphina* on Calibogue
Sound in South Carolina. He asked us questions about
how the boat worked and showed a genuine interest in
the answers. Taking a turn at the helm, he enjoyed what
he was doing. When I asked if he would like to spend a
week cruising with us, he eagerly accepted. And his
parents thought it was a good idea as well.

The year passed quickly, and Thackeray's anticipation
grew. So did mine. Remembering my first experience
away from home at summer camp when I was nine, I
hoped Thackeray wouldn't get as homesick as I had been.
Also, I wondered how it would be for me and Joan, not

used to having children aboard for more than a day at a time, to constantly monitor Thackeray's whereabouts and actions in case he inadvertently got himself in trouble in a strange environment. But then I thought he was a brave boy to go to sea for a week without the solace and protection of his parents. He'd get along just fine.

Before we went ashore, I wanted to try crabbing in Horseshoe Bend, so I baited the crab lines and put them in the water. The bait that I had bought in Hague had spoiled, but I had read that crabs like chicken really rank, so I thought I'd do well. But I caught nothing. Over on shore, about three hundred yards north of the College pier, a group of nine or ten kids was crabbing from a small public pier. Apparently, they were catching every crab in the bay. I quit in disgust and loaded all the bait in a bag to take ashore and throw away.

The tour of Historic St. Mary's City began at the Visitor Center, where we bought a ticket for all their exhibits and watched a videotape about the history of the town. Their brochure read, "We've had 355 years of experience with Maryland history. We began it." Not only true, but clever.

We rode our bikes to the Governor's Field Exhibit Area and left them in the parking area. Entering the grounds, we were confused about where to begin. Farthing's Ordinary, a replica of a colonial tavern, was nearby and was serving lunch, but we didn't want to eat.

Across the walkway from the Ordinary, I saw a table loaded with antiques. Behind the table, two lovely maidens in colonial dresses and bonnets were holding flowers in their dainty hands and talking to two tourists standing in front of the table. To the tourists' left was a man who looked as if he had just gotten off a ship, a very *old* ship: he looked like a pirate. The two damsels, talking like Eliza Doolittle, were trying to sell the goods on the table to the tourists. We walked over to watch the exchange more closely.

"Boot, suh, this is a royt foyn 'ammeh. Do ya a wuhld o' gude it wude," the girl in the pink dress said.

The pirate was nodding his head in agreement.

One of the tourists was a good sport.

"Okay, I'll buy the hammer," he said, smiling. "How much you want for it?"

"Ooh, suh, thanks evah so much! A 'ahlf-pound o' tobacca'll tyke 'er awhy wicha," the girl excitedly replied.

"But I don't smoke!" protested the potential customer.

"Sorry, suh, boot tobacca's ewl I kin tyke!"

The tourist had no idea how to continue this repartee. He shrugged and walked away with his companion. The three colonists looked at us expectantly. They were having fun and wanted it to continue. How I was tempted to be Henry Higgins! What a golden opportunity! Henry Higgins in shorts, polo shirt, and flip-flops! But I was too inhibited, damn it!

"What's all this stuff you're selling here?" I asked.

The pirate told us he was a merchant who had disembarked from the pinnace *Dove*, moored down on the river, and had some wares to sell before returning home to England. The only currency he recognized was tobacco. I told him we had no tobacco, only dollars and cents.

"Suh, whateveh they my be, Oy'm afride they wun't do me much gude back 'ome in England," the merchant said.

Knowing they couldn't sell us anything, the three started talking among themselves. They were discussing the crimes of a "John 'alf'ead," whose trial was scheduled for two that afternoon at the State House.

"Thaht bluedy pig-snatcha'll git wot's coomin' to 'im, Oy rekin!" exclaimed the yellow-clad girl gleefully.

The merchant told us to be at the State House at two for this important trial. Justice would be served!

We assured him we would make it a point to be there.

As we walked away, we heard them gossiping among themselves without changing character.

Continuing our tour, we visited the State House and then walked to the riverfront. Stepping aboard the *Dove*, we were greeted by our friend the merchant. "Well, ya see. Oy'm also the fihst mite on this splendid lit'le vessule!" he proudly told us.

Joan and I had a lot of questions about this ship, but we'd have trouble understanding his answers if he stayed in character. Pleading with him, and telling him we also came to St. Mary's City by water, we succeeded in loosening his resolve. He grinned.

"I've been first mate for over a year now. I enrolled in a program to learn how to sail one of these old square-riggers. Sure is a lot to know, but I'm getting there!"

He told us that he would be taking courses at St. Mary's College that year and eventually earning a degree.

"But this is what I love doing. This spring we sailed her up to Eastern Bay. Had a broad reach up and a broad reach back. It was incredible!"

On the tour he gave us of the boat, he covered how the boat was constructed, how the rigging worked, where the crew lived, and features unique to a square-rigged sailing vessel. He had learned well from the program he was enrolled in. I had no doubt he would someday have command of a square-rigger.

After eating the lunch Joan had packed, we returned to the State House for Halfhead's trial. Although the courtroom was packed, we got great seats two rows back from the action. The trial began, and it took an effort to remind myself that this was a re-creation, not the real thing. The actors, especially the one who played Halfhead, were immensely talented and played well off one another's words and actions.

As we walked back to the parking lot, I pointed to the

fences that we had been seeing all morning.

"Joan, this is the same kind of fence we've been seeing all over, even down in Virginia. I think they're put together without any nails or other fasteners."

After saying that, I lifted one of the railings to demonstrate. The whole section of fence came clattering down. In shock, I looked around me to see if anyone had seen this disaster. Joan, about to burst into a laughing fit, was the only witness. Quickly, I gathered the fallen pieces and put them where I thought they belonged.

"Will you be able to demonstrate other examples of colonial building methods?" Joan asked. "I see a barn over there. Will you show me how they put that together?"

The question was hardly worth answering, so I ignored it.

A short bike ride brought us to an archaeological dig, where the digging is done by a group of enthusiastic college students under the guidance of a professional staff. As we neared the dig, a young woman stopped her sifting and approached us. She was smiling.

"Good afternoon. Would you like me to show you what we're doing here?" she asked.

We told her we would. As she gave us a tour, she explained in detail what a dig is.

"Are you majoring in archaeology?" Joan asked.

"No, I'm an education major at a small school in Kentucky," she replied. "I'm spending the summer here and doing this work for extra credit hours. I'm meeting a lot of neat people and learning a lot. There's more to archaeology than just digging a hole!"

After our tour, our guide returned to the sifting she had been doing. As another couple approached the site, I saw a different student stop work to greet them. I wondered how the students had worked out the rotation schedule.

Archaeological dig at St. Mary's City

Although it was late afternoon, we still had two exhibits to visit: the Godiah Spray Tobacco Plantation and Chancellor's Point Natural History Area.

The tobacco plantation is the most realistic of the exhibits we saw. The house looks ancient with its weathered boards. As we approached the front door, the woman of the house was arguing with the hired field hand. The latter was the villain John Halfhead. Seeing us enter, the matron dismissed Halfhead and greeted us. After telling us about life on the plantation, she invited us to go outside and wander around the fields.

Tobacco was growing in the backyard; each plant looked as if it received individual attention. On the side of the yard is a weathered barn that looks as old as the house. We entered its gloomy interior and saw curing tobacco leaves hanging from the rafters.

Outside again, we walked to a field where the owner of the plantation, Godiah Spray, was tending his hogs.

Calling each by name—Chop, Bacon, Rib, Ham, or Sausage, he impressed us as being very fond of his animals. As we watched Chop wallow in his mud puddle and listened to his snorting and grunting, the farmer left to tend his tobacco plants.

As we were leaving the pigs, I looked toward the tobacco field and saw the farmer bending over one of his plants and caressing a leaf. I'm certain the man didn't know I was watching him: he was engrossed in this activity. The performers at Historic St. Mary's City certainly live the lives of the characters they portray.

At Chancellor's Point, we went to the reconstructed Indian Longhouse. Inside were a family of five and a guide. The father and the guide were having an animated discussion about Indians. The mother and the three young children looked bored and listless.

We sat down to listen to what the guide was saying. In less than five minutes, we realized that the guide was

Godiah Spray Tobacco Plantation at St. Mary's City

saying little, and the father, doing his best to impress the young guide with his vast knowledge of Native Americans, was a boor. Incredibly, the guide was showing interest, thus encouraging the man. One more minute of the discussion was all we could tolerate, and we left the Longhouse. I felt sorry for the mother and children. I wondered how long they had been silently suffering.

Chancellor's Point has a trail to the beach and the bluffs on the St. Mary's River, but we decided not to take it because of the late hour. Reluctantly we reentered the real world.

We returned to *Delphina* for a quick dinner. Afterwards, we returned to shore to attend that evening's bluegrass music concert on the waterfront, near the *Dove*'s wharf. Dixie Ramblers, a local group, was scheduled to begin at six.

Something about bluegrass music stirs the soul and taps the feet of everyone who listens to it. We hear it, and we feel good about ourselves and those sitting with us. Some people begin dancing with strangers in response to its vibrant beat. And so it was that evening, as we watched the sun getting lower with each tune. Although I knew no one there except Joan, I felt I was surrounded by family. The evening was very enjoyable, and we went home in good spirits.

Including the racing fleet rafted to the College docks, and other boats that had arrived that day, over a hundred vessels were in Horseshoe Bend that evening. We could hear music, laughter, and conversations coming from the anchored boats. These sounds mingled with sounds of gaiety on the pier as the crews of the racing fleet celebrated another successful race.

We had a quick nightcap and turned in. It was only nine, but we were worn out.

Around eleven, I awoke from a deep sleep. The sounds outside had become louder and included rock music coming from a stereo. Joan also was awake. We tossed and turned and tried to ignore the noise of the revelry. It was impossible. The noise continued for about an hour when, suddenly, the air was filled with the opening strains of John Phillip Sousa's march *Semper Fidelis.* Never had I heard such volume, not even in a concert hall. I popped my head out of the hatch to see if the Marine Corps Band were playing on our deck, but I saw only darkness. Surely, I thought to myself, God is announcing the imminent arrival of a contingent of Marines to still the noise!

The music continued until the last note of the march played. Then silence, as deep as the volume had been loud, settled over the water. In the distance, applause began; cheering followed shortly. The cheering continued for about thirty seconds, reached a crescendo, and abruptly stopped. There was no further noise; the party was over.

This experience overwhelmed me. My heart was beating quickly, and I knew I would have trouble settling down. I went into the galley, poured a double scotch, downed it in two gulps, and drank another more slowly. Following that, I was able to get back to sleep.

The morning brought rain to the anchorage and a small hangover to me. Boats were weighing anchor and leaving. The enormous raft-up on the dock began to dismantle.

Feeling ambitious, I left the dry comfort of *Delphina* and went ashore to get a newspaper. People were on the pier, but I heard no mention of what had happened at the previous night's witching hour. No way could I have imagined that rendition of *Semper Fidelis,* but I didn't want to bring the subject up either.

The sky had started to show signs of clearing, so after reading the paper, we went for a ride. The pleasure of having a paved shoulder to ride on made the afternoon most enjoyable.

Only one cruising boat was moored to the College dock when we returned to *Delphina*. I weighed *Delphina*'s anchors, and we went to the pier. The job of loading our bikes and Thackeray's gear would be much easier from the dock.

My brother Tom, his wife, Wendy, and their two boys arrived shortly after four, after a two-hour drive from Washington. As I had hoped, Thackeray was still enthusiastic about the trip. And so was his brother, John Austen, who is two years younger.

"I'm not afraid of boats anymore, Uncle Ken," he informed me.

"That's great, John Austen, because you'll be able to come with us in a few years," I replied.

Each member of our group carried some of Thackeray's gear from the parking lot to *Delphina*. Thackeray personally rolled his bicycle to the pier and made sure that its brilliant paint and chrome wasn't marred as I loaded it onto *Delphina*'s deck. The rest of Thackeray's things were placed below to stow later. Joan put the boys to work filling up the water tanks, and I mixed cocktails for the adults. Tom and Wendy invited us to join them for dinner at a nearby seafood restaurant.

After dinner we returned to the dock, and I wondered if Thackeray would change his mind about coming with us. But he was still excited about the trip, and as the moment of departure neared, he hugged his parents good-bye and said so long to his brother. Leaving his family for a week while he went to sea was no big deal as far as Thackeray was concerned.

Chance, on Deal Island, would be our next port of call. The island is across the Bay from the Potomac River, so Thackeray would experience good sailing at the beginning of the week—if there was wind.

Joan and I reviewed safety procedures and our plans

with Thackeray and showed him his bunk and locker. This small space would be his home for the next week. Besides his shiny, blue bike, Thackeray had brought a bike helmet and a seabag full of clothes, cookies, and comics. He was ready for an adventure.

CHAPTER EIGHT

Deal Island

The rain of Sunday made way for the sun of Monday. High pressure was building from the west. The air was crisp, and we had a brisk northeasterly breeze.

Joan showed Thackeray how to raise the jib and staysail and how to secure the halyards to belaying pins with a figure eight and a half hitch. We got the sails up before leaving Horseshoe Bend and rounded Church Point under full sail. If the wind held, the sail across the Bay would be splendid.

The itinerary for the week was ideal for a young boy. After we sailed across the Bay, we would ride our bikes down Deal Island. A leisurely cruise up the Wicomico River to Salisbury would start the next day. On Thursday, we would anchor in the Honga River before again crossing the Bay and going into the Patuxent River on Friday. Our final anchorage would be at Solomons. With all this activity, plus his comic books, Thackeray would be well entertained.

Early into the passage, Thackeray displayed more interest in the bike ride the next day than in the sailing. The night before, he had proudly shown us his riding outfit, consisting of a helmet, colorful riding outfit, and red sneakers. Treating them like treasures, he had carefully packed these items in his locker. His bicycle, like ours, was secured on deck to the lifelines, but unlike ours, his bicycle was gleaming and beautiful. It looked *sleek*. That morning, after he had had his cereal, he went on deck with a rag and wiped the dew off his blue beauty. I wondered whether he thought he was on a boat cruise or the Tour de Chesapeake.

"Thackeray, did your folks just get you that bike?" I asked.

"No, it's a year old. How old is yours, Captain Ken?"

Sometimes kids ask me questions that I really don't care to answer. Looking over at my bike, a worthy monument to the gods of rust, I couldn't come up with a reply that would save face.

"One year. Captain Joan and I bought our bikes in Florida. They rust quickly in salt air."

Not passing any judgment on my answer, he asked, "How long do you think the ride will be tomorrow?"

"About four miles, right down the middle of Deal Island to Wenona, where all the skipjacks are. Then back to Chance, for a total of eight miles. Should be easy. What's the farthest you've ridden?"

"About ten miles. My dad clocked me."

"Well, this'll be a piece of cake for you then."

He walked over to his bike, wiped some spray off its shiny paint, and stood against the foredeck railing. Looking out over the water, he seemed in deep thought. He was probably trying to work out a plan to pace himself the next day. At that moment, he may as well have been on a bus on Interstate 95 as on a sailboat on Chesapeake Bay.

After we passed through Kedges Strait, we entered Tangier Sound and altered course to the north. Deal Island was visible to starboard. The wind was barely a whisper, and the tide was going out, so I reluctantly started the engine, and we dropped the sails.

The same men who work the skipjacks were pulling crab traps as we motored past their workboats. I wanted to impress the watermen with *Delphina*'s grace and beauty under sail, but that demonstration would have to wait for another day. I concentrated instead on avoiding the many trap buoys that lay on our course.

The snug harbor at Chance is on the north end of the island. We had no trouble negotiating the channel, and we anchored in the middle of the little harbor. We used two anchors and set them well. Near us was the bridge that connects the island to the mainland. If *Delphina* dragged on her anchors, and one of her masts hit the bridge, she would lean over and take on water. She would sink. I am never comfortable around bridges.

We were definitely back in watermen's country. Workboats were coming in to unload at the packing plant. Shedding pounds came to the water's edge. Crab traps were stacked in a yard adjacent to a fuel dock.

A public boat ramp was next to the shedding pounds. We found the ramp to be a good place to unload the bikes and leave the dinghy.

After going ashore, we went to watch a woman working the shedding pounds. We had never watched this intriguing operation before. Hundreds of "pailers," as the watermen call peelers, were in different tanks, and the woman spent a few minutes at each tank as she pulled out crabs with a pair of tongs. She did this maneuver quickly, and I couldn't see why she would choose one crab and not another. Her intensity was such that I didn't want to interrupt with a stupid question.

Besides the job of picking the meat from steamed hard crabs at the packing plants, this sorting job requires special people if it is to be done well. Looking hour after hour at thousands of crabs slowly moving around in gurgling water requires tremendous concentration. I doubt that I could do it for more than a hour.

Thackeray was getting restless. He wanted to hit the road. By the time we got to the bikes, Thackeray had on his helmet and gloves. "Now, Thackeray, this is just going to be a short ride, so don't get all fired up. Remember to conserve your strength for tomorrow," I intoned. "Ooookay, Captain Ken!" I led the way as we rode single file on the edge of the road. Thackeray was in the middle, and Joan took up the rear. The ride was short, just long enough to see what the island is like. The land is flat, and along the main street of Chance are nice residential areas, a church with a well-kept cemetery, a general store, and an old, abandoned, brick bank building, small in size, with large windows behind massive bars. Many of the houses had mailboxes with ducks, geese, dogs, or boats painted on them. Some of the yards had extensive collections of birdhouses and lawn ornaments. An occasional skiff, with flowers growing in it, decorated a yard. Crab traps were stacked near some houses.

Satisfied that we were impressed with his appearance and with his riding skills, Thackeray readily agreed to returning for a ride around the harbor on *Flipper*. With slight trepidation, he allowed us to leave his bike on shore, after we had locked it between ours to a utility pole.

From where *Delphina* was anchored, we couldn't see how extensive the harbor at Chance is. Around a marshy point, another section of the harbor has docks that line the banks. We went to that area on *Flipper* and saw many moored workboats.

One of the boats was a skipjack. Although it was in the water, I couldn't understand how it could float. Many of its galvanized fastenings were bleeding through peeling paint. Some of the fastenings had rusted entirely and had released their holds on the wood. Rot was rampant. The boat was a sorry sight.

We moved ahead, past another marsh, and saw another mast that had the telltale rake of a skipjack. As we got closer, we saw that this boat was in similar condition to the first.

"Well, I guess the bulk of the working fleet must be down in Wenona, just like we heard," I said as I tried to sound optimistic.

A low, gray sky greeted us the following morning. Rain was on the way; the only question was when it would arrive. Thackeray's spirits were not at all dampened, and he eagerly got ready for the ride to Wenona. But first we had to go to the fuel dock for gas for the outboard engine.

The proprietor of the fuel dock helped us to secure the dinghy near the gas pump. This facility is used almost exclusively by workboats, and the bulkhead was high and awkward to climb over. While I mixed in the oil and pumped the gas, the owner and my crew went inside the dock building, which served as the office, a hardware store, and a bait-and-tackle shop. After I finished filling the gas tank, I went inside to pay. Thackeray greeted me excitedly at the door.

"Captain Ken, guess what!" he said. "They moved the whole building from where it used to be!"

I looked over at the owner. He was smiling and nodding his head. He walked over to a bulletin board that had a couple of old photographs affixed to it.

"Yessir, this old place used to be the hotel buildin' over at the steamboat landin' on the Sound. Long time ago a hurri-ken come along and destroyed the landin'. Didn't hurt the buildin' much though. You can see a picture of it here. Some time ago they hauled it over the marsh and put it here. Been here ever since."

He spoke of this old building with as much pride as Trump would speak of his Tower. He was in his fifties and had the rugged features I associate with watermen. A warmth and friendliness radiated from him. In no hurry to see us go, he continued talking.

"Your missus here tells me you come here to see some skipjacks. Well, we got nine left here on Deal—two here in Chance, six down in Wenona, and one somewheres down in the Tidewater, takin' folks out on rides. Should be back for the season, though."

"It looked to me as if the ones we saw here need a lot of work. Will they have them ready to go for the races?" I asked him.

The skipjack races held each Labor Day weekend off Deal Island are well-known.

"Oh, yes, they'll get 'em ready somehow. Always do. But seems to me that with the arster problems we've had the last few years, the boys ain't puttin' back as much inta the boats as they gotta. I tell 'em, too, but they don't listen. Spend the money on somethin' else, they do. It's a shame."

I didn't want to leave this man, and I think he was sorry to see us leave, but the rain was not going to hold off all morning. It was time to saddle up.

The road to Wenona wound through little clumps of forest that alternated with small neighborhoods and marshland. The traffic was light, and the lack of a paved shoulder presented no problem.

We were in Wenona in less than an hour. The road ended at the waterfront, where a street went past a general store and a cluster of decrepit buildings. A large, unpaved lot with various items of debris scattered around its periphery dominated the scene. A crudely lettered, hand-painted sign was propped up on a discarded engine block. It read "Parking $2." No cars were in the lot.

The harbor area features finger piers attached to bulkheads that line the basin. Jutting out from one end of the basin is a long pier on which sat a dilapidated crab shanty with a dirty, misshapen couch in front of it. Old traps and discarded appliances were scattered around the sides of the shanty. Moored nearby was a skipjack in the same state of repair as the two we had seen at Chance. Directly ahead of me, as I looked at this skipjack, was a boat, in fine repair, that had the name *Dunrovin* painted on its transom. I thought its name better fit the skipjack.

Since it was the middle of the morning, most of the workboats were on the Bay, and the harbor was deserted. Although the clouds had added a serene quality to the countryside, on the waterfront they added a feeling of gloom. My mood was somber. Even Thackeray appeared reserved.

We rode over to the general store and entered. Inside were two elderly men and five women in their twenties and thirties. The men and women were in separate

Wenona waterfront, Deal Island

groups, having lively conversations. Other than giving us a quick glance as we walked in, both groups ignored us. The store was exactly as I had pictured a general store in a fishing village would look: nets and other commercial fishing gear were displayed next to food, hardware, and durables. I walked back to where fishing tackle was displayed. I was curious about the groups' conversations, but the women were drowning out any chance I had of hearing what the men were saying. From the little I could understand of the women's chatter, I thought their talk was regular small-town gossip. Joan and Thackeray didn't seem interested in either the people or the store, so we went outside.

After leaving the store, we turned right and walked down the street toward the decrepit buildings. Rounding the corner of one of these buildings, I saw a sight that, at first, didn't register. I stopped and stared. A condominium building, with the type of architecture that some people call trendy, was at the end of the street. In front of the building, the developer had built piers for the owners' yachts, thus upgrading the development perhaps to upscale.

My disappointment was acute. Before coming to this building, I had seen houses, places, and things, including the discarded engine blocks and appliances, the old couch, the derelict boats, and the "Parking $2" sign, that belonged on Deal Island. Everything was in harmony and added to the island's character. The condominium building, a recent addition, wasn't in harmony and didn't belong in that setting. As we walked back up the street to our bikes, I had a strong feeling that Deal Island had been violated.

We were anxious to find some more skipjacks, regardless of their state of repair, and we did: we saw five, besides the one we had seen by the crab shanty. One was in someone's front yard and had gaping holes through the

Skipjack, Wenona, Deal Island

frames where new planks were to be placed. Two others were nearby; one was sitting contentedly on the mud bottom, and her sister was tied to a pier next to her. And two others were secured to a pier and had had recent restoration work done on them. None of these boats looked capable of withstanding the rigors of a boat race or a full season dredging in the winter. But it was only the last day of July, after all.

The rain held off on the ride back to Chance, but the threat was greater. In two trips with *Flipper*, I took Joan, Thackeray, and the bikes to *Delphina*. With luck, we could get to Whitehaven, on the Wicomico River, before the rain came.

Joan and Thackeray, Deal Island

CHAPTER NINE

Wicomico River

We left the harbor before eleven. The clouds were getting blacker, and if a full-blown Chesapeake squall hit, I would rather be on open water than near the bridge at Chance. The course to the mouth of the Wicomico River, although exposed, offered anchoring room off the channel in moderate depths if a squall forced us to stop.

We were nearly at the mouth of Wicomico when a squall bore down on us. We quickly got out of the channel and anchored. It was impossible for us to continue: the strong winds were driving heavy sheets of rain which obstructed our vision. Anyway, it was lunchtime.

The squall lasted about a half hour. After I raised the anchor, we got under way again under a slowly clearing sky. The broad mouth of the Wicomico stretched before us and beckoned us to enter.

Seven miles up the river is the village of Whitehaven, where we planned to stay and have dinner ashore at the Red Roost Restaurant. The following morning we would travel the remaining thirteen miles to Salisbury.

Waterfowl were numerous as we slowly motored up the river past marshy banks. Many egrets and herons waded near the tall grass, while other birds flew past us. Overhead, an osprey soared in a wide circle.

Nearly every aid to navigation on this river was crowned with a sprawling osprey nest. In one nest we saw three adults, and I wondered about their relationship. On two occasions, as we neared a nest, one of two ospreys in the nest flew off. Each time, the osprey that had flown off circled and constantly watched the nest. The bird left behind raised a hellish din, and its sharp beak flashed in the sunshine. The osprey in the air convinced me it would swoop down on anything that dared to try to disturb the nest and, with its vicious claws, would slash the intruder.

DDT decimated this magnificent species, and it's heartening to see the ospreys making such a strong comeback. Federal law prohibits disturbing their nests, and I'm always amused whenever I see that the Coast Guard, maintaining a navigational aid that an osprey family has built a nest on, has had to replace that aid with a buoy alongside it to avoid harming the nest.

Osprey nest atop aid to navigation (Note replacement buoy)

The river narrowed, and Whitehaven soon appeared. Whitehaven is an old community, settled in the mid-1600s. A cable ferry, one of the nation's oldest in continuous use, crosses the river at the eastern end of the village. The beautiful Victorian and colonial homes, nestled on the shore, add a storybook quality to the peaceful scene.

Although it was early afternoon, nobody was visible on the streets of the village. The only motion we saw was the ferry plodding across the river. Whitehaven looked like our kind of place. But where could we tie up?

The small marina was full of boats. The only available space was on its outer bulkhead, but that was the fuel dock. We couldn't stay there. Just before the marina was another bulkhead that fronted a small, well-kept park. Our chart indicated deep water right up to shore. In the absence of a "No Trespassing" sign, I decided to tie up to that bulkhead.

Whitehaven waterfront

After unloading the bikes, I went to find someone to pay for our dockage. The two-story marina building was a logical place to seek information. I found no office on the first floor, so I climbed the stairs to the second floor and tried the only door I saw. It was locked. Looking in a window, I saw that it was someone's home. Thankful that the door was locked, I returned downstairs. There was no sign of an office anywhere.

Thackeray came over and joined me, and we headed toward the ferry landing. The ferry was small, capable of carrying only a few vehicles. An elderly couple in a late-model car arrived at the landing as we walked up. The captain motioned the driver to drive onto the ferry. The driver did so, but hesitantly, as though he was frightened the ferry might sink from the car's weight. He parked the car at the forward end of the ferry and turned off the engine. The couple remained in the car.

Anxious to go to sea again, Thackeray spoke up.

"Captain Ken, can we go for a ride on it?"

The trip across the river and back would be fun for both of us, and the friendly-looking captain might be a good source of information.

"Good afternoon, Captain. May we come along for a ride?" I asked.

"Why, sure. Come on aboard," he answered from his tiny cabin on the side of the ferry.

I introduced myself and Thackeray. The captain introduced himself as Chuck Taylor.

Thackeray and I studied the features of the boat as we went across the river. The ferry soon arrived at the other shore, where a road led into the marsh.

The car didn't get off the ferry, and the driver kept putting the transmission in and out of gear with no result. I noticed the car had a rental sticker on its rear bumper. Captain Chuck, seeing that the car wasn't leaving, came over to the passenger side of the car. The woman looked up at the captain and rolled down her window. With a heavy French accent, she told him that her husband couldn't speak English very well.

"We have had no problem with this automobile before," she said. "Will you kindly help my husband?"

Captain Chuck smiled, walked around to the driver's side, and looked in the window. The man, looking puzzled, continued running through the gears.

Still smiling, and in a soft voice, the captain said, "Excuse me, sir, but I'm sure that if you turn the key to start the engine you won't have any problem gettin' the car movin' again."

Captain Chuck pointed to the key ring on the steering column.

The man looked up at the captain, nodded in grateful acknowledgment, and turned the key. The car roared to life and was soon off the ferry.

Captain Chuck looked at me as if to say, "All in a day's work."

A pickup truck boarded, and the captain got the ferry moving again. On the way back, he gave me directions to the Red Roost Restaurant and told me that he thought the bulkhead to which *Delphina* was tied was owned by the people in the house directly across the street from the little park. When we arrived back at the landing, Joan was waiting for us. No one was in line to go across the river, so Joan came on board and joined us as Captain Chuck talked about his work.

"Most of my life I spent crabbin' and tongin' fer arsters, then this job on the ferry come along, and I took it. It's a county job and has some good benefits. Now that I'm gettin' older that's important to me. Still go crabbin' though, one day a week. I'll be goin' tomorra."

"What kind of hours do you have running the ferry?" I asked.

"I run it sunup to sundown, six days a week. Makes

for a long day in the summer. Wednesdays another fella takes 'er. That's when I go crabbin'. Should do all right tomorra. Friend of mine got twenty-two bushels yesterday."

"How many trips do you make in a day?" Joan asked.

"Well, depends. One day, I think it was on Memorial Day weekend, I had a hundred and two trips. Usually it's not that many."

He told us that the other cable ferry on the Wicomico, at Upper Ferry, was in Cambridge being fitted with a diesel engine.

"They were runnin' it with an outboard. Kept burnin' 'm up, so they decided to go with a diesel."

Two cars pulled up at the landing for the trip across. The captain invited Joan to come along for the ride, and she eagerly accepted. He also let Thackeray and me ride again.

On the return trip, I had a great idea.

"Captain Chuck, is it okay if I take a picture of my nephew sitting next to you?" I asked.

The captain's whole face beamed his answer. He moved over to allow Thackeray entry to the little cabin and kept right on smiling. I thought he enjoyed our company as much as we enjoyed his.

Since we still didn't see any sign of life in town, we decided to go for a bike ride and find the restaurant. The directions given me by the captain were involved, and I didn't want to get lost on the way to dinner.

We had been told about the Red Roost Restaurant by a couple in Florida. The restaurant is a converted chicken house in the country and is enormously popular. Its menu features different dinners with all the steamed crabs you can eat.

The restaurant is located about three miles outside Whitehaven, and the ride took less than a half hour on roads through beautiful pastureland and forest. At the restaurant, we were told by the owner's son, managing in his father's absence, that someone from the restaurant would come to Whitehaven and pick us up for dinner.

"We do it a lot for people who come to Whitehaven by boat," he said.

When we told him we would be coming by bike, he said, "Well, give us a call if you change your mind, or if it looks like rain. Be a good idea if you get here when we open at five thirty. It'll save you a wait."

Back at Whitehaven a half hour later, we saw someone on shore. A man was digging a ditch on the edge of the little park near the marina. I walked up to him. Thackeray followed me.

"Good afternoon," I said, "that's our boat on the bulkhead there. Is it your bulkhead?"

The man was in his sixties. He stopped his work.

"No, it's not. It belongs to the people in that house. They don't seem to be home now. I don't see their car."

"Do you know if they'd mind our being tied up there?"

"I don't think so. You can check with them when they get back."

A car pulled up on the street next to us. The driver was a middle-aged woman.

The man said to her, "Dear, that lovely schooner belongs to these people."

The man told us that he and his wife, the woman in the car, had bought the marina a few years back and had moved to Whitehaven to "get away from it all." They had succeeded beyond their dreams.

"We haven't known any stress at all since we moved here," his wife added. "Everybody should find a place like this!"

I asked her if they lived in the house at the marina, and she said they did.

"Well, I almost walked right into your house. I thought it was the marina office. I'm glad you had the door locked!"

They both laughed, and she said, "That happens quite often. Maybe I should put a little sign up."

While we were talking, a car pulled up in front of the bulkhead-owner's house, and an elderly couple got out of the car, entered the house, and closed the door behind them. I excused myself and went to the house and knocked. The woman answered the door. She was in her eighties, at least.

"Good afternoon, ma'am. That's my boat tied up on your bulkhead. Is it okay with you for us to be there?"

"Why, yes, I suppose so."

"Thank you. How much do I owe you for the privilege?"

She was taken aback by this question and became flustered.

"Well, I don't really know. Why don't you ask the man who owns the marina what would be fair?"

I said I would and returned to the man working in the park.

When I explained what I needed to know, he smiled and said, "$15.00 is fair. That's what we get for a night."

I returned to the woman and gave her the money. She seemed embarrassed by the transaction. Either I was the first boater who ever moored to her bulkhead, or I was the first who offered to pay.

Dinner at the Red Roost that night was perfect. Thackeray, not excited at the prospect of cracking open crabs, chose a child's chicken platter. He also talked us into letting him have a Coke and a dish of ice cream. Joan and I ordered all-you-can-eat steamed crabs, fried chicken, clam and shrimp crisps, corn on the cob, and hush puppies, plus a large pitcher of beer. Dinner was terribly messy, absolutely delicious, and wonderfully fun.

We resumed the trip up the river early the next morning. After passing through more marshes, the river went through rolling farmland. Farmhouses and small landings, alternating with an occasional mansion, appeared on the shore. As we neared the outskirts of Salisbury, the homes became more numerous and more ornate. I couldn't recall ever having been on a more scenic river. Even Thackeray was engrossed in the sights.

We would have to tie up in Salisbury since our chart indicated no room to anchor there. Our guidebook said the city had recently completed building a marina, and we were planning to stay there for the night. We had the current with us all the way from Whitehaven, and the current would influence how we would approach the dock. Since a slight breeze was blowing off the dock, I wanted to turn the boat around and head into the current. This maneuver would allow me to place *Delphina*'s starboard side gently against the pilings.

Informing Joan of my plan, I swung *Delphina* around into the current while Joan waited to step off with a bow

House on the shore of the Wicomico River

line. As soon as she could, Joan jumped onto the dock with the line and put a wrap around a piling. At the same time, a gust of wind hit *Delphina*'s stern and forced it out into the river. No current offset the wind, and when I reversed to regain control, the stern went more to port. No way were we going to get *Delphina* to the dock on that attempt. I asked Joan to throw the bow line back onto *Delphina*. After tossing the line, she stayed on the dock. Meanwhile, the dockmaster had come out of his office and was walking toward Joan.

Fortunately, Joan had set up dock lines on both sides of the boat; I planned to approach from the other direction. Gravely, I informed Thackeray that he would be responsible for throwing the bow line to Joan when I gave him the word.

"Ooookay, Captain Ken, noooo problem!" he said.

His assurance filled me with confidence.

The second attempt went without incident, and *Delphina* was secured. I didn't want the dockmaster to think I was some idiot who couldn't maneuver his boat, so I explained what had happened with the wind and the nonexistent current. He chuckled.

"That happens a lot," he informed me. "The wind kinda funnels down here. People are always getting fooled."

I like dockmasters who understand the hazards we captains have to deal with.

The Port of Salisbury Marina is located within walking distance of the downtown area and the zoo, so we had no need to use our bicycles.

Salisbury's zoo has been called one of the finest of its type in North America, and we wanted to go there before seeing any other sights. On our way to the zoo, we strolled through the downtown area, which has been converted into a pedestrian mall. We came to the Chamber of Commerce and picked up brochures and a map. We studied them while we ate lunch at a deli in the next block. We had only that afternoon to see the sights in Salisbury, and we chose to explore the historic Newtown section of the city, which has many fine examples of Victorian architecture, rather than visit the Ward Museum of Wildfowl Art at Salisbury State University.

After walking through the spacious Salisbury City Park, where we watched a boy catch a large turtle on his fishing line, we reached the zoo. Many people were also visiting that afternoon, but we never felt crowded. Unlike major zoos, this zoo doesn't feature large animals, but it does have a collection of small animals that will please any visitor. The zoo takes great pride in their rare spectacled bears, but that afternoon the bears were bashful and didn't come over to greet us when we arrived at their cage. We spent some entertaining moments watching the antics of prairie dogs as they went about their lives in their large prairie-dog town. One of the little guys was

Pedestrian mall, downtown Salisbury

clever enough to get outside the fence that ran around his town, and he led the keepers on a merry chase until he was recaptured by a man wielding a butterfly net.

On our way to the Newtown district, we stopped at a convenience store for some cold, liquid refreshment. Thackeray and Joan got soft drinks; I got a beer. We went outside to enjoy our drinks, but halfway through drinking my beer, I was informed by a store clerk that I was breaking the law by drinking beer in public. I quickly chugalugged the remainder before the police came to haul me away, and we left.

The architecture we saw in Newtown was varied and intriguing. In addition to the Victorian houses, we saw the Poplar Hill Mansion, a Georgian-style house built in 1805. Despite his sore feet and tired legs, Thackeray also enjoyed the area and took great pleasure in photographing a fine example of a Gothic-style church.

When we returned to the boat late that afternoon, Thackeray asked permission to visit the dockmaster in his office.

"After you take a shower, you can visit until it's time to eat," I told him.

Thackeray left immediately for the marina's shower facilities.

While Joan was preparing dinner, I went to the office to find out what Thackeray and the dockmaster were talking about. Entering the office, I saw the dockmaster and two of his friends. Thackeray was in the next room playing a Nintendo game by himself.

"Captain Ken, I won! I won!" he shouted when he saw me.

I looked over at the dockmaster, smiling sheepishly behind his desk. He nodded.

"The kid's good, gotta give him credit."

Thackeray tried to get me involved, but I told him dinner was almost ready.

As Thackeray dried the last dinner dish, he looked up and saw the tour boat *Maryland Lady* returning to its berth after its dinner cruise.

"Captain Ken, is it okay if I go meet the driver?"

"Sure, but it's the captain, not the driver. Let's both go over."

Thackeray asked Joan to come with us, but she informed him that she would be doing laundry since there was a laundromat at the marina.

"Let me have any dirty clothes you want washed," she told him.

Thackeray gave Joan a few items of clothing. Then he reverently handed her his red sneakers.

"Please wash these, too, Captain Joan. They got dirty from that walk today."

Joan was stunned. I was amused. Thackeray was serious. The sneakers looked as clean as they had before the walk, but after all, they were part of his cycling outfit and had to be *pristine*.

"Thackeray, I hate to disappoint you, but I'm not washing your sneakers," Joan told him. "They aren't dirty! I'm only washing clothes."

"Ooookay, Captain Joan! Whatever you say!"

Thackeray is a most agreeable kid.

I walked toward the pier where *Maryland Lady* was moored. Thackeray, in his eagerness to meet the captain, had run ahead and was talking to the first mate on the dock. The captain, dressed in whites with shoulder boards denoting his rank, was talking to two of his passengers at the foot of the gangway. Arriving at the gangway, I waited until the captain was free. Meanwhile, the first mate had returned to the boat, and Thackeray joined me.

"Good evening, Captain," I greeted the captain as soon as the passengers had left. "My nephew wanted to meet the captain, so here we are. We're from the schooner tied up on the outside pier. I'm Ken Carter, and this is Thackeray Carter."

"I'm Dick Smith, and I'm glad you came! I noticed your boat out there. All the way from Florida, huh? We get very few out-of-state boats up here."

I asked him about the tours on *Maryland Lady*.

"Well, we have a ninety-minute sightseeing trip on the Wicomico, and longer trips when we serve lunch or dinner. We just returned from our two-and-a-half-hour dinner cruise. We can cover a lot of the river in that time, all the way down to the country club. Do you remember seeing that on your way up?"

"Yes, I do," I replied.

Thackeray had his mind on the economics of the tour-boat business.

"How many people did you have on your trip tonight?" he asked.

"Tonight we had only sixteen, but it varies a lot. Tomorrow night we're filled up with a hundred and twenty people."

Thackeray's interest turned to boat handling.

"Do you ever have any trouble docking up?" he asked.

Captain Dick laughed.

"I sure used to! On a lot of the trips we left on, I wasn't sure what slip I'd be tying up in when we got back. The boat didn't have big enough engines, and also the wind blew us around a lot. Then I had new diesel engines put in. Now, even if it's blowing twenty-five knots, I can dock without too many problems. Before the new engines, I would have had to cancel. Now tell me, how did you like your trip up the river?"

"I liked it," Thackeray said.

"You'll be here a couple of days, I guess," Captain Dick stated.

"No," I said. "We'll be pulling out first thing in the morning."

"Oh, no! Don't do that!" he pleaded. "You owe your-selves more than half a day in Salisbury!"

"I'm sure you're right," I answered, "but we have to be in Solomons on Sunday."

He seemed genuinely sad that we had to leave.

As we left the captain, he said, "Well, please come here again next time you're in the Bay."

We'd be in the Honga River the next day and far away from a city. I wondered if the people living in the communities along that river could possibly be any friendlier than the people we had met on the Wicomico River.

CHAPTER TEN

Honga River

The trip back down the Wicomico was as rewarding as the trip up had been. If the river wasn't so far from the boating centers on the Bay, I'm sure more boaters would visit this charming area.

As we passed Whitehaven, we looked for our friend the ferry captain. The ferry was tied to the landing on the Whitehaven side with no one aboard. Maybe Captain Chuck was taking a break. We continued on.

Some of the most remote watermen's communities are on the Honga River. On the river's western shore are the Hooper Islands and the villages of Honga, Fishing Creek, and Hoopersville; on the eastern shore is a peninsula and the village of Wingate. Far from the busy highways to the ocean, the roads leading to these areas go through desolate marshes that are often flooded in heavy rains. We were looking forward to going into the Honga River to see how watermen *really* live, in communities tourists never visit. Of course, *we* were not tourists; we were *travelers*.

After a careful study of our charts and guidebooks, I wasn't confident about entering any of the harbors along the Honga River with *Delphina*. Depths were questionable, and I couldn't tell, if we succeeded in entering a harbor, whether there would be a place to tie up or room to turn around.

I decided to anchor in seven feet of water near the channel leading to Wingate. The area was exposed, and we would have a long dinghy ride to the harbor, but the weather was settled.

With our outboard going full speed, it took only ten minutes to reach the harbor. A large fleet of workboats was moored there. Two packing plants, one on each side of the harbor, gave the place a distinctly commercial flavor. A pleasure boat would not have felt at home.

We tied *Flipper* to a bulkhead, scrambled ashore, and walked to the nearest packing plant. A dump truck was parked outside one of the plant's doors. The back of the truck was full of crab shells, the detritus from a day's pickings. Nearby, a worker was loading bushel baskets full of live crabs onto a large pickup truck. The area seemed so dry and desolate that I thought I was somewhere in the Great American West instead of Chesapeake Bay country.

We walked down the only road and came to a general store. I wanted a fresh salad to go with dinner and some fresh ground beef to add to the spaghetti sauce. The store appeared to be a good place to get everything. We went inside.

Two women were behind the counter. The store and the village looked like interesting places, and I hoped to learn something about them.

"Boy, Wingate's pretty far away from anything else, isn't it?" I said in a cheerful, friendly voice.

The older woman frowned.

The younger woman said, "WIN-get."

"I beg your pardon?"

"WIN-get. You say WIN-get," she explained patiently.

"Oh, I'm sorry! WIN-get. Well! Uh, may I please have a pound of ground beef?"

"It's all frozen," the older woman said.

General store, Wingate

"I'm sorry?"

"The ground beef's all frozen. I can't sell you just a pound."

Her patience with me was saintly.

"Well, okay then. How about a couple of tomatoes and a head of lettuce?"

I knew those wouldn't be frozen.

She reached under the counter and got two beautiful tomatoes. She picked up a large head of lettuce from a compartment near a freezer.

"Anything else?" she asked.

Inspiration hit me.

"Do you have any soft crabs?" I asked.

Her expression changed. She looked interested.

"Not here in the store. Got some at home though. Let me call my husband, and he'll bring 'em over. How many you want?"

Remembering our dinner of a dozen at Onancock, I

replied, "A dozen."

She phoned her husband and told him to bring a dozen crabs to the store. She hung up, and I smiled and began to wait for her husband. The woman had no desire to talk to me, and I didn't know how to talk to her. The younger woman was helping another customer find peach ice cream. Joan was busy monitoring Thackeray's efforts to select candy and cookies. I amused myself looking at the items stocked on the shelves.

A big, heavy man, rubbing sleep out of his eyes, came out of the back room to investigate the strangers in the store. He asked Joan where she was from, and they had a conversation about Florida. The man had vacationed there in the past.

About fifteen minutes after the older woman had called her husband, a man entered the store with a package, handed it to her, and left without looking at us or saying a word. I went to the register to pay.

"How much are the crabs?" I asked.

"$15.00."

I thought I saw a fleeting look of guilt and challenge on her face before her expression changed to deadpan.

I reached deeply into my pocket for the money and paid with a smile. This woman was not going to know that I knew I had been taken.

On the way back to the dinghy, I tried to justify my extravagance to Joan.

"What could I do after her husband went to all that trouble to bring them to the store? If I had any intelligence at all, I would have asked the price before I ordered them. Believe me, it won't happen again."

When we returned to *Delphina,* Joan opened the package of soft crabs. They were large enough for three meals, not at all like the small ones we had bought in Onancock. The woman had given us more than our money's worth.

We had dinner accompanied by swarms of houseflies that had come aboard during our absence. We had some flypaper, which I hung up without effect. Other than shooing the pests away, we had limited options for getting rid of the nuisance. We certainly didn't want the boat littered with fly carcasses. Fortunately, as we turned out the lights and went to bed, the flies quit bothering us.

The Patuxent River, across the Bay, was our goal for the next day. I was confident we'd get there, but I wasn't sure we'd have any wind to sail. For Thackeray's sake, I hoped we would.

CHAPTER ELEVEN

Patuxent River

The dog days of August settled over the Chesapeake. The coolness of dawn was quickly overtaken by the rising sun. For every degree the sun gained in elevation, the thermometer followed suit. Or so it seemed.

As *Delphina* slowly powered her way through the large fleet of workboats engaged in crabbing on the Honga River, I debated with myself whether to raise the sails. The winds were forecast to be light and variable for our crossing of the Bay to the Patuxent River, and that forecast almost always comes true. But this was also the last opportunity for Thackeray to reinforce his skills at hoisting headsails, to steer the boat under sail, and to use the knots he had learned and practiced all week. Also, he had not learned how to tack. I decided that we would sail.

Thackeray hoisted the jib and staysail and secured each halyard to a belaying pin with a figure eight and a half hitch. I was lazy in the heat; Joan was ambitious: she raised the remaining two sails. Although the wind was light, the sails filled nicely. I turned off the engine, and we moved slowly along.

Joan showed an avid Thackeray how to read the depths on a chart and how far we could safely continue on this course. After she explained to Thackeray what was involved in coming about, Joan let him take the helm while she handled the sheets. On the next tack, they changed positions. They were having a marvelous time. Then the ogre stepped in.

"I hate to spoil your fun," I said, "but at this rate we'll never get across the Bay. We have to use the engine."

After being obedient all week, Thackeray protested.

"But Captain Ken, I'm learning how to attack!" he said.

I nearly fell off the boat. In her patient voice, trying hard not to laugh, Joan explained to her pupil that the proper term is "to tack."

"I'm really proud of how much you've learned already, Thackeray," I said. "But we've got to get moving."

Reluctantly my crew agreed, and they furled the sails. The noise from the engine was most unpleasant as we motored across the Bay.

It was Friday. Thackeray wouldn't meet his parents at Solomons until Sunday at noon, so we were going to visit Sotterly Plantation, a former colonial tobacco plantation, located on the south shore of the Patuxent. We planned to anchor that afternoon at a place with the intriguing name of Cuckold Creek and ride our bikes to the plantation the next day.

As we entered the mouth of the Patuxent, I was surprised by the large number of sailboats we saw; most of them had their sails up. Just as the Chesapeake is a special body of water, it breeds a special class of sailors —those with infinite patience.

Douglass Wallop, in his novel *Regatta*, describes this characteristic with a description of a major sailboat race. The entire racing fleet, after a slow leg down the Bay, became becalmed. The current, which had been favorable, changed direction, and the boats dropped their anchors so they wouldn't be carried back up the Bay. This is the only circumstance I can think of that would cause all the competitors to come to a deliberate stop in the middle of a hotly contested race. It takes patience to race a boat while it's anchored.

The boats that were sailing were doing about one knot, but their sails were full of air and their crews were full of joy. Sometimes I wonder if, over the years, I have forgotten the simple pleasure of slowly sailing along while experiencing the harmony of wind, water, and boat. As a cruising sailor, I'm always trying to get somewhere, and if I can't get there under sail at four knots, I use the engine. The majority of Chesapeake sailors that we encountered on our journey don't have this compulsion. They truly understand what sailing is all about.

It was after three o'clock as we passed under the high fixed bridge that spans the Patuxent at Solomons. A couple of anchorages are up Cuckold Creek, and our guidebooks listed a couple of marinas. We anchored near Blackstone Marina. This marina has a bulkhead that goes around the property and that provides plenty of space to leave a dinghy without its being in anyone's way.

Flipper carried Joan, me and our bikes toward the marina, while Thackeray waited aboard *Delphina* for me to return for him and his bike. As we neared the bulkhead, a man in his sixties walked over with a big smile on his face.

"How may I help you?" he asked.

"Is it okay if we leave our dinghy here?" I asked him.

"Nope."

"Where should we leave it?"

"Nowhere here."

He was still smiling broadly.

"Even if we pay?"

"That's right. We don't allow anchored boats to leave dinghies here."

I was stunned.

"You know, this is the first marina I've ever been to where we weren't allowed to tie up, period," I said.

The man was enjoying himself immensely. His smile got broader.

"You have a logbook, don't you?" he asked.

"Yes, of course."

"Then you can enter this as a 'first,' can't you?"

He was full of glee. I expected him to start rubbing his hands together.

"I'm very sorry to have caused you this trouble," I told him.

As we pulled away from the bulkhead, I felt very depressed. What was going on? Had we entered an area where this attitude would be commonplace? Were we undesirables because we chose to anchor? Looking at Joan's face, I could see she also was depressed.

"Ken, let's just go to the other marina and see if we can leave the dinghy there. It's not much farther."

We headed directly toward Weeks Marina, about a quarter mile away. I saw Thackeray watching us from *Delphina*'s foredeck rail; he was probably as confused as we were. If Weeks Marina also rejected us, I didn't know what we'd do. Thackeray was excited about riding his bike to Sotterly. The twelve-mile round-trip would be a record distance for him. Not wanting to disappoint him, I had to find a place to unload the bikes and leave the dinghy.

We neared the marina. A man in his fifties was walking toward us. I dreaded a repeat rejection.

"Howdy, folks! You can just leave your dinghy here, or you might want to bring it around to the other side. There's less wake there," he said.

"Well, this is great right here. Thank you!"

Relief was evident in my voice.

The man turned around and walked back to the office building. Quickly we unloaded our bikes, and I left to get

Thackeray.

"What was that all about, Captain Ken?" he asked when I returned to *Delphina*. "I didn't know where you and Captain Joan were going!"

I told him what had happened, and we loaded his bike. While we headed toward the marina, I reminded him about the next day's bike ride.

"This afternoon's almost gone, so we'll just have a quick ride today to see what the roads are like. We don't want you getting all worn out."

Joan greeted us as we got to the marina.

"These are the nicest people here! The man who came down here is the owner. I went up to the office, and his wife told me that he would leave the showers open for us."

"That's great! What a difference from the other place! Well, let's get *Flipper* squared away, and I'll go see what we owe."

We unloaded Thackeray's bike and went up to the office. The owner, his wife, and another man were sitting on lawn chairs in the shade of the building.

Smiling at the owner and his wife, I said, "We sure appreciate your letting us tie up here! How much do we owe you?"

"Oh, you don't owe us anything!" the owner replied. "We're just glad we could help out! Now remember, you can move your dinghy around to the other side if you like."

Our map showed that Route 235 is the main road to Sotterly Plantation. We rode two miles to the road that leads to Route 235 and saw that the road has a paved shoulder. The traffic wasn't heavy, but it might be heavy the next day because of the weekend. Satisfied that the ride wouldn't be too difficult or dangerous, we returned to *Delphina*.

Thackeray's energy level was high, and Joan and I

helped him burn off some of this energy by having a sing-along with him after dinner. He was excited about the next day's challenging bike ride and had a little trouble getting to sleep.

The morning arrived with the promise of another hot, hazy, and windless day. We would have to pace ourselves riding. We discovered that a new Route 235 had been built, and the old route, carrying less traffic, is still in use. We took the old route until we came to Route 245, a country road with little traffic, that goes through farm-land to Sotterly Plantation. Arriving before the planta-tion was scheduled to open, we sat at a table under the shade of an oak tree and had a snack. Thackeray was still going strong and was confident he would set a new distance record that day.

Perhaps what sets Sotterly apart from other colonial plantations that are open for public viewing is that the visitor has the feeling of being in a home that has been allowed to age like fine wine. Built before 1730, the house has classic elegance. The original roofline is intact and is graced with massive chimneys. A formal garden and an adjacent orchard complement the surroundings. The lawn, groomed by a flock of sheep, rolls down to the river.

We were guided through the house by a woman wearing her normal street clothing. Well versed in much of the historical trivia of the plantation, she entertained us with anecdotes about the current and former owners. Asking all the members of our group questions about our-selves in a friendly way, she was as interested in us as we were in the house. An exemplary guide, she should write a how-to book.

After the house tour, we wandered along the same old road where hogsheads of tobacco once were rolled to waiting ships. We passed one of the many slave cabins that used to line the road. The only cabin left, it served into this century as the home of a woman born in it as a slave.

The plantation is a working farm, and its gift shop sells some of the products produced there. Thackeray, usually frugal, bought his parents a jar of strawberry jam and his brother a coloring history book. We tried to buy one of their country hams, but the foreman informed us the hams weren't cured yet.

We pedaled out the tree-lined drive, and I gave the grand, old plantation one last look. The place has an unmistakable aura of warmth and homeliness, as do the people working there.

Halfway back to Weeks Marina, we stopped at a convenience store to buy hot dogs and cold drinks. Although we were working up a sweat, Thackeray said he could just keep rolling along, "noooo problem!"

Soon we were back at the dinghy, and Thackeray posed for pictures. He had set himself a goal, worked hard to realize it, and was going to have something to

Sotterly Plantation

remember it by.

It was mid-afternoon when we got back aboard *Delphina* and stowed the bikes. We agreed, instead of staying in Cuckold Creek, we would go to Solomons and anchor in Back Creek. As I raised the two anchors I had set, people were waterskiing around us, and the boats' wakes caused *Delphina* to bob gently. We powered down Cuckold Creek to where it flows into the Patuxent. There we had an incredible and distressing experience.

A small sailboat, about twenty-two feet long and under power, was taking a shortcut across a shoal. The boat's course brought it close to a navigational light that was topped with an osprey nest, occupied by a lone osprey. When the boat arrived at the light, the four people in the boat, two men and two women, yelled at the osprey. The people so terrified the poor bird that it flew away. Apparently, the people thought that scaring ospreys was great sport, since the bird's flight was followed by howls of laughter from the boat. The bird did not return. The boat altered course and came alongside us.

Of course, I should have said something about their outrageous behavior, but I have learned that words don't register with such people. At best, they'd tell me to mind my own business; at worst, they'd pull out a gun and shoot me. I kept quiet.

The man steering, a quintessential example of a big, fat slob, yelled over, "Hey, did you people really sail that thing up from Florida?"

"Yes, we did," I said.

"Man, you gotta be nuts!" he hollered back.

Then he pushed his tiller over, increased the throttle, and moved rapidly away from us.

Our guidebooks did not prepare me for the sight that greeted us in Solomons. As we entered the harbor, we saw row after row of masts stretching ad infinitum until they disappeared into the haze. A *lot* of boats were there. We slowly motored up Back Creek and passed one marina after another. Despite all the boat slips in the harbor, we managed to find a lovely spot to anchor near the head of the creek between two waterfront condominium projects that had piers for their owners' yachts. The Calvert Marine Museum provides a floating dinghy dock for visiting boaters, and we left *Flipper* there when we went ashore the next morning. Joan and Thackeray were going to Mass, and Our Lady Star of the Sea Catholic Church was a short walk from the museum. I left my crew at the church and walked toward the south end of the island.

Solomons, unlike many of the communities on Chesapeake Bay, doesn't have a colonial heritage. It was founded in 1865 by Isaac Solomon, who bought part of a farm on Somervell Island and erected buildings for an oyster-processing plant. Much of what is Solomons today is built on the oyster shells discarded by the plant. From the oyster industry, ancillary businesses were begun, and Solomons became a prosperous maritime community. At the turn of the century, sailing vessels, engaged in the lucrative commercial fishing industry, were everywhere on the waters around Solomons. By the 1930s, however, the large sailing fleets in the area were greatly reduced in size, as many of the vessels were changed from sail power to engine power. As word about the excellent fishing in the waters around Solomons spread, sportfishermen came, and a charter-fishing fleet grew in response. By the late 1930s, Solomons had become a resort area.

During World War II, Solomons was a training center for amphibious warfare, and thousands of troops passed through the area. But the hardships caused by the war brought a decline in the number of tourists visiting the community.

By the late 1970s, however, people were coming to

Solomons in unprecedented numbers. The Governor Thomas Johnson Bridge was completed in 1977 and provided ready access to Solomons and the rest of Calvert County for thousands of residents of St. Mary's County, including military personnel from the Patuxent Naval Air Station.

Yachtsmen, discouraged by high-priced dockage and crowded waters in the Annapolis area, looked south and found a perfect natural harbor in Solomons and uncrowded cruising in the nearby waters. More and better highways made it easy for them to drive to the area. Existing marinas expanded in response to the demand. New ones opened. By the late 1980s, over fifteen hundred boat slips filled the harbor at Solomons, and more were under construction. Comfort Inn and Holiday Inn built large hotels with marinas for their guests who arrive by boat. Condominiums sprouted up to accommodate those seeking a vacation home away from an urban environment. And all this growth has occurred in a community of seven hundred permanent, year-round residents.

The boaters are happy, the marinas are full, the hotels are hosting tourists and conventions, exclusive gift shops are numerous, fine restaurants are crowded, the Calvert Marine Museum is bustling with visitors, the charter fleet is going out daily, and the three churches on the island are packed for services.

But some things have gone wrong. Not everyone is happy with the success. Culture shock has struck some of the longtime residents, as great changes have occurred in their quiet way of life. People who opened trendy shops in anticipation of an affluent clientele have found that the market may be growing, but so are the expenses and the competition. Some residents are worried that their lovely town may go the way of Ocean City—too much honky-tonk. Others, no longer able to pay the rent or the real estate taxes, are forced to move away. Of course, such problems are not unique to Solomons; they are the typical effects of rapid changes on a population and its community.

I turned around at the end of the island and walked back the way I had come. Spiritually refreshed, my crew met me on the steps of the church.

We took *Flipper* back to *Delphina,* and Thackeray packed his gear. The week had gone by quickly, and Thackeray had learned a lot. And so had we, of course. It is a rewarding experience to see life through the eyes of a child, and we were blessed with doing this for a week with none of the diversions most adults have. And Thackeray has such fine eyes to see through.

The dockmaster at the Holiday Inn Marina, though busy, was friendly and let us tie up there. Inside the hotel, hundreds of people were milling about. Still, we had no problem finding Tom, Wendy, and John Austen.

Catholic Church (left) and Episcopalian Church, Solomons

We were soon eating lunch as guests of Tom and Wendy.

After lunch, we went to the Calvert Marine Museum, a facility that has grown greatly since its inception in 1970. From one room of exhibits, it has grown to include the old Drum Point lighthouse (which was moved from the mouth of the Patuxent River to the museum's property in 1975), a shed full of original Chesapeake Bay watercraft, a boat basin, the former Lore Oyster House, a bugeye that is the oldest licensed passenger vessel on the Bay, and a large, modern building housing exhibits.

After the happy experience of touring the museum, we had the sad experience of saying farewell to our little shipmate.

"Don't be sad, Captain Ken," Thackeray said. "There's always next year, you know. Ooookay?"

When Joan and I returned to *Delphina,* the boat seemed terribly empty. Despite what Thackeray had said, I couldn't shake the sadness. But the next day we would be back on the Eastern Shore. Thinking about Dorchester County, the Heart of the Eastern Shore, cheered me up.

CHAPTER TWELVE

Little Choptank River

Anyone watching us leave Solomons would have thought we were being chased out by every sailboat in town. Having left our anchorage on Back Creek at first light, we were the first sailboat into the Patuxent from Solomons. About an hour later, the first boats of a race fleet left their moorings in Solomons and entered the Patuxent behind us. Our departure coincided with the first day of the Audi/Yachting Race Week. The wind was from the west, and many of the racing crews deployed colorful spinnakers as the boats left the harbor. We had to be content with only our foresail catching the breeze, so soon after we passed Drum Point, most of the racing fleet was catching up to us. From the air it must have looked like the posse was about to capture the bad guys.

After we had rounded Cove Point, we hoisted the other sails, and *Delphina* was soon barreling along. The sky didn't show any hope for sunshine; in fact, it looked as if it was going to rain. Soon the drizzle came and lowered visibility to a half mile.

Our destination was an anchorage in Church Creek, off Fishing Creek. To get to Fishing Creek, we had to go up the Little Choptank River about six miles. Entry to this river, for boats coming from the south, is around

James Island and requires careful navigation. Fortunately, we were able to find the aids to navigation despite the poor visibility, and we soon were at the mouth of Fishing Creek. Fishing Creek was our first opportunity to navigate a creek strictly by depth sounder and by what we could see on shore. The natural channel, down the middle of the serpentine creek, is bounded by shoal sides. Slowly we powered up the creek and counted each indentation on the shore. Without having touched bottom, we arrived at Church Creek, went in about a half mile, and anchored.

After we had set the second anchor, an officer of the Maryland Department of Natural Resources approached us in his patrol boat.

"Good afternoon! I see you folks are from Florida. Did you sail up?" he asked.

I told him we had, and he told us he also was a sailor and did a lot of racing during his off-duty hours. I was curious whether he also had heard the midnight rendition of *Semper Fidelis*. This man looked like a former marine.

"By any chance, did you finish a race at St. Mary's City weekend before last?" I inquired.

"No. Why do you ask?"

"Just curious," I said. "We were there when a big fleet came in. Do you know if there's a place where we can tie up our dinghy in either Church Creek or Woolford?"

Church Creek is a town at the very head of the creek. Woolford is a town off the creek about a mile before.

"There's a commercial pier at Church Creek that the watermen use. You could tie up there."

He wished us a pleasant stay and left. Joan and I discussed the idea of an exploratory dinghy ride and decided against it. It was late, and we were hungry.

The following morning we had a long, but enjoyable, dinghy ride up the creek.

As we passed Old Trinity Church, the sun came out from behind the clouds, and the early morning rays slanted through the trees and lighted up some of the tombstones in the churchyard. Built in 1675, Old Trinity Church is the oldest Episcopal church in continuous use in the United States.

Near the head of the creek, we saw a dock, but it didn't look commercial. Three workboats were tied to it, but it extended from the backyard of someone's large, new house. We saw a space where we could tie *Flipper,* so we went closer. I noticed someone working on the engine of one of the workboats.

"Good morning, sir. Can you tell me if it's okay for us to leave our dinghy here?" I asked the bent-over form.

A man stood up.

"Well, now this ain't my place," he said. "The owner lives in that house there, and he's out crabbin'. But I don't believe he'd mind."

I thanked him, and we tied up the dinghy and unloaded the bikes. As we walked our bikes off the pier, I saw a large "No Trespassing" sign on a tree in the backyard. Since we weren't in the backyard, I wasn't concerned. From the road, I looked back at the pier for a final check on *Flipper.* On the wall of a storage shed near the pier was another "No Trespassing" sign, situated so that it had to be seen by anyone going out onto the pier.

"Joan, I don't feel happy about this," I said.

"I don't either. But the man said it was okay. Where else can we go?"

I accepted this logic, and we began riding down a road through a forest. Many of the trees bore "No Trespassing" signs. After a few miles and a couple of right turns, we entered Route 16 and headed toward the town of Church Creek. Nearing town and the creek itself, we saw that many houses had "No Trespassing" signs. A door-to-door salesman would be challenged there. Seeing all these signs, I was worried about where we had left the dinghy.

We got to the head of the creek, where it met Route 16, and turned onto a street that ran parallel to the creek. A short way up the street, a large drainage pipe emptied into the creek. A piling was near the pipe.

"Joan, this is a perfect place to leave *Flipper,* and I think this is the same road that the pier is on. You stay here with the bikes, and I'll walk on and bring the dinghy back here, okay?"

She agreed, and I walked away. The pier owner's house was around the first curve. As I expected, the front yard, which we had not seen earlier, also had a "No Trespassing" sign. I walked around the house to the pier and got into the dinghy. As I was leaving the dock, the man working on the engine looked up. He looked surprised.

I'm just moving farther up the creek," I told him. "Thanks again."

The drainage pipe was located in a little cove which was too shallow for the outboard, so I tilted the engine up and rowed in. At low tide, this cove might have no water, and we'd be able to return to *Delphina* only at half tide or better. This limitation presented no problem since high tide would be at four that afternoon. And no "No Trespassing" sign was anywhere in view. Feeling much better, we started riding again.

Cambridge, the county seat of Dorchester County, was just six miles away, so we went there first. Cambridge has many fine, old homes and quiet residential streets. Arriving at the municipal boat basin, we stopped at the adjacent park and ate the lunch we had brought. After eating, we rode through lovely neighborhoods and then went to the downtown area. I asked a passerby for the location of the Chamber of Commerce and was given directions to its office on U.S. Highway 50. We went there.

Walking in the door, we were greeted by an effusive,

smiling man.

"Hi! Welcome to Cambridge! What can I help you folks with?"

We told him we were interested in getting as much information about the area as we could.

"Well, you've come to the right place! Where are you from?"

When I told him the Florida Keys, his reaction was immediate.

"You don't say! I lived in Key West for a couple of years in the early eighties! Well, worked there actually. I lived just outside Key West, on Big Coppitt Key, I think it's called."

He talked on and on about how much he loved the Keys and what a great place Key West is. His enthusiasm for the beauty of the Keys and for the things to do there was so great that I wondered if we had somehow come to the Key West Camber of Commerce. When I told him this, he laughed.

"I'm a native of Dorchester County, and I missed not being here, so I moved back. Now let me tell you what there is here!"

And he did, in wonderful detail. He concluded his presentation by telling us of his favorite places.

"There are two areas here in the County that you have to see—Blackwater National Wildlife Refuge and Taylor's Island."

He gave us numerous brochures and maps, including two maps that proved invaluable to us during our remaining time in Maryland: *The Maryland Bicycle Touring Map* and *A Fishermen's Guide To Maryland Piers and Boat Ramps*.

Most of the afternoon was spent wandering around Cambridge. Around four o'clock, we headed for Church Creek.

One of the houses in Church Creek had a little vegetable stand in its front yard, and we stopped for some salad ingredients. No one was in attendance at the stand, but nearby a "No Trespassing" sign kept silent watch. I noticed a smaller sign, propped against a coffee can on the stand: "Honor system. Please leave money in can." The two signs created a thought-provoking dichotomy.

All the signs we had seen in this town made me wary about leaving our bikes on shore overnight. Where could we lock them without trespassing? I looked for a suitable place on the ride to the dinghy, but found none until we came to the marsh near the drainage pipe. We locked the bikes to a utility pole about ten feet into the marsh. The marsh was muddy, but we wouldn't be trespassing.

The dinghy ride to *Delphina* was considerably faster and more comfortable without the bikes.

We went through all our literature and agreed that we had to see the wildlife refuge and Taylor's Island. We could visit both in one day with a bike ride about the same distance as our round-trip from Crisfield to Pocomoke City.

The weather continued fair the next day. After finding our bikes where we had left them, we left Church Creek and headed to Blackwater. Going through farm country, we had little traffic to contend with. Just before the turnoff for the refuge headquarters, I saw a pickup truck parked on the shoulder. A man, carrying a burlap sack and a crab net, was about fifty yards past the truck and was walking along the shoulder. Frequently, he would touch the ground with the net, lift the net to the opening in the sack, and drop something from the net into the sack. I couldn't tell what he was picking up. Maybe he was collecting snakes or frogs. As I passed him, I saw that he was about sixty years old. I shouted out a cheerful "Good morning," but intent on what he was doing, he ignored me.

The Visitor Center at the refuge was locked. A sign on

the door said "Visitor Center Closed Today." According to another sign on which their schedule was posted, the Center should have been open. We continued down the road to the headquarters building. The door was open, and we walked inside. A woman ranger greeted us.

"What can I do for you?" she asked.

"Why is the Visitor Center closed today?" Joan asked.

"It's closed this summer because of a manpower shortage. It will open again this fall when the geese begin to arrive."

She told us that the refuge itself was open, and we could ride our bikes on the Wildlife Drive for $1.00 each.

The Wildlife Drive is five miles long and goes along freshwater ponds, woods, fields, and marsh. At the beginning is a yellow caution sign with a picture of a goose and the letters "Xing." Along the drive are an observation tower and several short trails, affording opportunities to view wildlife in their natural habitats. We saw numerous waterfowl, some turtles, many squirrels, and two muskrats, but none of the bald eagles that call Blackwater home. The ride was peaceful and not once interrupted by vehicular traffic.

The drive ended farther south on the same road we had taken from Church Creek. We turned left and headed south. Soon we saw the same pickup we had seen earlier; it was again parked along the side of the road. I saw two large, transparent, plastic bags full of aluminum cans in the back of the truck. The mystery was solved.

The man was on the other side of the road, and this time he looked up as I passed. A beer can was in his net, midway to the burlap bag. Again I wished him a good morning, and again he ignored me. He looked directly at me, but his facial expression didn't change. One thing I knew for certain—enough aluminum cans were on the sides of the roads to keep him gainfully employed for a long, long time. I wondered what he thought of the

"Adopt-A-Highway" adopters. They could adversely affect his profits, if they had a mind to.

We stopped at the general store conveniently located at Riggins Corner. It was mid-morning, and we were thirsty. In front of the store was a line of fifty-five gallon drums, each with a basket of fruit or vegetables on top. I picked up two red delicious apples and went inside to pay and get a soda.

I was greeted by an ancient woman, bent over a walker, who was very slowly moving from behind the counter toward a chair next to a stove in the middle of the floor.

"What can I do fer ya?" she asked.

Her words were followed by a slow turning of her head so she could look at me. A faint smile came to her lips.

She was the oldest person I had ever seen. Her skin was attached to her bones in waxy, translucent folds that showed little evidence of flesh. Her knuckles and elbows were knobby, and her wrists and fingers were horribly twisted by some unseen force. She was alone in the store.

After noting her venerable age, I wondered how she could manage this business. My thoughts were interrupted by the sudden appearance of a much younger woman in a doorway at the rear of the store.

"I see you've met Mrs. Riggins!" she said with an amused smile. "I guess you were a little surprised! How can I help you?"

Mrs. Riggins had stopped moving and was regarding me with twinkling eyes and a mischievous grin. She was thoroughly enjoying my befuddlement. Managing to recover, I remembered I had come in with two apples.

"I'd like to get these and a Coke, please."

Joan entered the store, and I introduced her to Mrs. Riggins. Joan also was struck by Mrs. Riggins's age. Never one to hold back when her curiosity is aroused,

Joan asked Mrs. Riggins how old she was.

"Eighty-five," said Mrs. Riggins.

"Oh no, you're not!" the young woman scolded. "Now you tell these folks that you're ninety-five, like a good girl!"

Mrs. Riggins's smile got broader. She was having a good time. The younger woman helped her to ease herself into the chair.

"If you folks have a mind, you should set a spell and let Mrs. Riggins tell you some stories goin' way back. She sure knows a few!"

But Mrs. Riggins told us that she had had a long illness and was convalescing. These few words took her a while to say. Many thoughts were going through her mind as she talked, and these thoughts confused her. As much as we hated to, we said he had to leave; we had a long bike ride ahead of us. Just then a man came in the front door.

"I see you folks came by bike. You don't look nearly as weird as some of them bike-ridin' people do who come through here. They got those funny-lookin' helmets with little mirrors stickin' out of 'em, and funny lookin' clothes, too. Even your bikes look different."

I laughed and told him we approached the sport differently from those who took it seriously.

"Veteran bike riders want everything they can get to protect themselves on the road. There isn't much to protect you if you get hit by a car," I told him.

We started out the door, and Mrs. Riggins cried out, "Now please come back and see me real soon! Please come back again next week!"

As I mounted my bike, I wondered if Mrs. Riggins had any idea how much I would like to do that.

We left on a different road and headed west instead of south. Our plan was to go directly to Taylor's Island, but along the way we neglected to turn right where we

Riggins General Store, Dorchester County

should have. Blissfully unaware that we were going the wrong way, we rolled merrily along. About two miles down the road, we came to a historical marker and a quaint chapel. The marker informed us the building was Tubman Chapel, built about 1769. It served as a church for the local parish until 1872, when the Catholic congregation began worshipping at St. Mary's Star of the Sea Church, across the road.

There was no "No Trespassing" sign anywhere in sight. The front door to the chapel opened easily and we entered.

It could have been 1872 when we walked in. The interior looked as if it had recently been used. On the altar was a large, ornate, red missal. I went to the altar and looked in the front of the leather-bound missal. The date of printing was 1872. Reverently, I closed the book.

We stopped at the newer church to see what wonders awaited us inside, but we couldn't get to the front door, much less open it. The four-foot high, chain-link fence around the property had "No Trespassing" signs gracing it. I wondered if the church's pastor was aware of the missal in the chapel. If so, did he ever wonder why this treasure hadn't been stolen or molested?

Back on the road again, we saw a few small billboards advertising properties for sale on Hooper Island. I thought their presence was odd, since we were going to Taylor's Island, but I was becoming inured to oddities. Soon we came to a one-lane bascule bridge with large traffic lights directing the traffic.

"Ken, I think that's Honga on the other side of the bridge," Joan casually remarked.

"How'd we end up here?" I wondered aloud.

We studied the map together.

"We should have turned right, back here at Golden Hill," Joan said.

"But we never saw a Golden Hill."

"Whatever. But you can see we should have turned right onto Smithville Road."

"Well, as long as we're here, let's go over the bridge to Honga and have lunch at the general store."

Crossing the narrow bridge on bicycles was exciting. Before we could ride to the other side, the traffic light had changed, and cars were heading toward us. We stopped and let them go by.

On the other side of the bridge, we saw an old general-store building, but it was abandoned. Thinking that the store had been moved or had been replaced by something newer, we rode farther down the road. We were right: an enormous convenience store appeared on our right. We stopped and entered.

The store had none of the ambience of an old-time, cracker-barrel, pot-belly-stove kind of general store. I had read that general stores are favorite places for watermen to gather and converse, but I couldn't picture a group of watermen sitting inside that place and discussing anything. Progress had come to Honga. I wondered if any of the old-timers missed the old place. We bought a couple of hot dogs and sodas. After lunch, we headed back up the road; we still wanted to get to Taylor's Island. When we arrived at Golden Hill, we stopped and pulled out the map. We could see how we had erred so easily, and it was one mistake I was grateful to have made. Because of our error, we had seen the chapel, the missal, and Honga.

We took Smithville Road and headed north. In five minutes, we again encountered the man picking up the aluminum cans. He was covering a lot of territory. This time, I called out a merry "Good afternoon" and succeeded in getting a wan smile for my effort. We were becoming bosom buddies.

Ten minutes later we still hadn't seen anyone except the can man. Suddenly, the quiet was shattered by a roar. Something was approaching from our rear. Looking behind me, I saw a mega-tractor that was gaining on us quickly. It was pulling a mega-plow that took up both lanes of the road. Joan and I pulled off to the side and watched the machinery fly by. A young man with long, blond hair was driving. Going at least thirty miles per hour, he was ignoring the possibility of a vehicle coming the other way. Maybe he knew something we didn't: for the remaining five miles of Smithville Road, we encountered not one other moving vehicle.

"No Trespassing" signs were so numerous along Smithville Road that some owners had changed the messages in the apparent hope that someone would read the signs and, consequently, *heed* the messages. An example:

POSTED
No Poachin' No Trespassin'

NO NUTHIN'
This applies to friends, relatives,
enemies and YOU
SURVIVORS WILL BE PROSECUTED

Apparently thinking that some people might get bored reading signs prohibiting trespassing, regardless of the messages' literary merit, one owner had put up a sign to grab everyone's attention:

NOW ENTERING
SMITHVILLE HEIGHTS
POPULATION 2
CHARLIE WILLEY
MAYOR

A tree in his yard bore a second sign. The sign said "No Trespassing."

After riding on Smithville Road for over five miles, we came to Smithville, the most run-down community that we had seen anywhere on the Eastern Shore. It was residential; there were no businesses. Junk cars sat everywhere. Houses, bare of paint, appeared on the verge of collapse. People walking along the road, sitting on their porches, or working in their yards stopped what they were doing, looked at us, waved, and smiled until I thought their faces might break. These people knew a happiness that had nothing to do with any material possessions. But I could have been dreaming. Maybe they were just happy to see someone come down their road and wave to them.

Soon after turning left onto Route 16, we were on a bridge going over Slaughter Creek to Taylor's Island. At the end of the bridge is a roadside plaque and a cannon, called the Becky Phipps Cannon, which was captured by Taylor's Island militiamen from a British ship during the

War of 1812. Obviously, the residents of the island are proud of their heritage, and they want all visitors to know it as soon as they cross the bridge.

Farther down the road, we came to the Grace Episcopal Church, built in the 1870s. We found the door unlocked and walked in. In the vestibule was a guest book that was first signed in 1940. We added our names. Not often do I sign a guest book that is fifty years old.

Adjacent to this church is the Chapel of Ease, an Episcopalian chapel build in the early 1700s. It also was unlocked, and we entered. The gloomy interior was brightened by colorful paintings hanging on the walls.

A one-room schoolhouse, built in 1785, is on this same plot of land. An interesting feature of this building is a hole in each wall of the room so the stove pipe can be shifted with the wind.

Continuing our tour, we passed Ridgeton, a farmhouse constructed in 1857. A straight, tree-lined drive

Grace Episcopal Church, Taylor's Island

leads to this imposing house, and we saw two large chimneys and a widow's walk through the trees.

On our way off the island, we stopped at a general store near the bridge. We entered, and I was happy to see that the store had an ageless quality to it. Some of the stock on the shelves looked as if it had been placed there at the turn of the century and not touched, even by a dust cloth, since then. Arrayed on other shelves were items of more recent vintage. In front of the wood counter was a freezer with ice cream. One wall was lined with coolers of beer, soft drinks, and dairy products. The overall effect was that a museum had gone into the convenience-store business. Then I saw the dining room and bar at the rear of the store area.

It was the middle of the afternoon, and the dining room was empty. I peeked inside the room and immediately knew I wanted to eat there when all the locals do. But we were still eleven miles from Church Creek. Waiting until the dinner hour was out of the question. I bought a beer instead, but only after being assured by the woman at the register that I wouldn't be arrested for drinking it on their porch.

The first nine miles to Church Creek were mostly through marsh. Trees were nonexistent, and the sun beat unmercifully on our bare heads. By the time we arrived at Woolford, I was ready for another beer. The general store in Woolford had a large selection. I bought and quickly drank a sixteen-ounce single.

After the refreshment from the beer, I found the remaining ride to the dinghy easy. Loading the bikes into *Flipper* from the drainage pipe was not. As we struggled, a woman walking her dog came up to us.

"I wondered whose boat that was," she said. "There hasn't been a boat tied there for years, not since my son used to tie his crab skiff there."

She sounded wistful.

"And that was seventeen years ago, just before he went into the Navy."

Her voice trailed off. She had become lost in her thoughts.

"Oh, we wondered why there was a piling near the pipe," Joan told her.

The woman said nothing further and walked away.

After we returned to *Delphina*, we finalized our plans for the next day. We had visited Oxford in 1982, and we wanted to return. Several creeks off the Tred Avon River offer secure anchorages within biking distance of Oxford, and we chose Peachblossom Creek, as much for its name as for any other reason.

The next morning, it rained heavily. The rain continued into the afternoon, but we didn't care. We read books and got a good rest. And we didn't see one "No Trespassing" sign the entire day.

CHAPTER THIRTEEN

Tred Avon River

Navigating out of Church Creek and Fishing Creek wasn't any easier than going in, but again we didn't touch bottom. I was beginning to get cocky and this frame of mind worries me. On the water, I prefer to be humble.

The passage to Oxford was boring. Although the monsoon-like rains of the previous day had ended during the night, the sky was still overcast and hazy. The visibility was only a couple of miles. There was no wind, so *Delphina* was chugging along under power.

I can't imagine a cruise on the Eastern Shore that doesn't include a visit to Oxford, one of the oldest towns in Maryland. In 1694, along with Annapolis (then called Anne Arundel), Oxford was selected as one of only two ports of entry for the colony. Originally named Thread Haven, the town enjoyed great prosperity for nearly a hundred years as a center of international trade. Large tobacco plantations in the area brought great wealth to their owners. After the Revolutionary War, however, British ships no longer called to carry on trade with Europe. Oxford's fortunes and population declined.

The slump ended after the Civil War and the advent of railroading on the Eastern Shore. Oysters replaced tobacco as the cash crop, and the invention of better packing and canning methods for oysters brought economic prosperity back to Oxford. Unfortunately, the oyster beds couldn't produce enough to maintain the frenetic harvesting activity, and by 1910 the boom was over. Steamboats and trains stopped coming to Oxford, and Oxford's trade with outside markets came to a halt. As businesses closed, the resident watermen continued to pursue a living on the water, but the town settled down to a period of dormancy.

Although the completion of the Bay Bridge in 1952 opened Eastern Shore communities to hordes of tourists, Oxford has retained the atmosphere of a historical waterfront town. The town has not allowed outside influences to impinge upon its character. If you take away the paving and the cars, Oxford appears untouched by time. The marinas in the harbor contain many traditional craft, as if the owners of classic vessels throughout the Chesapeake know that Oxford is where their boats will feel most at home.

As we entered the Tred Avon River, however, I noticed that at least one developer had discovered Oxford. On the south end of town,we saw a new residential development with slips for the owners' yachts. We planned to tour the town the next day, and I made a mental note to visit the development. With relief, I noticed that the remainder of the waterfront was the same as it had been on our visit in 1982. After that visit to Oxford, I had regarded the town as being beyond the reach of a developer. After all, where in the town could a developer develop? A few lots were vacant, but none were large enough for a major project. Certainly no one would dare to knock down any of the historical buildings to make room for progress.

We anchored near the town pier and made a quick run ashore in the dinghy to get some water and to visit the post office.

When we're planning a cruise, we select post offices along our intended route and arrange for mail to be directed to General Delivery and held for our arrival.

This system had worked well for us in the past, and we had planned for three mail drops on this trip. Our first mail drop had been in Crisfield, and we expected more mail in Oxford. We weren't disappointed.

But we were disappointed when we tried to fill our water jugs. Oxford provides a dock for the temporary use of visiting boaters, but water is not available there. Maybe sometimes I expect too much.

Continuing our trip up the Tred Avon, we saw several of the large estates that Talbot County is known for. Huge mansions dominate manicured lawns that extend seemingly forever. Enormous trees are perfectly located, as though planted by someone with a sense of aesthetic balance. Occasionally we saw a satellite dish hidden strategically in some bushes. I found it difficult to imagine that the owners of these magnificent homes would sit in front of a television set. Surely they would spend their leisure moments reading Shakespeare or Wordsworth or *The Wall Street Journal*.

To starboard as we entered Peachblossom Creek were two spacious estates and a country club. I felt wonderful knowing that we had the right to enter this creek, anchor, and be at home among the wealthy for a while. One serious problem, though, was where we could go ashore with the dinghy. Many piers extend into the creek, but they are private. Our best hope for securing *Flipper* was the bridge that spans the creek; maybe one of its abutments would give us access to shore and a place to leave *Flipper*.

We anchored about halfway up the creek. I made drinks, and we sat in our deck chairs and wondered what the poor people were doing. The urge to call my stockbroker was strong, but then I realized that I didn't have one.

Talbot County estates, Peachblossom Creek

I didn't even have any stock. So magical was the opulent setting that it was easy to enter a fantasy world. I promised myself I would buy a lottery ticket the next day to make my fantasy world a real one.

The next morning I took an exploratory run on *Flipper* to see about the bridge abutments. Repairs were being made to the bridge, but since it was Saturday, no one was working. The only possible place I saw for securing a dinghy and going ashore was a boat ramp on the far side of the bridge. I couldn't tell if the ramp was private, but I saw no "No Trespassing" sign. A light drizzle began, and I returned to *Delphina*.

An hour later, the drizzle stopped, and the sky began to brighten. We loaded the bikes onto *Flipper* and went to the boat ramp. Approaching the ramp, we saw a man and a woman on a large powerboat moored on a nearby pier. The pier was attached to the lawn of one of the large mansions. The couple, by all appearances, lived in that house. I gathered all the charm I could.

"Good morning!" I said. "Can you tell me if it would be all right to tie our dinghy to that ramp?"

They smiled back at me.

"Good morning!" the woman said. "Sure, it's all right. Go ahead."

The ramp was accessible from the water, and unloading the bikes was easy. The hardest part of the operation was lifting the bikes over the three-foot guardrail on the side of the road. As we mounted the bikes, a distinguished-looking man, wearing athletic clothing and riding a bike, approached us and stopped.

After wishing us a good morning, he said, "So you're from the Keys. I have a place down on Cudjoe Key. Just got back from a diving trip there last week."

How did he know we were from the Keys? We had never seen this man before. I asked him.

"I have a friend who saw you come up the creek yesterday," he replied. "You're anchored across from his house, and he saw the home port on your boat."

"I guess you have an extensive neighborhood-watch system here," I said.

He laughed and said, "There isn't much that goes on here we don't know about. For instance, my house is right over there. You can't see much of it from here because of the trees, but I saw you dinghy in about seven thirty this morning. You seemed to be checking things out. Looks like you got squared away all right with your dinghy. Where're you going on the bikes?"

We told him we were going to make the loop that connects Easton, Bellevue, and Oxford.

"That's a great trip," he told us. "You'll really like the ferry ride over to Oxford from Bellevue. As for me, I'm just out trying to get some exercise. Say, if you're back early this afternoon, tie up your dinghy at our place and come on up to our house for a drink. We can talk about life in the Keys."

"We don't know when we'll be back," Joan told him, "but if we finish seeing the sights early, we'd love to come over."

We said good-bye to this friendly man and rode toward Easton. The light traffic and wide shoulder enabled us to have a nice ride to the town.

Easton calls itself the Colonial Capital of the Eastern Shore, a reflection of the pride the residents have in their history. The county seat of Talbot County, it has a population of eight thousand. The town grew around a courthouse built in 1700.

My impression on entering Easton was that it is a wealthy community. Spotlessly clean and free of litter, the streets leading to the downtown area are graced with many handsome houses, new and old. The downtown area has fine stores, restaurants, and numerous offices of members of the New York Stock Exchange. The atmosphere of prosperous gentility nearly overwhelmed me. I was getting hungry, but looking at the different restaurants on the outside, I knew that we couldn't afford their offerings on the inside. I suggested to Joan that we find somewhere to eat on Highway 50. She agreed.

After a bland and boring meal at a fast-food joint, we went back through town and looked for Route 33 to St. Michaels. After a few false starts caused by the lack of directional signs in town, we found the road.

The traffic was heavy on Route 33 as hordes of tourists drove to St. Michaels. The highway has a wide shoulder, so the worst part of the ride to the turnoff for Bellevue was the tremendous noise as the cars and trucks sped past us.

Once we were off Route 33 we were in a bike-rider's paradise. The traffic was insignificant, and the many trees that lined the road provided a canopy. We were sweating heavily in the heat, and getting out of the sun was a great relief. Soon other bike riders, heading in the opposite direction, appeared on the other side of the road. We smiled and waved, but these people didn't want any part of our carefree spirit. They were serious bike riders, riding serious bicycles and wearing the latest serious bike clothing, helmets, gloves, and shoes. Occasionally, one would nod in our direction or lift a hand in response to our wave, but none of them smiled back. Maybe frivolous gestures would destroy the image they so carefully cultivate at great expense. Or maybe they didn't deign to acknowledge obvious amateurs on rusty machines.

Of course, I have experienced this aloofness on the water many times. Traditionally, when boats are near each other, the people aboard the boats wave. Many people smile. Some yell out that you have a nice boat. But people have also looked at me, eyeball to eyeball, and not in any way acknowledged my greeting. Sometimes, depending on my level of frustration at being ignored, I violently wave my arm, smile broadly, and yell out "Howdy!" Usually, the recipient of this largess acknowledges my existence with a nod. If not, I get tempted to undertake more violent action, but I never do. I do get in such a foul mood that I promise myself I will not initiate any future greetings. Invariably, the next boat we pass is loaded with effusive sorts, waving madly, and my mood improves.

The road continued to be scenic, and the traffic continued to be light. Spurts of cars and bikes did appear every twenty minutes, coinciding with the ferry schedule. Apparently, the ferry was busy that day, and I was concerned that we might have a long wait.

When we arrived at the landing, the line of cars was long. Numerous people had parked their cars and were waiting to take the ferry without them. And there were at least ten bikes and their riders in line. But my fear about our having a long wait was groundless: the professional crew loaded all the people and vehicles aboard.

The Oxford-Bellevue ferry is the oldest continuously operating free ferry in the country. It's not the fare that's free, it's the ferry itself: it doesn't use a cable to guide it. Founded in 1760, the ferry is privately owned and operates year-round except for a hiatus from Christmas through February. The fares were once payable in tobacco; nowadays they are payable in cash and are quite reasonable. Our ride across the Tred Avon was a pleasure, and we had ample opportunities to watch the activity on the river.

Our first stop ashore in Oxford was the Customs House, a replica of the original building. Joan tried opening the door, but it was locked. An elderly gentleman came over and told us that, although the building is open on weekends, it was closed that Saturday because of the Annapolis-to-Oxford sailing race.

"But don't worry," he said. "I'll let you in."

He reached into his pocket for his key.

"Damn it! I don't have my keys on me. I must've left them home."

He was upset about not having his keys, but he continued talking.

"They have this race every year. This year, though, only about half the usual boats raced. The race started up in Annapolis Thursday afternoon, and they had a lot of rain. I suppose some people didn't want to race in all that rain. It's a shame."

I was surprised half the boats *did* race in those downpours. What the man said confirmed to me that die-hard racers will race in almost any conditions. Also, I knew they will spend any amount to gain a competitive advantage. It's not coincidental that Annapolis has one of the largest used-sail brokers in the country. Many of these racers buy new sails every year because their old ones stretched a little. Sailboat races have close finishes, and an improvement on a boat that increases speed by as little as a hundredth of a knot can make the winning difference.

We thanked the kind man for his information and rode down Morris Street.

Robert Morris Sr., a shipping agent for a Liverpool firm and the father of the financier of the Revolution, built his home in the 1700s at the north end of Morris Street. Today his home is part of the Robert Morris Inn. The Grapevine House, built in 1798, features a grapevine that was brought over from the Isle of Jersey and planted in 1810. The vine still produces wine grapes. The Academy House is an imposing structure, also located on this street. From 1848 to 1855 it served as the home for the officers on the staff of the Maryland Military Academy. Lining Morris Street are numerous interesting stores. I was tempted to enter each one, but I chose Bringman's Tred Avon Confectionery, which, in addition to looking like a neat place, was a lottery agent. They would sell me a winning ticket. We entered the store.

I didn't want to buy one of those instant tickets; I wanted to go for the big one, the one that would give us $13 million, the one that would give us the money for one of those estates on Peachblossom Creek. Only one ticket is needed to win, and I handed the man behind the counter a dollar bill and the card I had filled out with our magic numbers.

"Do you want to spend $1.00?" he asked.

Was he making fun of me because I only wanted to spend $1.00? How could I spend less? Lottery tickets cost $1.00.

"Why sure," I answered.

He ran the card into the computer and returned it to me with two tickets.

"Now that second ticket has numbers that I chose for

you, so you have to give me ten percent when you win."

A big grin filled his face. He couldn't fool me: I knew the computer had chosen the second set of numbers.

"I get two tickets for $1.00?" I asked.

"Yup," he replied, still smiling.

What an omen! No doubt the numbers chosen by the computer would be the winners! Carefully placing the tickets in my wallet and feeling very happy, I left the store. Tomorrow would be the lucky day.

We stopped at the Oxford Museum on Market Street and saw a collection of artifacts from the town's past. I was especially intrigued by the scrapbook of articles and photographs.

Riding our bikes once again, we went to the northeastern point of the town, where Town Creek meets the Tred Avon River. A modern house, designed on the lines of the Hooper Strait lighthouse, is located on the point.

We were happy to see that the weekend log-canoe races were under way. These races have been a tradition on the Eastern Shore for many years. Although the wind was blowing less than five knots, the boats were going fast.

Two features of these boats that add to the interest of watching them race are the large sail area and the hiking boards that the crew lie on to provide ballast. Since log canoes have no ballast keels, the hiking boards are essential for stability. In a stiff breeze, though, capsizes are common and add a great deal of merriment to the proceedings.

While we were engrossed in watching the boats, a young woman rode up on her bike and joined us.

"Enjoying the race?" she asked.

I told her we certainly were.

"When I was a kid, my dad had a three-log canoe. We raced it every weekend, just like these boats are doing. What a blast! But then my dad sold it. It's a lot of work and money to keep one up. Sometimes I wish we still had it."

She pointed out different boats to us as they passed and told us a little about some of the owners.

"As you can see, the boats come in different sizes depending on how many logs were used to build them."

We continued to watch the races for a while longer and then rode away to visit the new development that we had seen from the water.

The development, a mixture of town houses and individual homes, fits in well with the surroundings. The area is not near the historic district of town, and the buildings don't interfere with the charm of Oxford in any way. The impression I had of the development was that the homes are expensive, and the neighborhood is sterile. I didn't want to linger there.

We got on Route 333 to return to Peachblossom Creek and passed by the Oxford Community Center. The Tred

Log canoe race, Tred Avon River

Avon Players had a sign up advertising their summer production, opening the following weekend. Joan also saw the sign, and we both wished that we had come to Oxford a week later.

We had eight miles to go to Peachblossom Creek, and it was already four o'clock. Stopping at a store on the outskirts of Oxford, I bought a big beer to quench my big thirst.

"Joan, what are we going to do about that man's invitation for a drink? We won't get back until around five. And then we'll be all grubby and smelly. Are we going to be able to arrange to sit downwind of him? What'll we do if he invites us into his house? I really feel awful about this. I'd feel better if we brought some beer with us, but it'll be warm by the time we get there."

"I don't know what to say. It is pretty awkward. He invited us for early afternoon, so maybe he won't be home. We'll just have to wait and see, I guess."

Riding to Peachblossom Creek, my euphoria over the good omen with our lottery ticket was forgotten as I thought about how inconvenient living aboard a boat sometimes is. How nice it would be to get home, call the man who invited us, and ask him if five o'clock would be all right for us to arrive. Then we could take a hot shower, change clothes, show up with an ice-cold six-pack, and be ready for a good conversation.

My mood improved as I marveled at the many tree-lined drives we passed. Each had a small sign with the name of the mansion the drive led to and the year the house was built, but no house was visible from the road.

Finally we arrived at Peachblossom Creek and loaded the bikes on the dinghy. We took *Flipper* to the dock at the friendly man's house to see if anyone was home. We could see no one, and I was sure, based on the excellent system of vigilance in the area, that were he in his house he would have seen us. I was also certain, because of the way we now looked and smelled, that he wouldn't enjoy our company even if we brought Madeira wine and told him the meaning of life. With relief tinged with sorrow, we returned to *Delphina*. Maybe we would see him someday in the Keys, and we could invite him for a drink.

When I bought the lottery ticket in Oxford, Joan bought some fatback to use as crab bait. The store had no chicken, and a woman told her that fatback made better bait anyway. But we were so exhausted from the heat and the bike ride that we couldn't find the energy to bait any lines. We had a quick dinner. After reading some information on St. Michaels, our destination the next day, we went to sleep.

CHAPTER FOURTEEN

Broad Creek

As we motored past Oxford early that Sunday morning, the town appeared to be asleep. Even the weather seemed to be sleeping; no wind was blowing, and the sun was taking its time getting up.

As we left the Tred Avon River, we saw crabbers at work out on the Bay. The sight surprised me since watermen are serious about treating the Sabbath as a day of rest and a day to spend with their families. On the lower Eastern Shore, we hadn't seen this level of activity on a Sunday.

We entered Broad Creek around nine o'clock. A large power yacht that had passed us ten minutes earlier abruptly turned ninety degrees and came to a halt a half mile ahead of us. Had it run aground? I checked the chart and saw that the water is deep where the boat had stopped. A minute later, someone on the yacht put out an anchor, and the yacht stayed put. Curious, I thought; it didn't look like the type of boat that would anchor to fish. Then someone hoisted a large red flag, and I thought the yacht was a race-committee boat. Suddenly, I saw a fleet of about twenty sailboats powering down Broad Creek toward the anchored yacht. Soon the fleet was milling around the yacht, and several of the crews were hoisting sails. The air was so still that cigarette smoke would have drifted straight up without a ruffle. And these boats were going to *race?*

While I admire the spirit that prompts a sailor to take every advantage of a one-knot cat's-paw, I can't understand what prompts a group of intelligent and sober people to have a sailboat race when there is *no* wind. Of course, the boats can move a little with no wind—the current causes that—but all the boats move at the same speed. Where's the race?

Maybe each participant had a Zen koan to meditate on: who wins the race when the racers do not race? What is the sound of one hand clapping? But, in all likelihood, the racers were inveterate optimists, infinitely patient, searching for a few of those one-knot cat's-paws.

Powering *Delphina* slowly, and watching the depth sounder, we worked our way up to San Domingo Creek. Friends of ours, who had done some cruising in the Bay, had told us about this back entrance to St. Michaels. Not many cruising sailors going to St. Michaels use this anchorage, but by our doing so, we could avoid the crowded conditions that prevail in the harbor at St. Michaels.

The tree-lined shore was impressive. Very few houses were visible until we were well into Broad Creek, and the feeling of remoteness was delightful. We anchored near a few houses, as far up San Domingo Creek as *Delphina*'s draft allowed. The sense of remoteness remained, despite our being only a half mile from St. Michaels, perhaps the Eastern Shore's most popular tourist destination.

With few exceptions, whenever we told people in the Chesapeake area that we were sailing around the Bay that summer, they wanted to know if we had gone, or would be going, to St. Michaels. Having visited St. Michaels before, I could understand why they'd ask. The town, with the Chesapeake Bay Maritime Museum, his-

torical buildings, interesting stores, watermen's workboats, and outstanding restaurants, captures the flavor of
the Eastern Shore. To not visit the place is to not fully
appreciate the history of the Eastern Shore and the rapid
changes that are affecting the area.

St. Michaels has every kind of store to cater to each
visitor's every whim: two hardware stores, a supermarket, a pharmacy, a saloon, an ice-cream parlor, two laun-
dromats, art galleries, craft shops, marine stores, book-
stores, florists, real estate offices, clothing stores,
museums, a seafood market, and a liquor store. And
these places are busy. Our priorities, chosen from all
these options, were the museums.

We took *Flipper* to the public pier at the end of West
Chew Street in St. Michaels. Many workboats were
moored to this pier; the watermen had tied a bow line to
the pier and placed an anchor off the stern. We tied
Flipper with one bow line to the pier where the water
was shallow. No workboats were tied at that end. We
unloaded our bikes and rode to the St. Mary's Square
Museum.

Entering the building, we were immediately greeted
by a smiling man in his seventies.

"Good afternoon, and welcome to St. Michaels!" he
said. "Where are you folks from?"

We told him, and he told us about the museum and
how it was established. As he elaborated on the history of
the town, he escorted us to different displays to illustrate
his talk. Occasionally, we asked him questions about
himself.

"No, I'm not a native of St. Michaels, but I spent all
my summers here growing up," he replied to one question. "Met my wife here one summer. After I retired, we
moved here, into the same house where my wife was born
and raised."

In one of our guidebooks, we read about a colonial

mansion named Crooked Intention on the banks of San Domingo Creek. I asked if he knew where it was.

"I've heard of the place, but durned if I know where it is. Let me call my wife. She'll know how to get there."

He made the call and then told us, "It is on San Domingo Creek, on the west branch at the head of the creek. 'Can't miss it,' she said."

Joan asked him what changes he had seen in St. Michaels over the years.

"Oh, lots, lots. Something funny happened a while back. There was talk about the town commissioners wanting to return Talbot Street to the way it was in the last century—brick streets and brick sidewalks and all that. I had to laugh because back then there was no sidewalk, just ditches running down the sides of the street. People don't know the way it used to be."

James Michener, the author of *Chesapeake,* lived in St. Michaels while he was working on that book. I asked our guide if he had ever met him.

"As a matter of fact, I did meet him once. No, make that twice. The first time was at a cocktail party. Someone introduced me to him. He doesn't take any notes at all; the man has a phenomenal memory. Then a few weeks later, I was walking down Talbot Street, and I saw him walking with another man. He saw me too and walked toward me. As soon as he got close enough, he introduced me by name to his companion, Walter Cronkite. Yessir, that's my one claim to fame! But how did he remember my name with all the people he met? It's some memory he has, that man."

He finished showing us the exhibits. As we were signing the guest book, another couple came in, and he gave them the same enthusiastic greeting that he had given us. Not only was he ready to guide again, he was excited about it.

As we were learning in our travels, many of the towns

on the Eastern Shore have nicknames. St. Michaels is known as the Town that Fooled the British in the War of 1812. The residents heard that the British were going to attack their town to destroy the shipbuilding yards. On the night of the attack, all lights in town were extinguished. Lanterns were lit and hoisted into the treetops to trick the British gunners into aiming high. The ruse worked: only one house was hit. That house, called Cannonball House, is still standing.

We rode to Talbot Street, the main street through town. On both sides of the street are houses that are homes and houses that are businesses. Regardless of their function, they are interesting to look at from the outside, and I wanted to see how they looked on the inside. The homes we couldn't enter; the businesses, we could.

The first business we went to was the Book Nook, located in a house of undeniably humble origins. The house has Victorian styling, but its lines are simple and unpretentious. What paint remains on the house is green and peeling; no paint is on the shutters. On the porch is a small sign that reads "Book Nook." The effect of the place on someone who loves books is overwhelmingly positive. We had to go in.

The interior of the house, at first glance, appeared as disheveled as the exterior. Books were piled everywhere. Little wooden blocks on top of some of the piles indicated that the books in the pile were history, philosophy, religion, literature, and so forth. Small cards categorized other books in smaller piles: trains, hobbies, travel, foreign language, et cetera. Every book that I saw appeared to be used. The shop is a browser's nirvana. No one was present; I was going to spend the rest of the day going through all the books.

"May I help you find a book?" a woman asked.

Her voice was deep and resonant, and the words were

spoken with a slow, deliberate cadence. The inflection in her voice told me she wanted to find a book for us, not because she wanted a sale, but because she knew it would bring pleasure to us and to her.

I looked up from a pile I was studying. A short, stocky woman of indeterminate age was standing in a doorway that led to a kitchen. She was dressed in a plain, brown skirt and a tan blouse that would have been appropriate attire at anytime in the last four decades. Her long, dark hair, accented by a few brilliant white strands, was pulled back and tied. Her handsome face had a solemn mien; she appeared to take her business seriously.

With the aid of a cane, she walked slowly into the living room where Joan and I were standing. I gave her the standard answer of a bookstore browser.

"No thanks. I'm just looking."

"Please take your time," she said. "If you don't mind, I'm going to sit down. I'm seventy-three years old, and my feet get tired."

She sat down on a sofa. In that same rich voice, she began to tell us where all the different categories of books were located. It was difficult for me to concentrate as I looked at her while she spoke. An aura of timelessness and infinite wisdom enveloped her. Tempted to interrupt her and ask if she were psychic, I kept quiet; I was mesmerized by the rhythm of her dialogue. When she finished her speech, she waited for a reaction.

"Do you have Richard Halliburton's *Complete Book of Marvels?*" I asked.

"No, I sold one a while back and haven't been able to replace it. I do have two other books by him, though. His first, *The Royal Road to Romance,* and his second, *The Glorious Adventure.* They're both on that shelf behind you."

I turned around. They were in a stack by themselves. With awe, I picked them up. The first title had a copyright date of 1925; the second, 1927. One was priced at $5.00, and the other at $6.00.

She noticed my reaction to the books.

"I think they're both first editions, but I can't tell for sure," she said.

Her voice had acquired a tinge of excitement.

"I'll take both of these," I told her, with what I hoped was a steady voice. "I can't thank you enough for having these books."

Her solemn expression relaxed into an easy smile.

"I often have what people are looking for."

Back on the sidewalk again, and away from the woman's influence, I tried to put the incident into perspective, but I couldn't. Only the tangible evidence of the two books in my hand reminded me what had happened. Those books may be numerous (I have no idea how many were printed in those years), but to me they are as much a treasure as first editions of works by Dickens.

As we neared the St. Michaels Hardware Store, the traffic on Talbot Street was heavier, and more pedestrians were on the sidewalks. We didn't want to miss any of the interesting window-shopping offered by the stores on both sides of Talbot Street, so we locked our bikes to a pole and started walking.

We stopped at a real estate office because I saw an easel on their porch that displayed photographs and brochures of properties that were for sale. So convinced was I of the winning nature of one of our lottery tickets that I had to see what was available for us to buy. As we were reading a brochure for an estate, a man came out of the office and joined us on the porch.

"Is there a particular property you're interested in?" he asked.

Pointing to the brochure, I replied, "Well, I really like this place here."

"That's one of the finest properties available in Talbot

County at this time. As you can see, the main house was built in the 1600s and was completely restored last year. And with all the land on the estate, it's a bargain at $4 million. Would you like me to arrange an appointment for you to inspect the property?"

"It is quite a reasonable price," I said, "but the house is more than we want. I think we'll continue looking around for a while."

Did the man really think we could afford that place? Joan and I were dressed in shorts and polo shirts, she with sandals, I with flip-flops. Do multimillionaires dress so casually in public these days? Do any of them wear shorts and flip-flops when they shop for estates? Before I became too excited about any estate, I wanted to find out if we had won the lottery.

Since it was Sunday, the papers wouldn't have the winning numbers, so we crossed the street and went to Hudson's Pharmacy, where lottery tickets are sold. The winning numbers for $13 million were posted. They did not match our numbers. So much for omens. I probably wouldn't be happy living in one of those estates anyway. And I might have to buy a car again. Life is full of mixed blessings.

On our way to the Chesapeake Maritime Museum, we stopped at Justine's Ice Cream Parlour for a treat. I made the mistake of getting a cone with two scoops of ice cream, and most of the ice cream melted and dripped onto my hand as we walked to the museum.

Chesapeake Bay Maritime Museum is the crown jewel of St. Michaels. Founded in 1965, it has grown from one house to a sixteen-acre complex of twenty-six buildings and a number of vessels that are indigenous to the Bay. The old Hooper Strait lighthouse, moved to the museum in 1966, dominates the museum grounds and provides a centerpiece for the many exhibits. Of the many delights to entice the visitor to St. Michaels, this museum is the most popular.

We walked past the Crab Claw Restaurant and observed the boating activity in the harbor from the waterfront. Just as our guidebooks indicated, St. Michaels is one of the most popular cruising destinations on the Bay. Boats of all descriptions filled the marinas and the small anchorage area. We were thankful we had chosen San Domingo Creek. The creek was a lot more peaceful than what we were looking at.

We wandered back to our bikes and rode to the pier where we had left the dinghy. Since our plan was to ride the length of Tilghman Island the next day, we locked our bikes to a post and walked onto the pier.

When we got to *Flipper*'s space on the pier, we saw that she was lying on the mud like a beached dolphin. The tide was low. I would have to get in the mud and cajole her back into the water.

As soon as I stepped down, my foot and flip-flop sank

Chesapeake Bay Maritime Museum, St. Michaels

six inches into the muck. The only thing that kept me from sinking farther was the base of oyster shells under the mud. Trying to raise my foot and flip-flop required an extreme effort, but I finally freed them from the mud. After removing both flip-flops, I began the laborious process of moving the dinghy. I hoped no broken glass was beneath the mud; it was strange enough feeling all the pieces of shells between my toes.

After ten minutes of backbreaking work, I got *Flipper* floating, and she bobbed gently in thanks. I washed all the mud off my feet and climbed into the dinghy. Joan joined me immediately, and we left the pier.

Crooked Intention was where the wife of the museum guide said it would be. The mansion is truly magnificent; worn, whitewashed bricks, marvelously preserved, give it an air of ageless antiquity. The house is situated on the shore at such an angle that the late-afternoon sunlight, coming through the trees, was striking the front of the house and bathing it in a warm, suffusive glow of light. The lawn stretched to the water, and a pier extended from the lawn. Wanting to photograph the scene, I slowly approached the pier while I got my camera ready.

A pickup truck approached. I quickly took a picture before the truck came closer to the house. Apparently, the driver knew the picture I wanted because he stopped and then backed the truck. After I put the camera away, he drove forward and parked in front of the house. Such consideration should exist everywhere.

The next morning gave us a repeat of Sunday's weather: it was hot with no wind. Arriving at the public pier, I decided to secure *Flipper* in deeper water using the watermen's technique of squeezing in between two boats, dropping an anchor off the stern, and tying the bow to the pier. On the workboat to our right was a burly waterman, busily organizing his trotlines. He looked at me as I pushed off his boat.

"Will I be in anyone's way here?" I asked him.

"Naw, there's plenty of room," he answered.

The stern anchor grabbed hold of the bottom, and I gave the line some slack to bring the bow up to the pier. Soon everything was squared away, and we were ready to begin the bike ride. I thought it would be a major project to load the bikes onto *Flipper* when we came back, but I'd worry about that later.

We were on Route 33 for the entire ride to Tilghman. The return trip would be on the same route, but we had no choice: only one road goes the length of Tilghman Island.

When we arrived at the town of Tilghman at Knapps Narrows, we had a welcome change of scenery from what we had seen on the ride from St. Michaels: a waterfront community instead of farmland.

Knapps Narrows is a break in Tilghman Island that boaters use to go from Harris Creek on the east over to the Bay on the west. This break saves boaters considerable time because they don't have to go around Blackwalnut Point, the southern tip of the island. Several marinas, as well as packing houses, crab pounds, and restaurants, are located in Tilghman.

The first thing to catch our eye in Tilghman was a beautifully restored skipjack, lying quietly in a berth at a marina. After seeing so many skipjacks in rough shape, we were thrilled to see one in this condition in its natural environment. The boat looked so perfect, though, that I doubted it would be used for dredging. The vessel had neither a donkey engine on deck to haul the dredges nor metal plates on the topsides to keep the hull from being damaged by this equipment.

The fifteen-mile ride had given us large appetites. We decided to have a large breakfast rather than wait for lunch. We rode over the bascule bridge that spans the Narrows and stopped at a small general store. The woman behind the counter told us the Chesapeake House, located a half mile farther south on the left, served breakfast.

Following her directions, we continued our ride, and I soon saw a workboat basin on our left. Raked masts, a sure sign of skipjacks, jutted into the sky. I called out to Joan, and we turned left onto the road that led to the basin. In the basin was a magnificent fleet of skipjacks. Rafted together in several groups moored to a bulkhead were about fifteen skipjacks, two bugeye ketches, and a buy boat. All the vessels were in fine repair. With their jaunty bowsprits pointing the same direction, they gave the impression that they were impatient for the season to begin so they could get to work. The fleet perfectly reflected the proud heritage of Chesapeake Bay watermen.

A little farther down the road, we came to Harrison's Chesapeake House restaurant. Parking our bikes near

Skipjack, Tilghman

the entrance, we thought this place would satisfy our needs, although it might be expensive. It had the appearance of a turn-of-the-century inn that catered to the carriage trade. We climbed the short stairs, entered the enclosed porch, and walked to the foyer.

Framed pictures of celebrities and prominent politicians, proudly displaying fine catches of fish, hung everywhere. Rave reviews of the restaurant's fare were also framed and hung. What was this place going to cost us? For the first time on our vacation we didn't care; the spirit of the place had captivated us.

The entrance to the dining area led through the lounge. The ambience and lighting inside the lounge was what I imagine a Key West bar in the 1930s had had. I looked for Ernest Hemingway at the bar. A man, his back toward us, was sitting there, but he was not Papa.

The dining room, in marked contrast to the bar, was light and airy. Large windows gave a view of the water. We sat down, and the waitress came for our order. As we waited for our food to arrive, I kept looking around; I expected Ted Williams and Curt Gowdy to join us for breakfast.

For the quality and quantity of the food, the price was reasonable. The servings of hash browns and omelets were generous and delicious. We discussed coming back to this outstanding restaurant for an early dinner that day, but I knew I would have difficulty pedaling all the way back to St. Michaels after gorging myself. We paid and left.

Outside again, we were assaulted by the heat with a cruel vengeance, as though in retaliation for our rest in air-conditioned comfort. The heat killed any thoughts we had of riding the rest of the way down the island. We headed north.

About four miles north of Tilghman, a road leads to the village of Sherwood. We had passed the road on our way down Route 33 and had decided to visit Sherwood on our way back up to St. Michaels. We turned right and rode past the post office and antique store, the only evident commercial enterprise in the village. The main street is lined with beautiful homes, but not one could be called pretentious. The village has an atmosphere that made me feel at home.

The main street ends at a public pier that extends into Waterhole Cove on Harris Creek. The cove is an ideal anchorage, and the pier is perfect for securing a dinghy.

As I thought it would, the return trip to St. Michaels seemed to go on forever. Finally we reached West Chew Street and turned toward the pier and the dinghy.

The same waterman we had seen that morning was still in his boat, but he was cleaning it instead of working on his trotlines. Occasionally he looked up as we struggled to load the bikes. I wondered what he was thinking about our landlubbing efforts.

After I had tied the bikes to the pipes and had started the engine, Joan released the bow line. I put the engine in reverse, but we didn't move. I gave the engine more throttle. Still we didn't move.

The waterman looked at our transom and said, "Looks like you got a line on your stern that's caught on somethin'."

Of course we did. Like an idiot, I had forgotten the stern anchor. I pulled it up quickly, and we left the dock. The waterman had continued his chores with no change of expression. Joan was ready to explode with laughter, but she also was kind.

We returned to *Delphina* without further incident.

We were leaving the next day for the Wye River, and we pored over the charts and guidebooks to find out where we could anchor. All indications were that the Wye is one of the Bay's most beautiful rivers, and we decided to spend two nights and a full day on it.

From our anchorage in San Domingo Creek, the straight-line distance over land and water to the Wye River entrance is only four miles. The distance around Tilghman Island to the Wye is thirty-two miles. I hoped we would have some wind for the trip.

CHAPTER FIFTEEN

Wye River

The absence of wind the next morning gave us no choice but to use power to go to the Wye River. Rather than go around Blackwalnut Point, we could take a shortcut through Knapps Narrows, but that channel is subject to frequent shoaling. We didn't want to risk running aground.

It took us most of the day to get to Tilghman Point, the northernmost point on Tilghman Island. The wind refused to blow, and the constant drone of the diesel magnified the monotony. Once we were in Eastern Bay, our boredom was occasionally interrupted when a large crab, just below the surface, swam by us. If the crabs had been closer to the boat, we could have scooped them up with our dip net.

Several books we had read about Chesapeake Bay stated that the largest crabs in the Chesapeake are caught in Eastern Bay and the Wye River. Watermen who crab in that area firmly believe the large size is because of the water's low salinity, but scientists have no definite reason. We didn't care why the crabs are huge. It had been a while since we had done some serious crabbing, and we were ready to tackle the big ones. We had the fatback that Joan had bought in Oxford, and I had bought some chicken backs in St. Michaels. All we had to do was get to the Wye River.

Rounding Tilghman Point, I began a compass course toward a buoy that marked a shoal guarding the entrance to the Wye, and then I became confused. The chart shows that a neck runs north-south along the western shore of the Wye River and ends at Bennett Point. I was unable to distinguish Bennett Point, although I was headed almost directly toward it. Furthermore, where I thought the point should be, I saw a lighthouse, and the chart showed no lighthouse on Bennett Point.

Trusting the compass, I continued on the course I had set. Soon a sailboat came powering down the Wye, and I could make out the point as the boat passed between the lighthouse and the far shore. Somebody, probably not the government, had recently erected the lighthouse, which was not yet entered on the chart. At last I saw the small green buoy I was headed for. Leaving it to port, I turned into the Wye River.

Our anchorage for the night would be in Shaw Bay, a short distance into the Wye East River. The following day we would go up this river, also known as the Front Wye, to Wye Landing and a public pier. The plan was to anchor near the pier and take the bikes ashore for a ride to the famous Wye Oak, the Maryland State Tree, in the village of Wye Mills. Although the navigation up the river would be straightforward, I was worried. It looked *too* easy.

After daybeacon "3," the chart indicated no aids to navigation for the remaining four miles to Wye Landing. Negotiating the river without running aground requires staying in the middle of the river and counting each cove and creek as it appears so that the boat's position is always known. This attention to detail is what worried me: my mind wanders. But I'd deal with that problem the next day.

As we were motoring to where we could make our turn into the Wye East River, I noticed that a sailboat that had been behind us from Tilghman Point was starting to turn into the river, although the boat was about fifty yards behind us. I was certain the shortcut would result in a grounding, and it did. The boat came to an abrupt stop. The people on board weren't in any danger, and the tide was rising, so we continued on. We were soon anchored in Shaw Bay, in fifteen feet of water, opposite a large estate on Bruffs Island.

We immediately put baited crab lines in the water. The boat that had grounded, under way again, passed by us and anchored closer to shore.

The setting was perfectly delightful. A slight breeze had sprung up, and it cooled us considerably. But we weren't catching any crabs. The lines were at different depths, but the crabs didn't bite. An occasional giant crab, an inch or so under the water, swam by and wiggled his claws mockingly at us.

A man rowing a scull came near. As if he knew we were having no luck, he said we were anchored in too deep water—the ideal depth for crabbing was six to eight feet. This I couldn't understand. The watermen put their traps out in water fifteen feet deep, and they catch crabs. Dinner time was near, however, and I didn't want to move the boat, so I decided to wait until we got to Wye Landing to take the man's advice.

We left Shaw Bay at first light and cautiously motored up the river. The shore on our left was Wye Island, supposedly the first place in the country where wheat was raised. The State of Maryland owns most of the island and leaves it in its natural state as a park.

Joan was steering. Her mind doesn't wander, and she was paying close attention to the course. As I sat in the companionway and watched the scenery, I occasionally looked at the chart to see where we were. I had trouble finding our location on the chart. The serpentine nature of the river made navigating confusing. Suddenly something didn't look right. Although *Delphina* was in the middle of the river and the depth was adequate, the river was getting narrower. We were heading into Quarter Cove.

"Joan, do a one eighty!" I cried.

She immediately turned *Delphina* around.

"What's wrong?" she asked.

I pointed to Quarter Cove on the chart and said, "We were headed into this cove. Put her in neutral, and let's figure out where to go from here."

After studying the chart and recounting creeks we had passed, we agreed that we had been heading into Quarter Cove. Joan pointed to the entrance of Dividing Creek and said she hadn't seen it when we passed by it because of the angle of its mouth to the river. She could see the entrance only after having passed it, and she hadn't looked behind her. She had thought that the Wye River was Dividing Creek and that Quarter Cove was the Wye River.

Joan put the transmission into forward and got *Delphina* under way again. After that incident, we both identified each landmark as we came to it. When we arrived at Skipton Creek, we entered it and anchored in seven feet of water, the ideal depth for crabbing—according to the man in the scull.

To the south of us was Wye Heights, an estate with an impressive house with four large pillars, and to the north, on the river, was the public pier at Wye Landing. Although it was a Wednesday, the area was swarming with small recreational boats whose crews were engaged in crabbing. Most of the crabbers were using trotlines, while others were using traps.

Not wanting to miss all the action, we decided to catch a couple dozen huge crabs before we went ashore.

After getting ten lines into the water, we sat back and waited for them to jiggle. But all the action was about thirty yards from us, where other crabbers had their trot-lines and traps. I was reminded of Horseshoe Bend where all those kids were catching crabs from the short pier. What were we doing wrong?

An hour passed, and we had caught three crabs. At five inches from point to point, they just qualified as keepers. Where were the giants? My frustration level reached its peak, and I got into *Flipper*. If the crabs wouldn't come to us, by golly, I would go to the crabs.

Being careful not to interfere with the trotlines and traps, I put four lines in shallow water near the shore and waited. As the sun broiled my brain and flies bit my flesh, I continued to wait. Nothing happened. On the brink of insanity, I pulled up the lines and returned to *Delphina*.

"Let's have some lunch and go ashore," I pleaded.

Joan agreed. Putting our three crabs in a shady spot, we ate quickly. After we loaded the bikes into *Flipper,* we went to the public landing.

A boat-rental business is located at the pier, and all their boats secured in the water nearby gave the place a crowded look. A few workboats, including a skipjack undergoing restoration, were tied to the pier. Unloading the bikes was easier than it had been at St. Michaels, and we were soon pedaling away to Wye Oak State Park.

The Wye Oak is over four hundred years old. Ninety-five feet high and one hundred sixty-five feet wide, the tree is the largest white oak in Maryland and is magnificent to behold. Its massive trunk twists upwards and endows the tree with strength and permanence. When I looked at the oak from a distance, I saw that the symmetry of the branches is nearly perfect.

Tremendous efforts have been undertaken to protect the tree and keep it alive. Numerous cables have been secured to the branches to keep them from falling, rot has been removed and replaced with cement, and lightning protection measures have been installed.

As we walked toward our bikes, a woman who was looking at the tree called out to us.

"Did you see the snake?"

I thought I had heard incorrectly.

"What did you say?" I asked.

"Did you see the snake? There's a big snake coming down the tree!"

Joan and I looked at each other and went back to investigate.

A black snake, at least six feet long, was slithering slowly down the tree. As it came to the base of the trunk, it seemed to sense our presence and hesitated. Apparently satisfied that we meant it no harm, it quickly moved into the grass and disappeared into some thick shrubbery.

"Well, that was really something! Thanks for calling us back!" Joan said to the woman.

"I had a feeling you might want to see it," the woman explained.

We rode to Wye Mill, one of the two mills that the village of Wye Mills was named after. The other mill is no longer standing. Wye Mill was built in 1671 and was undergoing restoration when we visited it. During the Revolutionary War, the troops at Valley Forge were provided with flour ground at this mill and paid for by Robert Morris of Oxford.

After visiting the mill, we turned around and headed back to Wye Landing. It was hot, still, and muggy, and we lacked the energy to explore the countryside any further.

The busy crabbing activity of earlier that day had ended, and we had the idyllic anchorage to ourselves. We did manage to catch two more crabs, but they also were of minimum legal size. We began to think that the giant

Wye Mill

crabs of the Wye River were myths. Rather than steam the five we had, we decided to save them for the next evening, after we would have had a chance to try our luck in the Chester River. Also, if the wind was calm, we would have a chance to scoop some crabs off the surface of the water as we went down Eastern Bay.

CHAPTER SIXTEEN

Chester River

As we got under way that Thursday morning, I thought we were surrounded by a Japanese watercolor. The sun hadn't risen yet, but its light over the horizon was breaking through the heavy haze and was giving our little world a magical mauve glow. Vapor was rising from the surface of the river, as the warm water met the cooler dawn air. But the peaceful scene was abruptly shattered by the roar of an outboard, and I came back to reality.

The boat with the loud engine was soon beyond hearing distance, and the throb of our diesel was the only sound as we slowly worked our way down the river. I returned to my dream world. As the sun came up, the colors around us intensified and tempted me to turn off the engine and drift the rest of the way. But I couldn't let my mind wander! Quickly verifying that I was still in the middle of the river, I looked at the chart and started counting the landmarks. I wasn't in trouble yet.

Because the light was so different from what it had been the morning before, the trip downriver was a new experience. All the sights on shore had a fairy-tale quality. Even the boats that entered the scene had an unreal quality about them as the river mist enveloped them. It took all my effort to stay alert. I should have asked Joan to steer, but I was determined to get us out of the river.

At last, daybeacon "3" appeared, and with aids to navigation to focus on, I steered past Shaw Bay. As I looked back at the Wye East River, land of big crabs and scenic shores, I thought that the river, having captivated me with its spell, was reluctantly releasing me. And the ethereal atmosphere I had relished quickly dissipated. The haze thinned as the sunlight intensified, and the misty mauve color turned yellowish brown. As the air temperature rose to that of the water, the mists disappeared. Soon we were back at the Wye River entrance, and I was back in the real world.

The mirrorlike surface of Eastern Bay was frequently disturbed as crabs swam along on their way to unknown destinations. Joan took the helm, and I grabbed the dip net. Standing on the starboard side of *Delphina,* I could scoop up any crab that came close to that side of the boat. In a half hour I managed to scoop up seven, including three doublers—pairs of crabs engaged in the rite of courtship. This activity ended as we neared the southern point of Kent Island. Also ending was our visibility. As we rounded Bloody Point and entered Chesapeake Bay, we could see only about a quarter mile ahead. We were in fog.

We wanted to avoid the shipping lane because of the poor visibility. After passing the Bloody Point light, we veered to starboard until the depth sounder read fifteen feet. Then we steered north. We altered course as necessary to maintain the fifteen-foot depth.

For an hour we continued to navigate that way. By the time we reckoned we were halfway between Bloody Point light and the Bay Bridge, the visibility had improved to over a mile. Our nerves settled down. We entered the ship channel and increased our speed. After we went under the bridge, we headed toward Love Point, the northern tip of Kent Island. We reached Love Point light, passed it, and entered the Chester River.

Chestertown, our final destination on the Chester River, is twenty-eight miles upriver. It was almost three o'clock when we entered the river, and we discussed possible anchorages. Although not the closest or best protected, our choice was one inside the Corsica River because the Soviet Union maintains a retreat on the river for their embassy personnel.

In college, I had studied the Russian language for two years. In the years that have passed since then, I haven't had the opportunity to use what I had learned. If we anchored close enough to the retreat, I might be able to talk with some Soviets. After all, the Cold War is over.

Entering the Corsica River was easy. The beach and pier for the retreat are inside a cove near Town Point. Slowly we motored toward the beach and anchored when the depth sounder indicated seven feet. We were about two hundred yards from the beach, and we could see and hear the children playing on the sand and in the water. They were speaking Russian. Two women were watching the children. No men were in sight.

We baited the crab lines and put them in the water. I listened for any indication that the people on shore wanted to talk to us. I heard none. Going below to mix drinks for us, I decided to play Tchaikovsky's *1812 Overture* on the stereo to let the Soviets know I appreciate their culture. Turning up the volume enough so they could hear the music on shore, I went back on deck with the drinks to see how events would unfold.

Three men had come to the pier and were preparing to fish. The children and women ignored the music. If the men were listening, they gave no indication. But the crabs were responding. We pulled up one after another, and they were huge. Soon the cockpit was crawling with crabs.

The music ended, and still no reaction came from shore. I expected some applause at least, and maybe a "Bravo" or two. I put on Rachmaninoff's *Symphony No. 2* and turned up the volume even louder. Surely this music would trigger a reaction. The women and kids departed, but two more men joined the others on the pier. Apparently they were having no luck with the fishing, but they were having a spirited conversation. Our luck with the crabs was over, but we had about thirty crabs, including the ones caught earlier and the day before.

The symphony ended. The sky was dark, and the men ashore were speaking in low voices. They did not react to the end of the music. Not certain how these men would react to my starting a conversation, I decided to keep quiet. Perhaps *glasnost* didn't extend to the Chesapeake.

We spent the rest of the evening cooking crabs in the pressure cooker while we listened to Billy Joel at a volume only we could hear.

The next morning, the fog and heavy haze of the day before were gone, and the trip up the river to Chestertown was made in brilliant sunshine. We pulled into a marina to get fuel and to top off our water tanks. A dock attendant helped us with our lines.

"All the way from Florida, huh?" he said in greeting.

He was about twenty and had an athletic build and a deep tan.

We told him we were from the Keys and were cruising the Bay for the summer.

"Did you get to Onancock? That's where I'm from."

He handed us the fuel hose, and I told him about our visit there, but I refrained from asking him about cobia. Instead, I asked him what had brought him to Chestertown.

"During the school year, I'm a student at Washington College. I'm going into my junior year this fall. I got this job, so I stay here through the summer also."

"Do you know anything about the Soviet retreat on the Corsica River? We anchored there last night, and I got the impression the people there aren't all that friendly."

He grinned and asked, "Did you see all the KGB guys with machine guns walking around the place?"

I told him we didn't see anything like that.

"Well, last year some friends and I were riding around there on a boat, and we sure saw them. They didn't look very friendly to us!"

He told us a good place to anchor was in front of the public dock, between the bridge and the marina. We thanked him and went to anchor.

From the water, Chestertown is impressive. Large, elegant homes line the shore. Lawns and gardens come right to the water's edge. Piers project into the river with some large yachts tied to them. Even the drawbridge that spans the Chester River has classic lines and elegant features.

Now the county seat of Kent County, Chestertown was founded in 1706 as the Port of Chester. For nearly two centuries, Chestertown was a prosperous, bustling center of trade and commerce. As transportation by railroad and highway advanced on the Eastern Shore, the town's importance as a port waned. Today, however, the port is popular with cruising boaters.

We were soon ashore with our bikes. The houses away from the waterfront are as elegant as the ones we were anchored near and provide a fascinating mix of architectural styles. We followed High Street to the town center, turned right on Cross Street, and went to the Chamber of Commerce, where we acquired a walking guide, a biking guide, and an architectural guide—everything we needed to tell us about this beautiful place.

Although not listed as the beginning point on any tour, Washington College was our first stop. Founded in

Typical houses in Chestertown

1782, the College is Maryland's oldest institution of higher learning. George Washington gave permission for the school to be named after him and also served on its Board of Governors. The beautiful campus was deserted as we rode around it.

Returning to the center of town, we realized walking would be better than riding, so we locked our bikes to a post.

The heart of the town is Courthouse Square, a lovely park featuring criss-crossing brick walkways on its manicured lawn. The walkways are lined with benches, trees, and light posts. An ornate fountain crowns the center of the park. Near the square are old-fashioned stores that display a wide variety of goods to please the most sophisticated shopper. There is even a movie theater downtown, in the original theater building—a rare sight nowadays.

The afternoon had been spent riding or walking, and we were hungry. Thirty chilled steamed crabs were waiting for us back on *Delphina*. We bought six ears of corn and returned to the boat for a feast.

We studied the routes shown in *The Kent County Bicycle Tour* and decided to do a loop the next day into Queen Anne's County. None of our guidebooks or brochures offered any insight into what we were likely to see, but we thought the trip might be an interesting ride in the country. On Sunday, we would take *Delphina* downriver to Langford Creek, anchor in Shipyard Creek, and ride in a loop to visit Remington Farms, St. Paul's Church, and Rock Hall.

We began the ride to Queen Anne's County early the next morning. After walking our bikes on the Chestertown drawbridge, we were in Queen Anne's County, the Crown Jewel of the Chesapeake. Unfortunately, on our route, we saw none of the county's jewels. We were in farm country, and cornfields alternated with soybean fields and fields lying fallow. I know that some people

Residential street and telescoping house, Chestertown

consider farm fields to be jewels, but we had seen so many farm fields on our rides that they had lost their sparkle. No trees grew along the highway to give any cooling shade, and the sun beat down relentlessly. We turned at the little village of Crumpton, went over the Chester River again, and reentered Kent County. Back in Kent County, we saw a few trees; otherwise, we were seeing farmland.

The monotony of viewing fields was interrupted by the sight of the most interesting farmhouse I had seen yet in our travels around the Bay. The house reminded me of the Bates's house in the movie *Psycho*. The fenced drive leading to the imposing house on the hill looked inviting in an eerie sort of way. The house and the surrounding yard had no sign of life. I wondered about the people who lived there. Thinking about going to the house, I felt a chill. It would be an intriguing place to go trick-or-treating on Halloween.

We arrived back in Chestertown before noon. As we rode into town, I spotted a sign for the play *A Streetcar Named Desire*. I slammed on the brakes and read the sign carefully. Performed by the Actor's Community Theatre, it was scheduled to begin at eight that evening at the Norman James Theatre at Washington College. Joan joined me and shared my excitement at the prospect of seeing this classic drama. We made a mental note of where we could buy tickets and left immediately to buy them. We were not going to miss this play!

A gift shop off Courthouse Square sold us the tickets, and we grew more excited. A fine performance of a Tennessee Williams masterpiece is a theatergoer's dream.

Joan reminded me that I needed a new pair of boat shoes, so we looked for a place that would sell them. Houston's Dockside Emporium had what I was looking for. The store also had for sale *Chesapeake Country*, a book published earlier that year and full of spectacular color photographs. I couldn't resist buying it.

As I was paying for the shoes and the book at the register, the saleswoman asked if we had come to Chestertown by boat. I told her we had.

"How long are you planning to stay here?" she asked.

"We'll be leaving tomorrow morning. We're going to anchor in Shipyard Creek and then ride our bikes around that area."

"Oh, you'll love it there. I was born and raised on Langford Creek. I won't tell you how long ago that was! My husband and I live here now, but we keep our boat in Long Cove, just off Langford Creek. The creek is still one of the prettiest on the Bay, but the water isn't as clear as it used to be. Back in the sixties, the water was crystal clear. We could see all the way to the bottom. Now it's too murky."

"What caused it to get that way?" Joan asked.

"The biggest cause is the farms. There used to be a buffer zone of trees between the fields and the water. Now the fields go right to the water. Whenever it rains, all those chemicals the farmers use go right into the water. The same thing happens when people build houses too close to shore. You'll see what I mean when you go up there. Be sure you go to St. Paul's Church. Tallulah Bankhead's buried there, you know."

I told her we didn't know that, but we were planning to go to the church. We would definitely visit Tallulah's grave. We thanked her for the information and returned to *Delphina*.

We had an early dinner and prepared for our evening at the theater. We also had an opportunity to peruse *Chesapeake Country* and found that the text is as illustrative as the photographs and contains information we hadn't found in our guidebooks or brochures. The book not only brought back great memories of the places we had visited, but also got us excited about the places we were yet to see.

In our eagerness to find the Norman James Theatre, we arrived there an hour early. The early arrival allowed us a sneak peek at the interior of the theater and the opportunity to talk to the man selling tickets in the theater lobby. He wasn't busy yet, so we asked him about the Actor's Community Theatre.

"This is our twenty-second production," he told us. "We are a rather diverse group. Our members come from quite a distance, as do our audiences. We have somewhat of a different organizational structure from other amateur theater companies in that we have no officers and no board of directors. One person selects the plays or musicals we'll do each year, appoints the directors, arranges funding, handles publicity, and sells tickets. Of course, our members give a lot of help along the way. And we are very fortunate to have the use of this fine theater. Washington College is very supportive of our efforts."

We discussed other productions the company has staged since its inception. Then I asked about their production of *A Streetcar Named Desire.*

"We are proud of it. But I'll let you form your own opinions after seeing it. I think you'll enjoy it."

People began trickling in. We handed him our tickets and entered the theater. The seating was not reserved, and we got perfect seats.

The performance that evening was outstanding. The cast brought the play to life, and we were enthralled by their performances. The production was a demonstration of amateur theater at its best.

After returning to *Delphina,* we found that we were still under the spell of the performance. We couldn't stop telling each other about our impressions of different moments in the story. After a couple of drinks, we managed to get to sleep.

The trip down the Chester River to Langford Creek

was straightforward. After we entered the creek, I followed the aids to navigation and stayed out of trouble. But after we passed green buoy "7" off Drum Point, the navigational aids ended. I would have to keep *Delphina* in the middle of the creek and avoid the points.

After passing Cacaway Island to starboard, I steered toward Island Point. The readings on the depth sounder suddenly dropped. Before I could react, we hit bottom. Quickly, I reversed and gave the engine full throttle. *Delphina* responded by backing up. We weren't stuck. Returning to deeper water, I saw that I had cut too closely to the point. I had been daydreaming again. Luckily, the bottom was hard; otherwise, we would have been sucked right into the mud.

Going back to the middle of the creek, I rounded the point. A sportfishing boat, with the unlikely name *Oops* painted on its bow, passed us. The man at the helm hollered over to us.

"I saw you were going around too close. We tried to wave you back, but I guess you didn't see us."

"No, we didn't. Thanks for trying," I yelled back. "By the way, I really like your boat's name!"

He laughed and waved good-bye. Joan had kindly not said a word during the entire incident, and I silently vowed to show my thanks by not running aground the rest of the way to Shipyard Creek.

On the trip up Langford Creek, we didn't see many fields that came to the water. There were numerous trees on the shore, but we couldn't tell how deeply they extended away from the creek. We did see a lot of duck blinds. The creek seemed to have more duck blinds than any other creek we had visited.

We anchored in a little cove at the entrance to Shipyard Creek. Half a mile farther up the creek is a public landing. We loaded the bikes on *Flipper* and went to the pier. After a short bike ride through a cornfield, we turned right on Route 20 and followed the signs to Remington Farms.

At the entrance drive to Remington Farms, we were greeted by a sign:

REMINGTON FARMS
WILDLIFE MANAGEMENT AREA
Innovation-Demonstration-Education
Remington Arms Company, Inc.

At the bottom of the sign were silhouettes of a waterfowl and a rabbit, as well as the company's logo. A post with a carving of a duck on top was nearby.

As we rode a few more yards on the drive, we were confronted with another sign:

OPEN DURING DAYLIGHT HOURS ONLY
NO COMMERCIAL TOURS, HORSES,
BICYCLES OR MOTORBIKES PERMITTED

We were incredulous. What harm would a bicycle cause? I read the sign again. Were bicycles, horses, and motorbikes permitted if they weren't commercial? That's what the sign implied, and I was tempted to proceed. But then I thought that since this company makes guns and bullets, I had better not. Reluctantly, we turned away.

Riding toward St. Paul's Church, I recalled all the duck blinds we had seen earlier and reflected on the irony of an arms manufacturer's being concerned about the welfare of wildlife. Remington Farms, a pristine habitat for waterfowl, is in the midst of what must be, in the hunting season, a decidedly deadly environment for ducks and geese. I pictured each of the duck blinds being occupied by hunters totally dedicated to the demise of any waterfowl which appeared in their sights, and some of the hunters being armed with guns made by the owners of this wildlife sanctuary. But maybe I was missing the point, somehow.

And I was, of course. According to the U.S. Fish and Wildlife Service, there are over two million waterfowl hunters who are concerned about the threatened population of their prey. As waterfowl habitats fall victim each year to agriculture, urban development, and industry, the opportunities for the waterfowl populations to increase are diminished. And fewer birds to hunt might lead to fewer hunters needing fewer guns and less ammunition. So there's nothing ironic about a gun manufacturer owning a wildlife sanctuary; indeed, it makes good business sense.

Thoughts of killing birds were taken over by more spiritual meditations when we arrived at St. Paul's Episcopal Church, established in 1692. Situated amid venerable trees, it is in a shady and serene setting.

The churchyard contains many tombstones from the colonial era. The oldest tombstone we found bore the date October 20, 1729 and the thoughtful message:

> Behold and see now here I lye
> As you are now so once was I
> As I am now so must you be
> Therefore prepare to follow me

Wanting to pay our respects to a great actress, we visited the grave of Tallulah Bankhead, located in a family plot in a newer section of the adjoining cemetery. A withered flower on a stem lay on her tombstone, and a living carnation was planted at the head of her grave. She had a peaceful setting for her final rest.

We rode back to Route 20 to continue the loop to Rock Hall. We stopped at the Tolchester Marina to get a snack and something to drink. I opened the door to the small snack bar and found the place was packed with people.

Only later, after we had returned to Florida, did we learn from friends, who had made a ritual of going there, that the snack bar is known locally as Miss Virginia's, and that *Virginia* makes the best crab cakes in the world. If we had known that before our trip, we would have waited patiently to get a couple of those crab cakes. Instead, we bought soft drinks from a vending machine.

After the refreshment, we rode to the beach and looked out over the Bay—about a hundred yards out over the Bay. A thick fog was over the water. People were fishing from the beach and from some rocks that extended off the beach, and the people on the rocks were barely discernible. We planned to cross the Bay the next day, and we didn't want to have to face fog again. I silently prayed it would blow away.

When we reached the outskirts of Rock Hall, a quiet residential area, we were greeted by a sign:

WELCOME TO
ROCK HALL
NICE PEOPLE LIVE HERE

Thus assured, we entered the heart of the downtown area. Rock Hall is a town in transition. Some of the storefronts were empty. Others were boarded up. "For Rent" and "For Sale" signs decorated a few of the buildings. We headed for the harbor.

Until the 1960s, commercial and charter fishing for rockfish brought great prosperity to Rock Hall. When the State banned all commercial fishing for rockfish because of the decline of the rockfish population, the Rock Hall watermen turned to harvesting the plentiful clams in the nearby waters to make a living.

Today these watermen are facing challenges that have nothing to do with rockfish or clams. The character of their town is rapidly changing. Its proximity by road to the Bay Bridge and by water to Baltimore is turning the waterfront from a commercial fishing center to a haven for pleasure boats. Marinas are going up where packing houses had their wharves. Condominiums are sprouting up where warehouses once stood. The demand for slip space has made it very expensive for the watermen to dock their workboats. The place is experiencing gentrification and is going through growing pains. The process is the same that Solomons endured after it was "discovered."

Developers are applying pressure on the town government to allow the building to continue. In the Baltimore media, one developer advertises that a Rock Hall condominium is the ideal weekend retreat for harried, hard-working, stressed-out urban dwellers, and that they can get there in just minutes on a high-speed passenger ferry. The Rock Hall town fathers see economic benefits in tourism and pleasure boating, and they are allowing the building to proceed, despite vigorous opposition from longtime residents.

We locked up our bikes at the foot of the ferry pier and wandered around the waterfront. The air had a festive spirit, undoubtedly because of the music coming from the outdoor entertainer at the Waterman's Crabhouse restaurant, but I was sad to see piers rotting, buildings falling down, and derelict workboats lying neglected in the shallow water. Hundreds of sailboat masts, overshadowed by nearby trendy and upscale condominium buildings, were rising in the sky. The dock around the restaurant was full of fancy powerboats that had brought people to the restaurant to feast on crabs. The sights silently confirmed that the old way of life on the Rock Hall waterfront would never return. We walked to our bikes and pedaled up Route 20 to Shipyard Creek Landing.

During the afternoon the sky had become cloudier. A

cold front was coming. After we had returned to *Delphina,* it began to rain. It continued to rain during the night, and we slept fitfully in the stuffiness of the closed boat. The next day we would be going across the Bay to Baltimore. We didn't want rain for that passage, and each time I woke up I prayed the rain would go away.

But it didn't, not for three days.

CHAPTER SEVENTEEN

Patapsco River

The cold front that had brought the rain became a stationary front, a weather condition I have come to dread. Like an obnoxious houseguest, it hangs around until it sees fit to leave, and you can't do much about its presence except get in a foul mood.

The heavy clouds hung low, as though they couldn't support their own weight. The drizzle was constant and lessened the already poor visibility. We decided to leave our snug anchorage anyway and head downriver and across the Bay to the Patapsco River. If the rain stopped, and the temperatures remained in the sixties, we would have a pleasant stay in Baltimore's Inner Harbor. Certainly, cool and cloudy conditions would be preferable to Baltimore's usual summer weather: hazy, hot, and humid.

The trip down Langford Creek and the Chester River went quickly. The wind was directly out of the north, the current was favorable, and with just her foresail up, *Delphina* was doing seven knots. After we rounded Eastern Neck Island, we headed north to the Love Point light. Joan hoisted the remaining sails after she put a single reef in the main, and *Delphina* heeled heavily. We were sailing close-hauled, and we did a couple of tacks before reaching the Love Point light.

After we passed the light, we headed northwest to the Brewerton Channel Eastern Extension, one of the ship channels leading to Baltimore. The visibility on the Bay was less than a quarter mile, which was worse than it had been on the river. The drizzle had stopped, but a heavy mist remained.

When we reached the channel, we changed course to a westerly heading. The sailing immediately became less labored as we fell off the wind and no longer had the waves slamming into the bow. We stayed outside the channel to avoid confronting any ships that might be inside the channel. From the time we had left the Chester River, we had been sounding our foghorn at two-minute intervals, and we continued to do so.

Sailing in those conditions was not relaxing. The fog made it frightfully easy to become disoriented, and my mind played games with me. The wind screamed through the rigging and added a sense of urgency without telling us what was urgent. Sailing from buoy to buoy, we always knew where we were, but that knowledge provided little comfort. As we passed the buoy marking the junction with the Craighill Channel, we saw a pile of junk, to the right of the Brewerton Channel, that was not shown on our chart. It looked like a wreck and made us feel more uncomfortable.

As we passed North Point, at the mouth of the Patapsco River, the visibility improved dramatically. The huge complex of Bethlehem Steel, its many stacks spewing heavy smoke into the sky, appeared on Sparrows Point. The sight was depressing, although I was awed by the raw power the image conveyed. On the Patapsco's southern shore, near Orchard Beach, another industrial complex, probably a power plant, was sending enormous clouds of steam into the air. These scenes of man-made might, without any sign of humanity, gave me the chilling thought that machines had overtaken mankind. The gloomy sky reinforced the feeling of entering a netherworld.

Fortunately for my peace of mind, after passing under the Francis Scott Key Bridge, we began to see signs of life. Even the government seemed to want to dispel my fears: the Coast Guard has a buoy near the bridge, with the Stars and Stripes painted on it, to commemorate a very human deed, the writing of the "Star-Spangled Banner" by Francis Scott Key. A tour boat passed by us, and a few tugs scurried back and forth. A sailboat was coming up on our right and would overtake us, and I realized how ridiculous we looked. Both of us were wearing heavy parkas. Joan was wearing her hood; I was wearing my bright-red, wool ski hat. And it was August. As the boat passed us, we waved to the three people in the cockpit. All three, clad in foul-weather gear, looked at us without acknowledgement. How weird did we look?

Bethlehem Steel plant, Sparrows Point

The closer we got to the Inner Harbor, the less wind we had. We dropped the sails, started the engine, shed our parkas, and put on our foul-weather jackets. We were cold, but we looked more like sailors and less like arctic explorers.

Fort McHenry was directly ahead of us. The lawn surrounding the fort was an intense green and stood out like a brilliant emerald in the grayness of the sky and cityscape that surrounded it. We hadn't seen green that bright since we had been in Scotland.

We passed by Fells Point, a historic area of Baltimore that has undergone recent restoration. The row houses that Baltimore is known for gracefully line the waterfront. Except for the modern marine facilities that have been built in the area, Fells Point has the look of an earlier era.

At last we were in the Inner Harbor. Skyscrapers overlook a waterfront of ultramodern buildings that include an aquarium, a science center, an office building, and a shopping complex. Boats line the bulkheads that circle the harbor. The frigate *Constellation*, sister ship to the *Constitution*, lay at her berth to our left; the World War II submarine U.S.S. *Torsk* and the lightship *Chesapeake* were tied to the wharf on our right. We eased our way into a spot in front of the office building, the World Trade Center, and anchored.

Baltimore! I last anchored in this spot in September, 1981. The Baltimore City Fair was being held, and the area was bustling. Sitting in the cockpit, I watched as the people of this great city walked along the sidewalk only fifty yards from me. It was easy to catch their festive spirit, and I soon left the boat and went ashore to join the party at the fair. After that weekend, I had the indelible impression that the people of Baltimore know how to have fun and love having it. They collectively have a personality that gives "Bawlamer," as many of them affectionately call their home, a vibrancy not found in many other cities.

It was late afternoon by the time we settled down, and we decided to have dinner and wait until morning before going ashore. We already had a lot of information about things to do in Baltimore, and we spent the rest of the evening preparing an itinerary.

The next morning we were eager to go ashore. Our plan was to go first to the National Aquarium, which would open at nine. From there we would walk through the downtown area to Lexington Avenue and eat lunch at the famous Lexington Market, a collection of different vendors under one roof. After lunch, we would visit the Top of the World at the World Trade Center.

A few raindrops were in the air when we went ashore around seven thirty, and the clouds were ominous. We had left our raingear on *Delphina*, but we could duck into a store for shelter if we had to.

We walked around the periphery of the harbor. People were rushing past us on their way to work. They did not look happy; some looked angry. Maybe the gloomy weather was depressing them. As the angry-looking people approached us, they continued to look straight ahead, and I thought that, if I cheerfully wished them a good morning, they would hit me with their umbrellas. The uniformity of their appearances and moods was striking. These were not the Baltimoreans I had known.

Something else about these people surprised me: many of them were wearing jogging shoes with their expensive and fashionable business attire.

When I commented to Joan about this phenomenon, she said, "The trend started in all big cities just before I moved to the Keys. Women found it a pain to wear high heels on the city streets and the mass transits, so they wore sneakers to work and changed when they got to the office. Then some men caught onto the idea. It does look funny though, doesn't it?"

We arrived at the aquarium early and were nearly first in line. By nine o'clock, the line was long. After we entered the aquarium, the first creatures we saw were two beluga whales, swimming lazily in a huge pool. Like bottlenose dolphins, these gentle creatures have fixed smiles that make them look perpetually happy. But watching these captive whales, I thought they would probably be happier back in the ocean, where they would have more to see than tiles, glass, and staring faces.

We slowly walked around the many exhibits and the enormous tank full of many creatures of the sea. The crowds of children that were inside visiting the aquarium gaped in silent wonder at the colorful fish and screamed with a mixture of fright and delight when sharks appeared. In the tropical rain-forest exhibit, where brilliantly plumed birds flew free, I felt as if I were in the middle of the Amazon jungle.

After touring the aquarium, we walked to Lexington Market. Many buildings we saw along the way were new. I was overcome with exuberance as I sensed the city's vitality. The night before, we had listened to Gershwin on the stereo, and the powerful melodies kept repeating in my mind as I matched them with the scenes in front of me. The rush of the traffic, the blare of the horns, the scream of the sirens—all added to the rhythm.

The skyscrapers responded to my melodic mood. Looking up at the massive buildings as we walked along, I watched their reflections, bouncing back and forth in each other's windows or polished marble sides. In my mind, the reflections were phantasmic figures in a dazzling dance. The older buildings, with their weathered sides and fewer windows, stood by reprovingly as their younger colleagues played with tireless abandon. I spent more time looking up than looking ahead, and three times Joan had to grab me so I wouldn't cross a street against a light.

We managed to get to Lexington Market without my getting killed. Established in 1782, this marketplace, with over one hundred thirty-five merchants selling ethnic meals, produce, meat, and groceries, has become an institution.

Inside the large building housing these merchants is an atmosphere that reflects Baltimore's vivacity. At lunchtime, crowds pour in to partake of a riotous ritual as people engage in the merry madness of trying to get something to eat. The stress accumulated from a morning at the office melts away. Those who are preparing the food create a cacophony by yelling out their offerings to all who will listen and pause only long enough to collect a payment from a customer. It's a marvelous place to have a meal.

The greatest difficulty we faced was deciding what to

Skyscrapers, Baltimore

eat. I quit this laborious process and decided to stuff myself. I got a Polish sausage, a Greek pastry stuffed with spinach, some Chinese egg rolls, a Japanese sushi sampling, and a cup of beer. Joan got a slice of pizza and a Pepsi. Just as I thought I had everything I wanted, I saw a stall that offered soft-shell crab sandwiches. I got one and gave half to Joan.

While we enjoyed this spread, we entertained ourselves watching the crowds of people. The spirit that I had seen at the city fair years ago was still alive. Even the executive types who had appeared so sour on their way to the office were laughing and joking with each other.

Absorbing the sights and sounds on the streets, we walked back to the World Trade Center. I was absorbing the smell also. Downtown Baltimore had a wonderful aroma unlike anything I had smelled before. It was similar to the smell of bread baking.

Inside the World Trade Center, we bought our tickets for the Top of the World, the twenty-seventh floor of the thirty-two-story, pentagonal office building. An express elevator whisked us up, and we were greeted by a woman as we exited.

"Hi! Welcome to the Top of the World! Let me tell you what we have here."

Not only did she explain how the floor is laid out and what there is to see, but she also told us a lot about the city itself. It was from her we learned the first umbrella manufactured in the United States was made in Baltimore in 1828. She gave us brochures for some of the attractions in town and maps for the mass transit system and told us we could ride the trolley to Fells Point or to the historic Mount Vernon district of the city. This woman's pride in her city and her enthusiasm infected us. She must greet hundreds of people a week, but she seemed in no danger of getting burned out.

Another couple got off the elevator, and she excused herself to welcome them.

From the windows on this floor we looked at an unobstructed panorama of the entire city. Although it was cloudy, we could see to the horizon. At one viewing spot, we were almost directly over *Delphina*. From that height, she looked like a toy in a tub.

The history of the city is told in a series of panels and exhibits. One display shows that much was learned about the early life of Baltimore from the excavating for the new buildings in the Inner Harbor. As the foundations were dug, amateur and professional archaeologists screened out artifacts from the different layers of sediment. From a study of these artifacts, the archaeologists interpreted conditions and ways of life in former times.

From such a high vantage point, we could see construction all over the city. This city is growing! Looking out over the Patapsco River, we saw Bethlehem Steel on Sparrows Point and the many shipping terminals and wharves that line the river. Much of the waterfront still contains dilapidated buildings and rotting piers, but that blight is being removed as more marinas and condominiums are built.

From the World Trade Center we went to Federal Hill, directly across the Inner Harbor. From the top of this municipal park, we had a commanding view of the Inner Harbor. I spotted a monument that I couldn't identify, on the near side of the harbor from where we stood, and we walked down to it.

The monument is the memorial to the schooner *Pride of Baltimore* and those of her crew, including her captain, who were lost at sea on their return from a goodwill voyage to Europe. The monument is starkly simple and invites the visitor to stay awhile and meditate on what it memorializes. In the center of the little park is a wooden mast. A polished stone block, adorned with a plaque showing the vessel's lines and rigging, bears this inscription:

On May 14, 1986, the *Pride of Baltimore*,
her captain, and three members of her
crew were lost at sea.

The *Pride* now rests at the end of a goodwill
journey that covered 150,000 miles and
touched 125 cities around the world.

Yet her precious cargo—the spirit of the
people who sent her forth and of those who
received her—will never be lost.

What affected me most, as I reflected at this memorial, was the thought of the unselfish and courageous actions the captain and crew took in attempting to rescue their shipmates. The sadness at the loss of lives was with me, of course, but also the happiness of knowing that a great city and its people can put such a tragedy behind them and start anew.

The *Pride of Baltimore II* was built on the banks of the Inner Harbor, almost a stone's throw from the memorial, shortly after the loss. I could imagine the joy in the hearts of the city residents as they watched the building of this ship and the rebuilding of a dream. Not many cities in the world have a classic sailing ship for a goodwill ambassador, and for Baltimore to have one that truly reflects its pride, spirit, and heritage is a priceless treasure for all people, whether they are Baltimoreans or not. And I'm certain that Baltimore would have it no other way.

Before leaving the memorial, I wished the *Pride II* success on her current goodwill voyage, far from the shores of the Chesapeake. The dream lives on.

We spent the rest of the afternoon browsing through Harborplace, the two pavilions at the heart of the Inner Harbor. Completed in 1980, they contain over one hundred forty shops and eating places. Across the street, but connected by a skywalk to one of the pavilions, is The Gallery, an elegant multi-tiered atrium that sets a standard for urban retailing. We finished our window-shopping and returned to *Delphina*.

The following morning we awoke to an intermittent drizzle. On our agenda were visits to the grave of Edgar Allen Poe and to the house where he lived while he was in Baltimore.

Located in the Westminster Churchyard, the grave is a short walk from the Inner Harbor and easy to find. The old church, dating to the 1700s, is situated amid higher and newer buildings, and when we arrived at the site, I had the impression the church was about to be overwhelmed by progress. And in a corner of the property, surrounded by the constant sounds of construction, the earthly remains of Edgar Allen Poe seek an eternal respite.

At the foot of Poe's weathered tombstone lay withered flowers, perhaps the remains of the three roses placed there annually by the Mysterious Stranger, who leaves also a bottle of fine French cognac. The bottle of cognac does not remain at the grave: it becomes part of a collection at the Poe house.

Since 1949, the Mysterious Stranger has been making visits on the anniversary of Poe's birthday. Dressed in a dark, hooded cloak that reaches to the ground, the Stranger comes in the night and has never been identified.

Several pennies were on a ledge that goes around the gravestone. The pennies are left by Poe's admirers to perpetuate a fund drive undertaken by Baltimore's schoolchildren in the last century. Believing that the body of the great author should have a more prominent resting place in the churchyard than where it had been buried, the children collected pennies until they amassed enough to cover the cost of moving the coffin. The move was made in 1875. The pennies left nowadays are periodically collected by the Westminster Preservation Trust and used to preserve the grave.

The original burial site has not been forgotten: it is marked by a monument and surrounded by brilliant blooms. Each spring, the Trust's president personally plants red coleus and dusty miller around the site. The effect is stunning.

The burial ground contains many old graves. Some of them have horizontal marble plaques over the graves. Some type of force, never completely understood or identified, has caused these plaques to sag in the middle. The force was so great on one plaque that the plaque broke into two pieces. We have not seen this phenomenon in

Poe's first burial site (left) and gravestone, Baltimore

other old graveyards.

Getting to the house where Poe had lived was a challenge. All of the street maps we had of Baltimore were for the downtown area only. The best map we had, the *Official Landmark Map of Baltimore*, indicated the house was approximately one block west of Fremont Avenue, outside the boundary of the map. We knew the address was 203 North Amity Street, so we thought we would be able to find it.

After we crossed Martin Luther King Jr. Boulevard, a major artery, we entered a different world. Old row houses, ranging in condition from well kept to dilapidated, and ugly high-rise housing projects, looking more like prisons than apartments, defined the neighborhoods. The typical tourist doesn't see or walk around these areas. The territory didn't look friendly.

But we couldn't turn around and still keep our self-respect. We were nervous, certainly, but to give into the fear of a possible attack by a mugger was out of the question. We wanted to see the Poe house, and by gosh, we were going to.

After fifteen minutes of walking farther into this area, we still hadn't found the house and had no idea where to go.

"I don't know what to suggest, Joan," I said. "But I do know that in this neighborhood, I don't want to ask anyone if they know how to get to the Poe house."

"I think I see a sign for the house on top of the next street sign," Joan said.

The sign was for the Poe house and had an arrow directing us to turn right. We turned and found ourselves entering a more run-down neighborhood. Gamely, we kept on to the next sign, on Amity Street, which also pointed right. A half block away, on a corner, was the Poe house, a two-story, brick row house.

The author lived in the house from 1832 to 1835 and

wrote in the little garret. I looked at the roof and saw a small dormer window, the same one he must have looked out as he wrote. What was this neighborhood like then, I wondered. Today it is a poor one: across the street are decrepit row houses with boarded-up windows; next to the Poe house, the houses are in need of repair; on the street and sidewalks, weeds sprout up. One quaint touch is the old-fashioned street light on the corner.

The neighborhood was quiet, eerily so for the middle of the day in a major city. Unfortunately for us, in August the house is open to the public only on Saturdays. After spending a few minutes in silent reflection, we left the area.

It was late morning. We wanted to have lunch at the Lexington Market again. As we crossed the Martin Luther King Jr. Boulevard, light rain began. We walked faster. About a block from Lexington Market, a man with two umbrellas hanging from his forearm approached us

Amity Street, Baltimore (Poe house on right)

with a large smile on his face.

"You folks are gittin' all wet! How 'bout buyin' dese umbrellas?" he asked.

Suddenly his face lit up even more. Doing a quick two-step, he bounded up to me and put his forearm bearing the umbrellas next to mine.

"Sheeeee, man. Yo' tan's bettah dan mine!" he cried. "Wheah'd you git all dat colah?"

This sales approach was too much for Joan. Recovering quickly from her initial surprise, she started to laugh loudly.

Not sure what to say, I answered, "We're from Florida. The sun shines all the time down there."

"Well, Ah guess you ain't gonna need no umbrella, den!" he said as he stepped back.

"No, not really. This stuff won't last will it?"

"Naw, man. Only 'til Ah sell dese last two umbrellas, and dat won't be long. Stay dry, now, bro!"

With that, he danced down the street. Joan was still laughing, but managed to recover enough to continue walking to the Market.

After a lighter lunch than the day before, we went to the B&O Railroad Museum. My grandfather was a career terminal manager for the Missouri Pacific Railroad in Texas, and some of my fondest childhood memories are of freightyards and trains. I couldn't pass up the opportunity to visit this museum and relive some of those memories.

The museum is actually located on the site of the first rail terminal in the United States, established in 1829. Inside the roundhouse, we looked at twenty-two restored steam and diesel locomotives, some of which date back to the dawn of railroading in this country. Outside we saw another sixty cars and locomotives, including a couple we could climb onto.

Locomotive, B&O Railroad Museum

The man with the umbrellas must have been success-ful with his sales effort; the rain stopped before we left the museum. It was mid-afternoon, and we caught the trolley to take us to Fells Point.

Although Fells Point has been undergoing restoration for a number of years, some places have yet to be restored. As I looked at what had to be done to some of these buildings to make them habitable, I marveled that people would take on such a project and see it through to the end. The houses that have been restored are lovely and justify the work and expense.

Baltimore's oldest surviving house, the Robert Long house, is in Fells Point. Built of brick in 1765, its restora-tion is so perfect that I thought the house was new until I read the historical plaque.

We took the trolley back to the Inner Harbor and then took the Charles Street trolley to Mount Vernon Place, site of the nation's first architectural monument to

Robert Long house, Baltimore

George Washington. The Washington Monument in Washington, D.C. was designed by the same architect who designed the one in Baltimore. Many elegant town houses grace Mount Vernon Place and complement the picture of gentility that we saw on Charles Street.

Back on *Delphina* for the evening, we decided, as much as we had enjoyed two days of city life, we should move *Delphina* and anchor in Middle River, east of the city. My parents live a few miles north of Baltimore and were hosting a family get-together that weekend. Middle River would be a convenient place for us to use as a base from which to visit their home. Another advantage to the move would be seeing friends of ours, Norman and Margaret Edwards, who own a marina on Hopkins Creek, off Middle River. We decided to leave in the morning.

CHAPTER EIGHTEEN

Middle River

The weather forecast in the morning promised the stationary front was finally moving west and would leave sunny skies behind. But, as we went out the Patapsco River, the sky was still overcast. The wind was from the northeast at fifteen knots and impeded our progress as we motored along.

Our course to Middle River would take us around North Point and past Hart-Miller Island. We would anchor in the west branch of Hopkins Creek.

As we rounded North Point, the full force of the wind and seas struck *Delphina* head on. Her speed was reduced to three knots over the bottom, and the ride was bumpy. To starboard we saw the pile of metal that we had seen in the fog earlier that week. It was a wreck.

Slogging along as we were got tiresome quickly. We could have raised the sails and tacked to Middle River, but our batteries needed charging. That's the excuse I use when I'm lazy.

As we neared Hart-Miller Island, we saw the enormous project the State is undertaking on the island. Bulkheads were erected to the southeast of the island in a rough oval shape. The area formed by this dike is being filled with spoil from dredging Baltimore Harbor. Years from now, when the area behind the dike is filled, the island will be a park of over a thousand acres.

As soon as we headed on a northwesterly course to the mouth of Middle River, we picked up speed over the bottom. The tide was coming in, and the waves no longer slammed into the bow. Joan, always eager to sail and never lazy, hoisted the sails for a reach to the river. I turned off the engine.

Both shores of Middle River are lined with houses built close together. Most of the houses had piers with boats. Up each creek that we passed were many more boats, secured to slips at marinas.

We wanted to anchor opposite the Edwardses' marina, and when I had called Margaret Edwards from the Inner Harbor to let her know we were coming, she had given me directions to their marina from Middle River. We found Hopkins Creek without a problem. The creek, however, confused us because of its several coves and forks. Thinking we were in the right place, we anchored near what looked like a small marina.

A man walked to the end of his pier as we got into *Flipper* and waved to us to come over.

"Good afternoon, and welcome!" the man said in greeting. "We don't see too many Florida boats up here! Where are you going?"

"We're looking for Snug Harbor Marina, the Edwardses' place. Know where it is?" I asked.

"Oh, that's on the other side of this little peninsula. They're almost directly across the street from me, but you have to row around that point to get there by dinghy. You can just tie up here and walk over."

Thanking him for the offer, I explained the Edwardses were friends of ours, and we would be coming and going at different times throughout the weekend.

"Well, suit yourselves. But if you get tired of rowing,

tie up here and cut through the yard. We're sailors, too, as you might have guessed from our boat. Anything we can do to help you out, let us know."

Thanking him again, I rowed toward the point. We were greeted at the point by two vociferous Dobermans, one of which had a stiff rear leg. That handicap didn't restrict his aggressive moves. Fortunately for us, the dogs didn't go into the water.

When we got to the marina, we tied up our dinghy at an outer pier. No one was around the dock area, so we walked up to the street and the front door of the house. I knocked, but no one answered. Joan pointed to the car in the driveway and said that someone was probably home. Knocking again, I listened for movement, but heard nothing. We left the house.

It was late afternoon. Our map showed a highway about a mile away, and we walked to it. Finding a phone, I called my brother Patrick and made arrangements to meet the next day. We had a quick meal at a fast-food place, bought a six-pack of beer at a convenience store, and walked back.

The next morning, I rowed around the point again, and we went to Snug Harbor. Although it was early, Norman was working on a project outside.

Norman is in his eighties, but he has the vitality of someone much younger. A welterweight boxer when he was younger, he still has the build of an athlete on his stocky frame. He made a career out of the Merchant Marine, and after World War II, he and Margaret bought the marina and adjoining house and settled down to a life ashore. An inventive man, Norman finds this life perfect because he has infinite opportunities to use his mechanical genius. Fixing things for his marina customers, as well as working on a variety of projects for the marina, keeps him busy.

We met the Edwardses in Florida in 1984 when they

chartered us for a sail. Norman entertained us with humorous stories of his years in the Merchant Marine and his experiences with sailboats. Occasionally, Margaret entered the conversation with an observation or a wry comment. She provided a perfect counterpoint to Norman's effusiveness. A delightful couple, they won our hearts, and we became friends. We renewed the friendship every year when they came to the Keys. We hadn't seen them, however, for the past three years; driving down had become too difficult for them.

Norman greeted us with his usual ebullience. As he vigorously shook my hand, I clasped his right shoulder, which was still rock hard as though he lifted weights every day. He gave Joan a big hug and led us up to the house.

Margaret met us at the door.

After hugging Joan and then me, she asked, "What happened to you? I thought you would be here yesterday afternoon."

Joan told her what happened.

"Well, he couldn't have knocked very loud, because I was here. I was taking a little nap for a while, but I would have heard him if he had knocked louder."

I took all the blame. After all, Joan had pointed out the car in the driveway. We sat down and swapped news. I wasn't surprised to learn that Norman still works seven days a week at the marina and has no thoughts of retiring. It's tough, Margaret pointed out, just to get Norman to go on vacation.

We told them about our trip and that our next port of call was Havre de Grace. Margaret sat up.

"What's gotten into you, Margaret?" I asked. "I've never seen you get this excited before."

"I lived in a lighthouse there until I was three years old!" she said. "It's on an island just before you get to Havre de Grace. They haven't used it for years. A while back, a woman who's doing a book about lighthouses on the Bay called me to see if I could remember anything about it. Then she told me that somebody's looking into restoring the house and starting a bed-and-breakfast place. When you're up there, will you see what you can find out about it? I'd sure like to know."

We assured her we would. It was almost time to meet my brother. After agreeing to getting together again before we sailed away, we left the house.

That weekend is a hazy blur. Everything happened so quickly. In the car borrowed from my parents, we were traveling on land at much greater speeds than we are used to. After catching up on family news with all the gathered relatives, we spent the weekend eating delicious meals and home-baked goodies, playing with the kids, watching television and video movies, reading magazines, and playing golf. Although we hated the drive back in the dark, we returned to *Delphina* each evening around ten and enjoyed the serenity of being on an anchored boat.

On our third morning in Hopkins Creek, as I rowed around to Snug Harbor, yet another man came to the end of his pier and told us we could tie up at his place. We were being overwhelmed with kindness.

It seemed that no sooner had we anchored than we were under way again. We had made a final visit to the Edwardses, thanked them for their hospitality, and tried to figure out when and where we would see them again. We hoped it would be in Florida that winter.

Ahead of us was Havre de Grace, at the very beginning of the Bay.

CHAPTER NINETEEN

Susquehanna River

The weather pattern that had become established with the passage of the latest warm front was firmly entrenched. No wind blew, and the haze hung low over the Bay. A strong flood tide was helping the engine to speed us north. The navigation was routine, but as we entered the broad body of water named Susquehanna Flats, we had to make certain we stayed in the well-defined, but narrow, channel. Periodic booms from weapons being tested at the nearby Aberdeen Proving Grounds helped to keep us alert.

We could see a number of islands ahead of us. Joan looked through the binoculars for Margaret's lighthouse and found it on the island with the strange name of Fishing Battery. As we neared the island, I became excited by what I was seeing.

"Joan, it's beautiful!" I cried as I looked at the island through the glasses. "I've got to get ashore and take some pictures!"

When we were abeam of the island, Joan put the engine in neutral. I rowed *Flipper* to the island and tied her to a wharf.

The house was a long way from becoming a bed-and-breakfast inn: it had been neglected for years. The house, of brick construction, had peeling whitewash. All the windows were broken, and the inside was a mess. The cupola that had contained the original light stuck up from the roof. The Coast Guard, with no concern for esthetics, had erected a monstrosity of a derrick in front of the house. The current light was mounted atop this derrick. The old house would make a beautiful inn, but something would have to be done about the ugly light structure.

Although the island was overgrown with weeds, some lovely trees provided shade and decoration. Within a week, the island could be returned to a state of natural beauty.

I took several pictures to send to Margaret. Even with the overall appearance of being run-down, the island's charm would radiate from the photographs, and she would be pleased.

Back on *Delphina* once again, I took the helm, and we continued to Havre de Grace. We passed by the Concord Point lighthouse, built in 1827 to serve the increasing traffic coming down the Susquehanna River.

After we passed the lighthouse, modern condominium buildings came into view. They and the town's four marinas dominate the waterfront. We found a spot to anchor opposite the public fishing pier at Hutchins Memorial Park. Using the engine, we ensured the anchors were well set. The mighty Susquehanna provides half the Bay's fresh water, and the current can be powerful. The four bridges that cross the river at its mouth created an imposing sight from our anchorage.

Of the towns we visited in the Chesapeake Bay area, only Havre de Grace has a French name. One of our guidebooks explained how the town was named. In 1782, General Lafayette stopped in the town on his way to Philadelphia from Mount Vernon. Commenting on the beauty of the spot, he was told that a fellow Frenchman, upon seeing the town, had been reminded of a town in France and had cried, *"C'est Le Havre de Grace!"* The general agreed with his countryman's assessment and suggested the name of the town be changed from Lower Susquehanna Ferry to Havre de Grace. And it was, in 1785. In English the name means Harbor of Mercy.

The British showed their appreciation of the town by sacking it in 1813 and destroying two-thirds of the buildings. We wanted to see how the city was rebuilt. Also, our guidebooks reported that Havre de Grace is an ideal layover for cruising boaters: all amenities are available within walking distance of the waterfront, the city is rich in history, and the people are friendly and hospitable.

Since we could walk to everywhere we wanted to go, we rowed *Flipper* ashore without our bikes. At the Chamber of Commerce, we picked up three self-guided-tour brochures. We walked first to the restored canal lock on the north side of the city.

The Lock House, constructed of brick during the Canal Era, served as the lock keeper's home and as an office for collecting tolls from northbound vessels. The pivot bridge that allowed mules and wagons to cross the canal was reconstructed in 1984, and the outlet lock was de-silted in the late 1980s. Because of this restoration work, we had no problem understanding how the locks operated when the canal was in operation.

During the period from 1830 to 1860, the linking of the railroad and the canal brought great prosperity to Havre de Grace. After the Civil War, the town's economy faltered as the canal become obsolete, but by 1910, new industry and vegetable canneries had brought an economic resurgence to the city.

In the early part of this century, multitudes of sportsmen discovered that the Susquehanna Flats, with its vast flocks of waterfowl in the fall and bountiful fish, was an ideal area for pursuing their recreational goals. But in

Lock House, Havre de Grace

1972, Hurricane Agnes roared through and caused the Susquehanna River to dump tons of silt onto the flats. The grasses needed to sustain the delicate ecological balance of an estuary were buried.

As we wandered around the commercial downtown area, we noticed that the people on the streets were laughing and joking among themselves. The merchants have a wonderful collective sense of humor, evident in two of the brochures we obtained; one guide is a map with funny little drawings all over it, and the other is a folder entitled *Historic Havre de Grace*. On its cover is a question: "Why on earth should I spend a day in Historic Havre de Grace, Maryland?" Also on the front cover is the answer: "101 Reasons why you should spend a day in the city by the Bay!!" Inside are the reasons. Included among them are:

7. See Harford Memorial Hospital, birthplace of

the Baltimore Oriole's [sic] Ripkin brothers
—Cal Jr. and Billy.

35. Catch a fish or two at the Frank J. Hutchins
    Memorial Park at the foot of Congress Avenue.

69. Find out why collectors and carvers of duck
    decoys are considered intelligent people.

74. With 16 dentists and 65 doctors to serve you,
    you're always in good hands in Havre de
    Grace.

The residents of Havre de Grace take the art of decoy
carving seriously. Every May, the Decoy Festival is celebrated, and the Duck Fair is held every July. The Havre
de Grace Decoy Museum features the work of master
decoy makers, and fine examples of the decoy-makers' art
can be purchased at several stores in the city. Every time
I looked in a store window, I saw some reference to duck
decoys. At least it seemed that way.

One task we had to accomplish while in town was
mailing our absentee ballots for the primary election in
Florida. We had never voted absentee before, and we
were surprised when we completed the ballots that
morning: our signatures had to be witnessed by two
people or one person if that witness was a notary. Neither
of us is a notary, so we could witness each other's signa-
ture, but we needed another witness. We thought a postal
clerk could witness for us when we went to the post office
to mail the ballots.

We entered Havre de Grace's stately post office and
approached the clerk behind the window.

"Good morning," I greeted the young woman. "We
have to mail our absentee ballots today. Will you please
witness our signatures before we do?"

"Oh, I couldn't do that."

"Why not?"

"Well, it just wouldn't be right."

I didn't know if she thought we were trying to get her involved in an election scam, if fulfilling our request was against postal regulations, or if she refused to witness because we were strangers, but I did know the reason wasn't worth pursuing. We thanked her and went looking elsewhere for a witness.

We found one at City Hall, across the street. Joan Scarlato, the secretary to the Mayor and City Council, was so friendly with her greeting and her willingness to help us that I wondered whether we were in the City Hall or the Chamber of Commerce office. Without hesitation, she got out her notary seal and witnessed our signatures. If every city government had someone like Joan Scarlato working for it, no one would ever want to fight city hall.

Encouraged by her helpful manner, I asked her if she could tell us about Fishing Battery Island and the lighthouse.

"I'm afraid I don't know the latest. But I can give you the name and number of a local historian who would know."

She gave us the name and number of Ellsworth Shank, and we thanked her for all her help. We went outside to a pay phone and called him.

"Yes, I'm familiar with the property," Mr. Shank said. "A committee has been formed to see what can be done to make the best use of it. A number of years ago it was a county park, but that led to problems with garbage disposal and the like, so the park was closed. There has been some talk about opening a bed-and-breakfast inn, but nothing definite has been decided."

I thanked him for the information and hung up. We bought a postcard, and I recapped the phone conversation for Margaret. I also wrote about the pictures I had taken. We returned to the post office and mailed our ballots and the card.

We walked around the historic district. Not all the buildings have been restored to their original condition, and the self-guided-tour brochure invited us to "Mentally undress the structures with stucco, tar paper, asbestos shingles, and aluminum siding. Discover our historic district." We found we could fully appreciate the beauty, elegance, and origins of most of the buildings without having to mentally undress them.

We returned to *Delphina* and discussed our plan for the next day. The Sassafras River, on the Eastern Shore, would be an ideal place to anchor the next night. Near the Mount Harmon Plantation are an anchorage and a bulkhead. After a visit to the plantation, we could ride to Chesapeake City, located on the Chesapeake and Delaware Canal.

The trip to the Sassafras would be our shortest passage across the Bay, and it would take little time—unless we ran aground in Susquehanna Flats.

CHAPTER TWENTY

Sassafras River

As we left Havre de Grace and headed for the Sassafras River the next morning, we were beginning our trip home. Of course, we would be making more stops on the Bay, but they would all be south of Havre de Grace.

We powered *Delphina* through the Flats without incident and continued down and across the Bay. The weather forecast that morning had warned of potentially severe thunderstorms in the late afternoon, and we wanted to reach our anchorage without any delays.

The Sassafras presented no navigational problems. This river and the one to its north, the Bohemia, are very popular with boaters from Pennsylvania and Delaware. We read in one of our guidebooks that weekends are uncomfortably crowded, and that wakes from numerous passing boats can make life miserable. But in midweek on the Sassafras, we experienced a peaceful cruise amid a panorama of meadowlands and forests sweeping down to the river's edge. Occasionally, a farmhouse or mansion accented the scenery. On some stretches of the river, high bluffs, the products of erosion, rose from the shore.

It was only mid-afternoon, but the sky was darkening to the northwest when we approached Knight Island. I became apprehensive about our plan to sound our way into Back Creek on the east side of the island. If a severe squall struck, and *Delphina* were to drag anchor there, we could end up hard aground. A better plan was to anchor on the west side of the island. Although we would have less protection from the north, the likely direction of the wind in a squall, we would have time to set a storm anchor if *Delphina* started to drag. And we still wouldn't be far from the Mount Harmon pier.

We anchored on the west side and waited to see what would happen.

As forecasted, a severe thunderstorm threatened just after four o'clock. The sky's color changed in minutes from yellowish brown to black. Heavy raindrops fell. Suddenly, a strong wind roared in and caught *Delphina* on her port beam. In response, she heeled over. From inside the boat, we saw that the portholes on the cabin side were nearly in the water. Quickly *Delphina* rounded into the wind and righted herself. It's always a comfort to us when she behaves that way.

I had neglected to remove the awning over the main deck, and from the racket that suddenly started above, I knew a corner of the cloth had ripped. We had to get the awning down before it acted like a sail. Joan joined me on deck.

The wind had torn out the two aft corner grommets of the awning, and the awning was furiously whipping the deck. The resultant noise was like the rapid fire of an anti-aircraft gun. The rain was so heavy we couldn't see the end of the bowsprit. *Delphina* was thoroughly enjoying herself as she danced madly around her anchor. We crawled to the shrouds where the awning was tied. With a loud ripping sound, heard above the screaming wind, the last two grommets gave up their fight to keep the awning attached to the rigging. We grabbed for the awning and wrestled it into submission before the wind could blow it overboard. Rolling the cloth into a large ball, we dragged the awning aft and took it below.

During nine years of sailing in the Florida Keys, we have experienced our fair share of thunderstorms and severe squalls. But this squall was exceptional, as though the Bay, having spared us from its legendary summer thunderstorms for our whole cruise, was making up for lost time.

Standing in the galley, we felt utterly at the mercy of the elements. *Delphina* continued her wild gyrations, but her moves were predictable: she would heel, round into the wind, and right herself. We took comfort in these movements—if the anchor weren't holding, she wouldn't be rounding into the wind.

As is true with many squalls, this one ended as abruptly as it had begun. The rain stopped, and we opened the companionway hatch and went outside. To the northwest, from where the storm had come, the sky was beginning to clear. To the southeast, the sky was a dark gray color and was accented with frequent lightning flashes. And to the east was Knight Island. The anchor had done its job.

We had already changed into dry clothes. Hauling up the wet awning and spreading it out on the deck to dry, we again got soaked from water trapped in the folds of the cloth. All four corners of the awning were torn to shreds, and some of the seams were coming apart. But no damage had been done to *Delphina*.

The air the next morning was fresh and crisp. The weather was great for a bike ride. We got to the bulkhead at Mount Harmon Plantation a little after seven and unloaded the bikes. The bulkhead is the site of the original wharf to which ships moored while they loaded tobacco for export to England. The tobacco prize house, overlooking the river, still stands near the bulkhead. At this house, tobacco was pressed tightly into hogsheads by using a lever to compress the leaves.

The plantation wasn't scheduled to open until ten, and we decided to ride to Chesapeake City in the morning and return to tour the plantation in the afternoon.

The plantation's access to the highway is a two-mile lane lined with Osage orange trees that provide a dense canopy the length of the lane. The plantation is a wildlife refuge, and the sounds of birds, celebrating the day with their songs, filled the air. The perfume from millions of wildflowers in the surrounding meadows added to our sensory pleasure.

About halfway down the lane, the overhead branches suddenly exploded as a magnificent owl, with a wingspan of at least three feet, burst into flight. I watched him fly about fifty feet and then land ahead of me on a branch at the top of the canopy. He looked directly at me and seemed to be waiting for me to catch up. Obliging him, I rode farther and stopped to take his picture. He flew off before I snapped the shutter. He landed again, farther ahead of his previous perch. This game continued until he flew away at the end of the lane. I didn't see him land. I was disappointed because I thought we had become friends; also, he had never let me take his picture.

We rode into Cecilton and turned onto Route 213. Shortly after, we came to the Anchorage, a classic example of a telescoping house, so-called because each addition to the original house is smaller than the preceding one. The original brick house was built in the early 1700s, and the expansions were completed in 1835. Trees and shrubbery are planted throughout the lawn and create a landscaping effect that is as striking as the house.

Riding across the bridge that spans the Bohemia River, we were treated to a scenic view of the river, winding toward the Bay, and the sight of pleasure boats tied to their moorings. As we neared Chesapeake City, we began to see signs of civilization. One sign, a large billboard, exclusively advertised dump-truck insurance. As I

The Anchorage, Cecilton

read the sign, it did occur to me that we had seen an unusual number of dump trucks on that road. Obviously, the insurance agency knows where their market is.

Our first sight of Chesapeake City was the bridge that crosses the Chesapeake and Delaware Canal. When we got to the bridge, we could see how it dominates the sky as it towers over the town. Work was being done on the bridge, and traffic was reduced to going one way. The restriction had caused traffic to back up for a half mile. Fortunately, the historic district of Chesapeake City is located on the south bank of the canal, and we didn't have to cross the bridge.

Chesapeake City traces its origin to that of the canal, which opened for traffic in 1829. As we rode around the streets, I sensed something different about this town from other waterfront towns we had visited on the Bay. Then I realized that the predominant architectural style is Victorian, and with only a few exceptions, the buildings are astonishingly well preserved. With its colorful houses and stores, Chesapeake City looks the way I imagine a town on the Mississippi River looked in the 1800s.

The importance of the town is linked directly to the importance of the canal, which connects Chesapeake Bay to Delaware Bay. Each year the town extends its hospitality and services to the thousands of boaters who transit the canal. A lock was located in Chesapeake City until 1927, the year the Corps of Engineers completed a major expansion of the canal and eliminated all locks. Today the town is the transfer point for the pilots of ships negotiating the canal, as well as the location for the Corps of Engineers operations center.

On our way out of town, Joan noticed a stairway that went from the street to the roadway on the bridge. We parked our bikes and climbed. From the center span, we looked down and saw the town far below us and the canal stretching to the horizon.

Houses, Chesapeake City

We took a different route back to the plantation after we crossed the Bohemia River. The road went through farmland to Earleville, a small farming community. We got to the plantation gate just before two.

As we entered the lane under the canopy, the owl reappeared to continue his game. The owl was indeed wise: he knew how to play me. No sooner would I stop, get the camera out, and prepare to shoot, than he would fly off. I was convinced his goal was to get me so wrapped up in watching him that I'd run into a tree, but I didn't. Finally, he tired of the game near where he had begun that morning, and I saw him nevermore.

Mount Harmon Plantation started in 1651 as a land grant to Godfrey Harmon and prospered as a colonial tobacco plantation. The Georgian manor house, built in 1730, sits commandingly atop a small hill. From 1963 to 1975, the house was completely restored by a direct descendant of the family who had owned the plantation from 1760 to 1810.

We were greeted by a gushing guide who took us through the house with the zeal of a real estate agent about to make her first sale. Although she has shown the house to the public since 1975, she treated us as if we were its first guests and explained every detail in each room she showed us. She informed us that deeds for houses used to be placed inside the first balustrade of the stairway going to the second floor. In bygone days, guests visiting a house looked for the telltale cap that sealed the chamber in the balustrade. If the cap wasn't there, the property was still mortgaged, and the deed wasn't inside the chamber. I wondered if any home owner had ever placed a cap on the balustrade with no deed inside.

After showing us the rooms on the second floor, our guide invited us to take the stairs to the widow's walk. She stayed behind as we went up and marveled at the views. To the northeast, we saw another large estate, and to the west, we saw the Sassafras. The setting was breathtaking. I imagined I was a lord surveying my fiefdom.

We returned to the first floor. Another couple was waiting for a tour, and our guide went to show them the house. We went outside to wander around the formal gardens. Occasionally, we could hear the guide's voice coming through an open window. It had lost none of its alacrity.

When we got back to the wharf, we saw that the tide had dropped about a foot. Getting the bikes back in the dinghy was difficult, and I almost fell into the water twice. After some fancy footwork by Joan, we did get squared away and back to *Delphina*.

The next day we would be going directly to Annapolis, about forty miles away. The trip would be nice if we had the wind to sail the distance; otherwise, it would be a monotonous passage under power.

Mount Harmon Plantation

CHAPTER TWENTY-ONE

Severn River

The highlight of our uneventful passage to Annapolis was seeing the stately schooner *Lady Maryland*, sailing past Sandy Point light as she headed for Baltimore. The wind was all but nonexistent; the vessel was progressing more from engine power than sail power, but she looked elegant nonetheless.

We passed under the Bay Bridge, and immediately we began to see more boating activity. From looking at the chart, I knew that an attempt to shortcut the course to the mouth of the Severn River could easily result in a grounding. Controlling my eagerness to see the city, I kept *Delphina* well outside the extensive shoal areas guarding the entrance to the Annapolis harbor. After entering the Severn, we headed toward Spa Creek.

The anchorage area in Spa Creek near the town dock was full of anchored cruising boats, and the surrounding waters were full of other pleasure craft going in all directions. As is usual for this area, a sailboat race was under way south of the Naval Academy bulkhead and added to the confusion. We managed to work our way through all the traffic as we scanned the anchored boats to see if any of our cruising friends were in Annapolis. We saw no one we knew.

We circled around the area and headed back to the Severn River. Friends of ours, Joyce Myers and Ed Kroll, live near Weems Creek, and when they were in Florida that past winter, they told us Weems Creek is a good place to anchor. What they hadn't told us, and we had failed to ask, was where we could leave our dinghy.

As we entered Weems Creek, we saw expensive homes on heavily wooded lots. The people who live there wouldn't want the general public tying dinghies to their piers. *A Fishermen's Guide to Maryland Piers and Boat Ramps* listed no public facility on this creek.

The Naval Academy has placed a number of moorings in Weems Creek for their use when storms threaten their fleet, and we had to maneuver around and between the mooring buoys to find a place to anchor. The spot we chose was directly opposite a freshly tarred road that ended at the water.

After placing both anchors securely, we went in *Flipper* to the road and tied her to a nearby piling. Our friends' house was on the street that that road apparently led to.

But we soon learned the road wasn't a public road; it was someone's private drive. As we approached the beginning of it, we saw a closed gate across the entrance. As we climbed over the fence on the front of the property, I noticed that the road we had taken was part of a U-shaped drive. The other end of the drive also ended at a gate, but that gate was open. Hoping we would have no problem getting back to *Flipper*, we went to our friends' house.

Joyce was home, and after exchanging happy greetings, we sat down to discuss plans. Joyce wasn't familiar with the spot where we had left our dinghy, but she told us she had permission to use a neighborhood pier nearby. We could leave *Flipper* there in the future.

We made arrangements to return to the house to take

showers and to go out for a Friday night of fun and frolic with Ed and Joyce. Ed was at his office at the Oak Grove Marina on the South River, and Joyce would drive the three of us there to join him.

The fun began at the marina with an impromptu beer party funded by the marina owner, Sid French. The marina is large, and I commented to Sid that it was filled with powerboats.

"That's right," he said. "We used to have more sailboats here; now there're only two left, and one of them is leaving at the end of the week. Sailboaters just don't buy any fuel!"

The usual sailboat-versus-powerboat discussion followed this remark, and I soon realized that Joan and I were in enemy territory, albeit the enemy was most friendly: they kept giving us beers.

I pointed out to the group that on our sailboat we had gone from the Florida Keys to Beaufort, North Carolina, in five days and had used only thirty-five gallons of diesel.

"That just proves my point!" Sid exclaimed.

"Sailing is boring!" Ed added. "When I want to get somewhere, I want to get there and get there fast! I want to hear the roar of those engines!"

Ed sells and charters powerboats, and he was adamant in his feelings about them.

Joyce, who is the owner of the American Powerboat School, didn't rush to our defense, but was at least sympathetic.

"I haven't been sailing in a long time now, but I did enjoy it, especially the quiet; I remember that."

Of course, no one was converted to the other side, but the conversation was fun.

Just as the beer was about to run out, Ed suggested that Joan and I join him and Joyce in his boat for a run across the Bay to Kentmorr Harbour, on Kent Island, to get some steamed crabs. The round-trip would be twenty miles, and Ed would have a chance to make his point: we'd get there fast.

It was dark, but Ed knew the river channel well and made good time going downriver. After entering the Bay, he opened up. The boat surged forward and planed over the waves. Steering the boat from the fly bridge, Ed was in his element. A big smile filled his face, and his hair was blowing straight back. He looked at me, huddled on the port seat.

"Isn't this great, Ken?" he shouted.

Hearing him over the roaring of the engines and the screaming of the wind was almost impossible.

"Sure, Ed!" I screamed back.

Hoping to be more sociable, I climbed down the ladder to the cockpit, where Joan and Joyce were riding. Getting out of the wind was a relief. The women were doing their best to carry on a conversation, but each could shout only a few words at a time. Soon they surrendered to the relentless engine noise and became silent.

Soon after we arrived at Kentmorr, we had the boat secured in a slip. We took seats at a picnic table on the restaurant's outside deck. The waitress came for our order and told us all the jumbo and large steamed crabs were gone.

"We do have some mediums left for $28.00 a dozen," she added.

I almost fell off the bench.

Ed calmly said, "Then I'll have a dozen of those."

The rest of us ordered dinners that would not require bank financing. When I told Ed that in Whitehaven we had had all the steamed crabs we could eat for $13.95, he was unperturbed.

"Ken, it's a well-known fact that the closer you get to Annapolis, the more you're going to pay for crabs," he patiently explained.

Entertainment for the evening was watching Ed tackle those crabs. His hands worked so quickly they were almost a blur as he scooped out big chunks of meat from all parts of the crab. He left no meat on any piece of shell.

"Ed, where did you learn how to do that?" I asked him.

"Years ago, an old crab picker down in Crisfield taught me how to pick. She was good, and she was patient. Now it's second nature to me."

Seeing me drool as I watched him eat, Ed, under the pretext of teaching me how to pick out the meat, gave me two of his crabs. Powerboaters do have their good sides.

The ride back to the marina was a repeat of the ride over. The comment Ed had made about sailing being boring puzzled me because I found the powerboat ride boring. Not able to carry on a conversation, all I could do was watch the water race past. I thought what Ed must find so exciting about powerboating is what he does when he gets where his powerboat takes him.

It was nearly eleven o'clock when we returned to the marina. Joan and I could hardly keep our eyes open, but for our friends the night was only beginning.

"Let's go up to the lounge," Joyce suggested.

A restaurant and a nightclub are at the marina. A band was playing in the lounge. The place was packed with people having a good time dancing or lounging about. I found the smoke-filled air hard to breathe. The volume of music was ideal for dancing, but impossible for conversing. After having a beer, all I wanted to do was find a bed in a quiet place. I asked Joan how she felt.

"Let's get a cab and go back to *Delphina*," she said.

When I told Joyce we were leaving, she said a friend of theirs who lives on their street was getting ready to leave and would be glad to give us a ride back to his house. We immediately accepted the offer.

Despite not getting to sleep until after midnight, we were up at dawn. Both of us reeked of cigarette smoke, so our first priority, after getting our bikes ashore, was to take showers. Joyce had given us a spare key to the house.

Not surprisingly, Joyce and Ed weren't at home. We learned later they had gone to their boat after the night-club had closed and had slept there. After taking showers, we began the bike ride to the city dock.

From where we were anchored, I had seen the swing bridge that crosses Weems Creek, but I hadn't seen the bridge open. As we rode across the bridge, I saw sailboats on the other side that would need the draw open to get out of the creek. No bridge-tender's shack or bridge tender was visible. I found this absence strange: who opens the bridge? I left this mystery for another day and pedaled on.

We rode into the heart of the city, where the city dock is located. We locked our bikes to a street sign and walked to the Naval Academy. Although both of us had been to Annapolis before, we had never toured the Academy. We went to the Visitor Center and picked up a self-guiding map and brochure.

The Naval Academy was founded in Annapolis in 1845 and had an original enrollment of sixty midshipmen. Currently, the Brigade of Midshipmen is comprised of forty-six hundred men and women working toward bachelors' degrees and commissions as ensigns in the Navy.

Being sailors, we wanted to see first the Academy's famed racing fleet, which is moored in a basin off the Severn River. The sleek, blue, forty-foot sloops and yawls, their bows thrust toward the bulkhead, were nicely lined up in their slips. The name of each boat was painted on both sides of the bow.

Assuming a professorial tone of voice, I informed

Joan, "*Fearless, Active,* and *Restless* are raced by the men's teams. *Dandy, Frolic,* and *Flirt* are raced by the women."

She almost threw me in the water.

As we walked toward the Chapel, we noticed a crowd gathered in front of its steps. Getting closer, we saw a wedding party coming through the main door. On the stairs leading to the entrance were two rows of Navy officers in white uniforms. Two officers were on each step, and their sabers were raised to form an archway. The bride and groom were descending the steps, or trying to. With each step the newlyweds took, the two officers on that step lowered their sabers and prevented the couple from passing until they had kissed each other. The ceremony was romantic and traditional and great fun. In the finest manner of a paparazzo, I scurried to the front of the onlookers to photograph the happy couple. After they passed the gauntlet of officers, the pair walked away from all the commotion, and I followed to return to where I had left Joan.

Suddenly, not aware that I was behind them, the groom looked at his bride and said, "Thank God that's over! Where do we go from here?"

The question was rhetorical. The bride said nothing.

The rest of the morning, we visited some of the Academy's buildings that are open to the public. Bartlett Hall, the massive granite building that dominates the campus, is the dormitory for the entire Brigade of Midshipmen. Preble Hall is the Academy museum and contains the most comprehensive collection of Navy memorabilia in the country, as well as a collection of some of George Washington's personal belongings. In the rear of the Chapel is the mausoleum where the remains of John Paul Jones, Father of the United States Navy, are interred.

We walked back to the downtown area and had lunch

as we watched boats come and go in Ego Alley, the appropriately nicknamed boat basin where the town dock is located.

The weather was perfect for leisurely strolling, and we decided to spend the afternoon wandering around the streets. The heart of the city is a National Historic District containing many homes and buildings from the colonial period. Based on a street plan that was laid out by Governor Francis Nicholson in 1694, the streets in this district radiate out from hubs at Church Circle and State Circle.

As we walked along the crowded streets, I noticed that little had changed since our last visit in 1982. The fashionable stores were attracting swarms of shoppers, restaurants were overflowing with patrons for the midday meal, and the saloons were bustling. The atmosphere was still that of a friendly, small town, yet a sense of cosmopolitan sophistication was also present. Later, I read in a brochure that the residents' cultural leanings are reflected by an opera company, a symphony orchestra, two theater groups, and a summer concert series performed by the Naval Academy Band. Such artistic diversity would infuse any city with a special aura.

The residential streets are lined with old homes built close together, but the neighborhoods exude a feeling of intimacy rather than congestion. One such street, paved with bricks and lined with brick sidewalks, led us to the Maryland State House at State Circle.

This building, the capitol of Maryland, was completed in 1779. For a brief period, the building served also as the nation's capitol when the Continental Congress met there in 1783 and 1784. When we went inside, I did a double take when I looked in the Old Senate Chamber. A realistic, life-size figure of George Washington, in his general's uniform, stood inside. The figure was a statue, of course, a replica of the one created by Houdon, a French sculptor.

Residential street, Annapolis

In this room, in 1783, Washington resigned his commission as Commander-in-Chief of the Continental Army.

Our legs and feet were tired from the walking, and we returned to our bikes and rode back to *Delphina.*

The next morning, as we rode our bikes over the Spa Creek bridge into Eastport, we looked down and saw many crews readying their boats for a day of racing or cruising on the Bay.

Eastport is the heart of the marine industry in Annapolis. Numerous marinas line the shores of the peninsula. The Annapolis Sailing School, the oldest commercial sailing school in the country, is located in Eastport. The school is responsible for teaching thousands of people the intricacies of handling sailboats of all sizes.

We rode around the quiet residential streets and occasionally watched the boating activity on Back Creek. We stopped for lunch at Marmaduke's Pub, also located in

Eastport. The establishment does resemble a neighborhood English pub and is a sailors' hangout, where friends can swap lies and boast as they watch videos of the latest local sailing races.

Crossing back over Spa Creek, we locked our bikes to the sign again and sat down at the foot of the boat basin to watch the activity. We could sit there day after day and not get bored. The place is always crowded with interest-looking people, and entertainment is constantly provided by the boats prancing around in Ego Alley.

It was mid-afternoon when we headed back to *Delphina*. As we neared the Weems Creek bridge, the barriers across the road descended. The bridge swung open. Arriving at the bridge, I saw a woman in the center of the swing span. She was waving to the occupants of a sailboat that was passing through the opening in the bridge. Was she the bridge tender?

As soon as the bridge closed and the traffic cleared, I

Downtown, Annapolis

approached her. Joan was behind me. We introduced ourselves, and she told us her name was Ann Bellinger. She
was the bridge tender.

"Where abouts are you from?" she asked.

"Marathon, down in the Florida Keys," Joan told her.

"Marathon! You don't say! Why, I used to live there
back in the seventies! I worked at the Idle Hour Lounge.
Ever hear of it?"

The Idle Hour Lounge had been one of the most
popular, and roughest, bars in Marathon. It had closed in
the mid-1980s.

"Yeah, I heard of it, but I was never brave enough to
go in," I told her.

She thought this was funny. I was serious.

"Hey, if you folks aren't doin' anything, come on down
to my place for a while. It's not much, but it's shady, and
there's a cool breeze. We can talk some more about the
Keys."

"Where is your place?" I asked.

"Under the bridge."

An image of a Norwegian troll flashed in my mind.

"We'd love to!" Joan said.

On our way down to her place on the creek's bank, she
told us that she had tended other bridges, on the Waterway in South Florida.

"But I've been tendin' this one since 1983 under contract to the State. Yessir, sunup to sundown, seven days a
week, May first 'til the end of October."

"Good grief!" I exclaimed. "Don't you ever get any
days off during that period?"

"Only if I pay for a substitute. And sometimes I have
to work later than sunset, if a boat captain tells me he's
comin' back late. It's all in the contract."

As we stood on her porch in front of the little shack
under the bridge, she pointed to some plywood sheathing
nailed to supports on the concrete bottom of the bridge.

"The State had to put that in for me because chunks of concrete kept falling down. Luckily, none of them hit me on the head. I don't know what the lumber cost, but the labor alone cost $1200. Can you believe it?"

From the few sheets of plywood and the two-by-fours that were in place, I had trouble believing the project had cost that much. I had no trouble seeing where chunks of concrete had fallen off the bridge sections that were over the water.

She led us to the door of the shack. Inside were a television, a telephone, a couch, a refrigerator, and a table with a hot plate. She picked up the only chair and brought it outside. We all found places to sit, and in response to a couple of our questions, she started telling us about herself.

"I'm sixty-eight and the mother of six. I got divorced a number of years ago. Now, I like to date whenever I have a chance. That reminds me of a little story. I used to keep my finest silk dress down here, ready to change into if I got asked for a date that night. One day, one of my dogs fell into the water, right over there. You can see how strong the current runs through here. Well, it was really strong when he went in, and he was gettin' carried away by it. I jumped right in the water after him, got ahold of him, and swam back. Well, I was one wet girl, I'll tell you! I got out of my wet clothes, and the only thing I had to wear was that silk dress. So I put it on. Right after that, I saw that one of my boats was comin' in and would want an openin', so I went out. My, was that man ever surprised to see me all dressed up in my finery! You know, after he docked his boat, he came over here to make sure I was all right!"

"Did he ask you for a date?" Joan asked.

"No, he's married. Such luck!"

"Over the years I guess you've gotten to know some of the boat owners pretty well," I commented.

"Oh, yes, I'll say. We're like family. A lot of the people bring me treats from time to time."

"How many boats are on this side?" I asked her as I pointed upstream of the bridge.

"I think there's twenty-two. I call them my boats."

"Have you ever had any problems with the operation of the bridge?" Joan asked.

"Oh heavens, yes!" she cried. "Let me tell you! When I first took the bridge in '83, it would stick closed if the temperature got over ninety-five. I saw what the problem was—the steel apron was just a bit too long when it expanded with the heat. All they had to do was shorten it a little. I kept tellin' them that's all they had to do, but they did nothing. Meanwhile, every time it stuck I had to call the fire department to come over, and they would hose the bridge down to cool it off. Can you imagine? Then one really hot day I managed to get it open for a boat, but I couldn't get it closed again. The first car in line waitin' to get across had three men in suits sittin' in it. They didn't look too happy. They wanted to know what the problem was. Said they were from the State Highway Department. Well, did I ever tell them! Next day, they had a crew down here and fixed it just the way I told them."

"Has the bridge caused any problems since then?" I asked.

"Not a one. I knew what I was talkin' about!"

"How do you get back and forth from your house?" Joan asked. "I didn't see any car parked up there."

"Oh, I only live a couple of miles from here, so I just walk. My dogs need the exercise. If it's rainin', I just call a cab. Oh! Here comes one of my boats! I'll bet they had a good day sailing with all this wind!"

We followed her up to the controls. As the sailboat passed through, Ann and the people on the boat exchanged greetings. It didn't take much imagination to sense the warmth these people shared. The relationship has to be unique—tender and tendee.

We went back under the bridge and spent some time talking about Florida. Dinnertime soon arrived, and we got up to leave.

"Ann, it's been great!" I told her. "We sure hope you can find some way to come down and sit a spell with us. And you could look up friends from your Marathon days!"

"I'll do my best. You come back and see me again, okay?"

She walked us up to our bikes.

We went to our friends' house, returned the key, thanked them, said good-bye, and returned to *Delphina*.

Solomons, our last stop in Maryland, was over forty miles away. At first light the next morning, we got under way and powered down the Severn River. Motivated by the nice breeze, I hoisted the sails as soon as we entered the Bay.

CHAPTER TWENTY-TWO

Great Wicomico River

We sailed with a moderate easterly breeze to the Thomas Point lighthouse, in the Bay just south of Annapolis, but the wind lightened and veered to the south soon after we passed the light. Reluctantly, we started the engine. We powered south to Solomons and anchored again in Back Creek. We didn't go ashore.

We left the following morning for the Coan River, on the Virginia shore of the Potomac River. When we neared Point No Point light, in the Bay between the Patuxent and Potomac Rivers, the wind came out of the northeast at ten knots, and we started sailing again. The wind gave us a delightful sail all the way to the entrance light for the Coan River.

According to our guidebooks and chart, getting into the Coan River would be straightforward except that marker "12," opposite Walnut Point, is very near the shore. One guidebook informed us that steering past Walnut Point provides a real test of the helmsman's nerves.

Fish stakes were numerous in the entrance to the Coan. Although stakes are used primarily to mark oyster beds and have nothing to do with navigation, I was nervous seeing thin sticks placed in water the chart indicated was over ten feet deep. And my unease was compounded when I discovered that red marker "12" had been replaced by a green marker "13," almost *on* the shore. And between us and that marker was a phalanx of those oyster stakes. I really wasn't looking forward to testing my nerves.

I slowed the engine to bare steerageway while Joan watched the depth sounder. As we passed the last stake in the phalanx, the reading on the depth sounder dipped alarmingly, but quickly jumped back. We passed green marker "13" and Walnut Point. We continued a little farther to a bight and anchored. By leaving from this anchorage early the next morning, we could have an early afternoon arrival at Reedville, Virginia.

Going past Walnut Point the next morning was again nerve-racking. When we reached the open Potomac, we had a nice breeze out of the northeast, and I hoisted the sails. As we approached Smith Point light, we must have made an impressive sight because two men fishing from a pleasure boat waved, grinned, and gave us a thumbs-up.

After passing Smith Point, we altered course and sailed for the buoy that marks the entrance to the Great Wicomico River. We were able to keep sailing into the river. After we entered Cockrell Creek, we headed into the wind, dropped the sails, and went the rest of the way to Reedville under power.

Reedville is one of the waterfront towns on the Bay that was founded after the colonial era. In 1867, Captain Elijah Reed, a fishing captain from Maine, found the area suitable for establishing a commercial center to process menhaden, a herring-like fish caught in huge numbers along the East Coast. Soon plants sprouted up along the banks of Cockrell Creek, and Reedville became the Town Spawned by a Fish. So successful was the industry that, by the early 1900s, Reedville had the highest per capita income in the country.

The harbor in the creek is a busy one because of two fish-processing plants, on opposite banks, and large fleets of menhaden boats. As we motored up the creek, we could see the ruins of a number of old plants. The two that are still functioning continue to process enough fish for fertilizer, protein supplements, and pet food to rank Reedville as one of the top fishing ports in the United States. Our interest in coming to Reedville was not to see these plants, but to see the stately homes the town is known for.

We found a place to anchor just north of an ice plant. A long pier nearby looked promising as a place to tie the dinghy. We felt like walking that afternoon, so we went ashore without our bikes.

A machine shop is located near the pier, and a man working inside said we could leave our dinghy tied to the pier. A few steps away was Main Street. We started

Menhaden boats, Reedville

walking.

A pickup truck suddenly stopped opposite us, in the center of the far lane. A man in his sixties popped his head out of the window.

"Where'd you park your boat?" he asked.

I looked at Joan. How did he know we had come by boat?

"In the creek, by the ice house," I told him.

The man grinned. I could see another man was in the cab, and he was grinning, too.

"We're the two old codgers you saw fishin' out at Smith Point," the driver said. "Can I give y'all a ride somewhere?"

"No, thanks," I told him. "We're out for a walk around town."

"Well, don't miss seein' the old captains' houses," he said. "And the Fishermen's Museum, too."

None of our guidebooks had mentioned a museum in Reedville.

"Where's that?" Joan asked him.

"Oh, a little ways down Main Street here. It just opened this spring. Keep walkin' down that sidewalk, and you can't miss it."

The driver asked us a few questions about *Delphina* and our trip. His friend listened to our answers, but stayed silent. After satisfying his curiosity, the driver wished us a pleasant stay and drove off. During the time we talked, about five minutes, no other vehicles had driven by us. Reedville is a quiet town.

Reedville has the flavor of a community of sea captains. The serene setting is what a seafaring man would want after being away for weeks. The large, elegant homes provide a sense of stability and permanence, not at all like a pitching deck on an often stormy sea. And the families left behind would have no trouble being comfortable and secure in the spacious surroundings.

Albert Morris house, Reedville

Also on Main Street, looking out of place amid the elaborate architecture of the houses, was an unpretentious frame building and a sign that said "Reedville Market." Like the grocery we had seen in Kinsale, this market had been closed for some time. I made a note to learn why.

We walked as far as the museum and saw that it was open. We entered and were greeted by four people. The four were volunteers, giving their time to staff the museum, and we had arrived at the change of shift. Two of the people left, and a man and a woman remained to assist us.

The man, a retired captain of a menhaden boat, had spent forty-eight years earning a living from the sea. A more authoritative guide we couldn't have had. I was impressed by his enthusiasm, the same enthusiasm that the volunteers at the other small museums we had visited had shown. In addition to the exhibits that he explained to us, he regaled us with stories of life on a menhaden boat.

"We traveled all over the East Coast and into the Gulf of Mexico and, of course, the Bay. Wherever the fish were, we were. Fished in all kinds of weather. It could get pretty exciting in one of the net boats, closing up the net. Back in the days before hydraulics, the net was hauled in by pure muscle power, and the crews would chant songs as they worked, getting a rhythm to it."

As he spoke, I had the impression he wanted to be back on his menhaden boat.

"Once, in a storm, we had to duck in the Intracoastal in the Carolinas. We didn't have a chart and it was kinda scary, navigating that big boat down the Waterway from marker to marker. Got tight a few times. Funniest thing was when we bought a chart from some fella on a big yacht. He couldn't believe we were there without one."

The last exhibit we looked at was a series of photographs of the captains' houses. This exhibit summed up for me everything I had seen in the museum, as if the old captains were saying, through the photographs, "Yes, we lived a rough and dangerous life at sea, but look what we came back to!"

As we thanked our host for his time and attention, I studied his face more closely than I had earlier. His many years at sea had carved lines on his features that reflected the hardships he had faced, but his eyes had an unmistakable twinkle that told me he had loved every minute of his life. If the man had ever known serious worry, I couldn't tell it from his face.

"Please come back and see us. And tell your friends," he said as we left.

We walked the rest of the way down Main Street and admired the houses as we went. At the end of the street were two modern convenience stores. I wondered if they had caused the demise of the grocery store we had seen earlier. We turned around and headed back. We had passed the museum when a car pulled up alongside us. Our museum guide was driving.

"Can I give you folks a ride anywhere?" he asked.

I hated to say no, but we only had a couple of blocks to go. He understood.

Less than a block farther, a voice from behind startled us.

"I hope you're enjoying your visit to Reedville!"

We turned around. The voice belonged to a middle-aged man on a bicycle.

"This is a wonderful place," Joan told him. "We are enjoying our stay. We went to the Fishermen's Museum, and we've been admiring the houses."

"Is there anything you'd like to know about the houses?" he asked.

"Yes," I replied. "I noticed that several of the houses have the look of being recently restored, but no one seems to be living in them. Are they for sale?"

"Some of the houses have been bought by retirees from Baltimore and Richmond, and they have fixed them up with the idea of moving here. Many retirees, particularly those from Maryland, have roots here in Reedville. You know, in the days before all the roads and bridges were put in, people traveled almost exclusively by steamboat, and folks living here had closer ties to Baltimore than to any city in Virginia because the steamboats came from Baltimore. Ah, those must have been great days! You could get on the boat in the evening and wake up the next morning in Baltimore. Coming back would be the same thing. Back then they even had musical shows and plays traveling on the steamboats. It was a big occasion whenever a troupe visited with a show."

"Wouldn't it be wonderful if those steamboats were still making their trips?" I asked. "They're doing it on the Mississippi with great success. By the way, do you know why the Reedville Market closed?"

"It closed about a year ago. From what I hear, the cost of insurance got too high. The owner was going to have to make extensive repairs to the building to keep the premiums down. Since he was planning to retire soon anyway, he closed down. Say, would you folks like to visit my church? I'm Carlton Casey, the pastor. You must have seen it. It's the Bethany United Methodist Church."

We introduced ourselves and said we'd love to see it.

"Great! Well, I was on my way to mail these letters. You can start walking up there, and I'll meet you at the church."

As he unlocked the front door, he said, "I had to start locking up this year. I really didn't want to, but I didn't have much choice. Things were disappearing. Not much, but enough to add up."

The interior of the church was lined with rich wood paneling. The pews were arranged in an arc formation that faced the altar. I had never seen this arrangement before, but the pastor informed us it was common.

"If you get a chance, you should visit Christ Church in Lancaster County, near Irvington. It's a colonial church, and hasn't been changed since it was built around 1730. You'll find it's different from other churches you've seen," he told us.

Joan told him we were planning to go to the Rappahannock River and anchor in Carter Creek. Christ Church was definitely on the agenda.

In our travels around the Bay that summer, we had seen numerous M.E. churches and United Methodist churches. In Chestertown, we had seen an M.E. church and a United Methodist Church across the street from each other. We didn't know if they were the same religion. Joan's curiosity about this matter wouldn't rest, and she asked the pastor what the difference was.

"The two names are now the same Methodist religion

and have been since the late sixties. That's when they joined together and formed the United Methodist Church. But back in the 1700s, John Wesley, the founder of Methodism, sent Francis Asbury to preach in the Colonies, and the Methodist Episcopal Church was formed. They went through many splits, particularly in the Civil War, and the groups didn't start to reunite until well into this century. Many of the old churches still use the M.E. name, and in Hampton, where there was a large Methodist group, there is a Francis Asbury public school."

We thanked the pastor for his kindness and the information he had given us. On the walk back to the pier, Joan was happy that her curiosity had finally been satisfied.

"Ken, I don't know if you remember, but the Francis Asbury school is where Suzi Lowrey is a teacher's aide."

"No, that slipped right by me. But do you realize, as small as this town is, three people came to us, perfect strangers, and extended invitations for rides or to visit them? There's something special about the people here, and it has nothing to do with fish."

As we listened to the weather forecast that evening, we became excited at the prospect of some exhilarating sailing the next day. A small-craft advisory was in effect for winds of twenty-five knots from the northeast with seas four to six feet high. We would be going to the Rappahannock River, fifteen miles farther south. The forecast made me think we would be flying there.

CHAPTER TWENTY-THREE

Rappahannock River

Cockrell Creek was smooth as we motored out. Passing the menhaden plants, we saw one menhaden boat entering its berth and another coming up the channel. After we left the harbor, Joan headed *Delphina* into the wind, and I raised the foresail and the jib. That would be all the sail we would need in the strong wind that had been forecasted.

After we passed the lee of Fleeton Point, at the mouth of the creek, the full force of the wind struck us, and *Delphina* heeled heavily. The wind was coming from forward of the beam, and I eased the sheets to trim the sails. The angle of heel remained the same, as the bow literally plowed forward into the seas. Spray flew in all directions. Joan turned off the engine.

The sailing was bone rattling, rather than exhilarating, as we worked our way out the Great Wicomico River. The current was against us, and the steep seas, only about ten feet apart, tried repeatedly to bar our forward motion. They were succeeding: our actual speed over the bottom was about one knot. The heavy, overcast skies added a feeling of foreboding, and we were anxious to get to the entrance buoy. Once there, we could begin to head more off the wind and the seas. The current would still be against the wind, a condition that causes short, steep waves, but the seas would no longer be on the bow.

Carefully watching the depth sounder after passing the buoy, Joan steered a more southerly heading. A shoal was off to starboard, and we had to get past that before we could head directly for the Windmill Point light, at the mouth of the Rappahannock River. Gradually the motion on board became less chaotic. The sailing was exhilarating, and we were having a marvelous time. Even the leaden skies added to the drama.

We rounded Windmill Point light, jibed, and sailed into the Rappahannock River. The ebb current, which had begun about an hour earlier, slowed us, but as soon as we were inside the lee of Windmill Point, the seas improved considerably. Ahead of us we saw two groups of sailboats racing.

The racers were having an exciting time. Most of the boats had full sail up and, on the weather legs, were heeled over considerably despite the weight of the crew sitting on the weather deck. Occasionally, a strong gust of wind would hit a boat and cause a near knockdown. The crew of the affected boat would react with whoops and hollers of glee.

Navigating to Urbanna, a town sixteen miles upriver, was easy, and so was negotiating the channel into its protected harbor. The harbor was lined with boats in marinas on our right. On our left was an anchorage area full of moored boats. We proceeded to another anchorage area that had room and anchored in a spot between a newly constructed series of piers and the town's waterfront area.

We rowed *Flipper* to a small float tied to a slip in a marina. Two women were sitting in the cockpit of an adjacent sailboat. One of them said we could leave our dinghy there; they would even watch it for us. Thus assured, we walked up to town.

Urbanna is a great town for a cruising boat to visit. Not only are all marine services available, but also reprovisioning is convenient since all stores are within walking distance of the waterfront. And it has a colonial heritage that dates back to 1680, when the General Assembly of the House of Burgesses ordered the town established.

We didn't need any provisions, so we just strolled along the streets and looked at some of the historic buildings. Near the water's edge is the Customs House, now a private residence with a beautifully landscaped yard of dense vegetation. Immediately across the street is a restored tobacco warehouse, currently used as a public library. In the heart of the commercial center of town is the Old Courthouse, which has been renovated and is used by the Middlesex Women's Club.

We returned to *Flipper* and thanked the two women for watching her. As we prepared to leave, another woman approached us.

"I see that you're from Florida," she said. "Welcome to Urbanna! Isn't this a great place? We don't get that many cruising people visiting here, but when they do, they hate to leave. How long are you here for?"

Joan told her of our plans to leave the next day for Carter Creek.

"Oh, my husband manages a marina over there. We live here, though, on a powerboat in this covered slip."

Her husband came from inside the covered slip and joined us. She introduced him as Carroll and herself as Dana Davies. We introduced ourselves. We all talked a while about the different places we had cruised.

As we got in the dinghy, Dana added, "You really should stay longer, if you can."

We returned to *Delphina* and started to read some literature on the Carter Creek area. Our reading was interrupted by a voice calling out.

"Ahoy, *Delphina!*"

I popped my head outside and saw a middle-aged man rowing a dinghy toward us. He stopped and grabbed our rub rail.

"Hi! I'm with the Urbanna Creek Yacht Club," he said. "We're having a beer bust this evening, with crabs and corn on the cob, and we'd like to have you folks join us."

My response was immediate.

"Sure! We'd love to! When and where?"

"Whenever you can get there. It's right over there."

He pointed to a grassy area near a marina building. Some people were already there.

"We'll be there in about half an hour. And thanks!"

"See you then," he said and rowed away.

We washed up, changed our clothes, got into *Flipper*, and went to a landing near the party area. About thirty people were gathered around a couple of picnic tables. A large cooler was filled to overflowing with beer and ice, and another was full of wine. Two bushel baskets of steamed crabs sat nearby, and a charcoal fire, with corn roasting on top of it, was glowing brightly. About half the people were sitting at the tables; the other half were standing and talking in small groups. Dana came up to us.

"Hi again! I should have told you about this party earlier, but it slipped my mind. Then I told our commodore about you, and he's the one who came out and invited you. We're so glad you could make it!"

Boaters as a group, and individually, tend to be friendly people, but not often are they so friendly that the commodore of the local yacht club rows out to an anchored boat to invite the people on board to a party. The members of this club are special people. Dana told us to help ourselves to the food, introduced us to a couple of her friends, and went to find Carroll. We got some crabs, corn, and beer and sat down.

Throughout the evening, we managed to meet most of the people, drink a respectable quantity of beer, and stuff ourselves with crabs and corn. I was reminded of the parable of the loaves and fishes—the more crabs we ate, the more there seemed to be.

At one point during the party, I got into a conversation with Carroll. He was born and raised in Urbanna; his mother had been born in the Customs House.

"What's the oyster festival like?" I asked him.

Urbanna is famous for this festival, held annually the first weekend in November, and the Rappahannock is known for being rich in oysters.

"The one last year, we had sixty thousand people here over the weekend. Everybody had a great time. But I hope people start paying more attention to conservation. The number of oysters coming out of the Rappahannock is declining."

Dana came over and listened in.

"Did you tell them about the condos going up on the other side of the creek?" she asked her husband.

He told her he hadn't.

She looked at us and said, "You must have noticed all those docks over there. Well, those are all for the new condos going up on that shore. That farm was sold to some developer a while back. It's in Middlesex County, not under Urbanna's jurisdiction, and the county's letting them build on it. Look at how nice the creek looks now. For years I've been looking over and seeing those lovely meadows; now I'll be looking at condos instead. It sure won't be the same."

The commodore joined us.

"Make sure you get enough crabs," he said. "We've got plenty. By the way, feel free to use our showers. They're in the building right there."

It was just before ten. The party was still in full

swing, but we were getting sleepy. We tried to thank everybody individually and returned to *Delphina*.

We took leisurely showers the next morning; we had no need to hurry: Carter Creek, our next anchorage, was only six miles away.

A strong breeze was blowing and an hour was all it took for us to sail to Carter Creek. After furling the sails at the mouth of the creek, we motored up to a spot between the Tides Inn and the Tides Lodge and anchored. These two resort facilities highlight the affluent atmosphere around Carter Creek. *Lady Ann*, a large, elegant yacht, is moored at the dock of the Tides Inn and gave us the impression of 1920s-style opulence. The scenery around our anchorage was lush. Trees with heavy foliage grew right to the water's edge. We felt we would be comfortable there.

We were unsure what we would find on shore, but our highway map showed a potentially interesting loop through the towns of Irvington, White Stone, and Kilmarnock. The ride would be about sixteen miles and would take us past Christ Church.

The dockmaster at the Tides Lodge and Marina allowed us to tie *Flipper* to one of their floats. The ride to the road was through the Lodge's beautiful golf course. When we got to the road, we turned right and soon came to Christ Church.

This church was funded entirely by Robert "King" Carter, a plantation owner of immense wealth and stature. The conditions for his generosity were that the church be built on the same site as the original church built there in 1669, and that the bodies of his parents remain in their family grave inside the church. The conditions were met, and the parents' remains are still interred in the chancel under a large stone slab. Robert, however, is buried, alongside his two wives, outside the church. The church currently is used for services in the summer.

The church is cruciform in design and is the only colonial church in Virginia with the original pews. These pews are different from any I had ever seen. With square shapes and high backs and sides, they were effective in keeping cold drafts away from the occupants and in isolating family groups during the service.

The ride around the loop was scenic and varied, and we saw many large estates set back from the road. In Irvington, I saw a sign that read "Private, Please" on a gate leading to a mansion. I thought this message was more civil than "No Trespassing". Farther along the road, we passed by a bed-and-breakfast inn called the King Carter Inn. The man's influence lives on.

On the road between White Stone and Kilmarnock, we saw several abandoned buildings and mobile homes that had large numbers painted on their sides. They seemed slated for demolition, although some weren't in

Christ Church, Irvington

bad condition.

As we rode back through the golf course and passed the pro shop, I noticed a sign that said the course is open to the public. If it hadn't been late afternoon, we would have played a round. Golfing would be a prefect way to enjoy the serene beauty that is evident everywhere around Irvington. But we went back to *Delphina* and enjoyed the scenery from our deck chairs while we sipped our cocktails. The scenery seemed just as nice from that vantage point.

Sarah Creek, on the north shore of the York River, would be our anchorage for the next couple of days as we explored the Yorktown-Williamsburg area. On the chart, this anchorage looked like an ideal place for access to Yorktown and the Colonial Parkway. The only obstacle, if it could be called that, was the large U.S. Highway 17 bridge across the York River. But how hard could it be to cross a bridge?

CHAPTER TWENTY-FOUR

York River

A favorable current helped to speed us out Carter Creek and the Rappahannock River, and we quickly reached the Bay. The strong northeast wind we had had two days previously had moderated and veered to the east, so we waited until we were heading south before raising the sails and turning off the engine.

The sail down the Bay to the York River was pleasant and relaxing. We passed Wolf Trap light, marking the hazardous shoal that trapped the British frigate H.M.S. *Wolf* for five days. We sailed upriver to the entrance light for the channel into Sarah Creek, dropped the sails, and motored the rest of the way.

Three other sailboats, two at anchor and one on a mooring, were in the anchorage area. The swinging room was limited, and we would have to use a Bahamian moor. As we pulled up between the two anchored boats, I saw a man working in the cockpit of the boat to our left. Undoubtedly, he would be watching us to see if we anchored too close to his boat.

I dropped the first anchor, and Joan used the engine to back down. She continued reversing until two hundred feet of chain were let out. At this point, the man on the nearby boat should have been nervous—we were in such a position that, if we stayed on the one anchor, we would swing into his boat when the current or wind changed direction. I looked in his direction and saw that he was watching us. I waved, and he waved back. He was probably praying that we knew what we were doing.

I stopped the chain and motioned for Joan to reverse at full throttle to ensure the anchor was set. As she throttled up, *Delphina* went astern and continued going astern after the chain became taut. The anchor was dragging; it would have to be reset.

To haul up two hundred feet of muddy chain, even with a windlass, is a nasty job. To do it with an audience does not make the exercise more enjoyable. As I came to the end of the chain, and the anchor came out of the water, I saw that the chain had fouled around a fluke. Never before had this happened when I placed an anchor.

The current, meanwhile, had carried us away from where we wanted *Delphina*, so we circled around the anchorage and repeated the procedure. This time the anchor held. After I placed the second anchor, Joan powered *Delphina* forward a hundred feet, and I took in the slack on the first anchor chain. After I snubbed the second anchor rode on a cleat, I motioned for Joan to power *Delphina* forward to set the second anchor, and she throttled up. The anchor didn't set. Rarely has the second anchor failed to set for me after setting the first; I couldn't understand why I was having so much trouble.

We had to pull up both anchors and start again. This time I chose a different spot to begin, and I once more placed the first anchor. It held. I placed the second anchor. It held. We were home. I expected applause from our neighbor, but got none.

Cocktail hour followed in minutes. I couldn't recall when gin had tasted better or had had a more soothing effect.

Wanting to avoid the rush-hour traffic on Highway

17, we were up at dawn the next morning. The York River Yacht Haven, located across the creek from our anchorage, has an excellent reputation for service and hospitality, and we tied *Flipper* to one of their piers. At that early hour, the marina was closed; we'd check with the dockmaster later.

Although it was only a little after seven, the traffic was already heavy on Highway 17, but a paved shoulder enabled us to ride to the bridge. Just before the bridge, the shoulder ended, and we dismounted. Joan saw a sign.

"Ken, that sign says pedestrians aren't allowed on the bridge! What are we going to do? I'm not going to ride over the bridge!"

A curb, about thirty inches wide, was on each side of the bridge. Although not a sidewalk, it could serve as one.

"Let's walk our bikes over," I said. "If a cop stops us, we'll just ride the rest of the way."

Joan was game, so we began pushing the bikes on the curb. Many vehicles, including large trucks, exceeded the speed limit as they went over the bridge. The noise was deafening. We plodded bravely along, up and up, until we reached the top. Although the bridge is sixty feet high over the water at its center, it has metal spans that swing open to allow the passage of big ships. As the cars and trucks roared over these spans, the noise became a scream. We looked through the metal ribbing at the water far below. The effect was unsettling. I realized why the authorities didn't want pedestrians on this bridge: anyone walking over could be driven insane before reaching the other side.

A state policeman flew past in his car. Either he hadn't seen us or hadn't cared. Soon another trooper passed by and also ignored us. Maybe they knew they would cause a three-hundred-car pileup if they stopped on the bridge, and they were waiting off the bridge for us.

A pleasant thought to have as we walked down the other half.

The bridge is slightly over a half mile long, but the distance seemed more like ten miles by the time we finally reached the other side. The journey had been most unpleasant and disquieting.

I looked at Joan and said, "One down, three to go."

She smiled weakly.

No roadblock had been set up to facilitate our capture. Not one police officer was waiting to arrest us. We quickly got off the highway.

On our way to the Visitor Center at the Yorktown Battlefield, we rode through the streets of Yorktown. The early morning sunlight, unobstructed by any clouds, was striking the fronts of the historic houses on Main Street. The effect dramatically emphasized their elegance.

We stopped at the Victory Monument. Its white marble was ablaze with the warm sunlight, and the column's long shadow added depth to the scene. Signs attached to a fence around the monument warned of instability. Lightning had struck the monument that spring and had weakened the statue. Looking up at Victory, I saw that she was missing a hand.

We were the first visitors to the park headquarters that morning. While the light was beautiful, and the redoubts were empty of tourists, we walked around the gun emplacements and wondered about the conditions faced by the British gunners that fateful last day of the siege in 1781.

Although this was the final defense line of the British, the earthworks we were looking at dated from the Civil War. Little remains of the original earthworks constructed by either the British or American forces.

Inside the headquarters building, we picked up a self-guiding battlefield map and a map of Yorktown. The park features two tours for the battlefield area: the battlefield

Victory Monument, Yorktown

tour and the encampment tour. We planned to do both and began with the battlefield tour.

As most American schoolchildren learn, the Battle of Yorktown was the decisive battle of the Revolutionary War. After a siege by American and French forces under the command of General George Washington, the British forces under General Charles Lord Cornwallis lay down their arms in surrender.

The Park Service has reconstructed the fortifications used by both sides, and at numerous stops along the road, we read the descriptive plaques explaining what had happened at that site. At Surrender Field, the Park Service has constructed a building overlooking the field where the British and German troops laid down their arms. A tape recording in the building vividly re-creates the sounds of the troops.

As we did the encampment tour, I was struck at the beauty of the peaceful meadows. Full of aromatic wild-flowers, they are surrounded by majestic trees. The still-ness was broken only by the sounds of the many birds flying overhead. We were on hallowed ground.

The road winds through the countryside and lead us to the sites where the French and Americans had had their rear areas. Virtually nothing remains to indicate that thousands of troops camped in the area over two hundred years ago. At the French Artillery Park, however, weathered remains of the original fortifications are still visible.

When we returned to the Park Headquarters, we agreed the sixteen miles of roads that comprise the two tours had given us the best bike ride we had had that summer. After a quick break to eat the lunch we had brought, we rode away to tour Yorktown.

Overlooking the York River, Yorktown was an impor-tant seaport in colonial times. Two of the town's most prominent merchants during this period were "Scotch

Tom" Nelson and his son, William. Together, they owned many of the ships that called at the port, and they traded tobacco and other goods for products from Europe.

William's son, Thomas Nelson Jr., grew up amid this wealth and influence and became Governor of Virginia and a signer of the Declaration of Independence. During the siege of Yorktown, he was the commander of the Virginia militia. In one engagement, according to legend, he believed British troops were inside his residence, and he directed his troops to fire their cannons at his house.

We visited this house, the most impressive of those on Main Street. Now owned by the National Park Service, it is open to the public. The places where cannonballs had struck the brick walls were clearly visible. One former owner had even cemented a cannonball into one of the holes so no one would forget Nelson's sacrifice.

Not far from the Nelson house is Grace Church, where the patriot's body is interred. The inscription on

Thomas Nelson Jr. house, Yorktown

his tombstone reads, in part, that he "gave all for liberty." Indeed he did; the Revolutionary War cost him not only his wealth, but also his health.

Before we ventured across the Highway 17 bridge, I suggested we get some liquid courage at the pub on York-town's beachfront. Joan immediately agreed, and we each bought an ice-cold draft beer.

Unfortunately, the beer didn't make the bridge crossing any easier than it had been that morning.

At the center of the bridge, neither of us was cheered when someone, speeding past us in a pickup truck, yelled out, "Hey, you're breaking the law!"

But we did cross to the other side, and our crime remained undetected by the police.

The dockmaster was busy when we returned to the marina. A man on a boat near where we had left *Flipper* told us she was in no one's way, and we decided to wait until the next day to check with the dockmaster. We left the bicycles locked to a fence post and went to *Delphina*.

Despite arising even earlier the next morning and getting to the bridge before seven, we still found the traffic heavy. This time, however, we saw no state troopers. We got to the other side and gave each other the thumbs-up. Three down, one to go.

Our goal for the day was Williamsburg, thirteen miles from Yorktown by way of the Colonial Parkway. Williamsburg is best known for Colonial Williamsburg, the re-created colonial capital that has numerous exhibits of life in the colonial era. But it is also the home of William and Mary College, the second oldest college in America, chartered in 1693. We wanted to visit this campus and also ride around the part of town that is not part of Colonial Williamsburg.

The Colonial Parkway is a scenic road that follows the York River and offers many views of the river as it winds through marshes, meadows, and forests. Designated as a route for bicycles and noncommercial vehicles, the roadway is comprised of three lanes; the one in the center is used for passing only. The parkway has no paved shoulder, but the center lane allows ample room for cars to pass bike riders. The only problem with the road, from our point of view, is the surface: the pavement, made up of little stones embedded in cement, added greatly to the friction on our tires. The added friction increased the effort required to pedal and significantly slowed our speed when we coasted downhill.

Colonial Williamsburg has a large Visitor Center outside the Historic Area. The building is surrounded by enormous parking lots where the visitors leave their vehicles. After visiting the Center, purchasing tickets, and watching a film, the visitors are carried to the Historic Area by shuttle buses.

After entering the Center, we saw controlled chaos. The place was packed with eager people waiting to see history come alive. Management has everything well under control, however, and the layout of the building is a study in efficiency.

We learned it was going to cost us a minimum of $21.00 each to see the sights. The ticket-information brochure Joan picked up was headed:

How to Visit

Colonial Williamsburg

─────────────

Each Individual Needs A

General Admission Ticket

Explained in the contents was everything visitors needed to know about the cost of their visit to Colonial

Williamsburg.

We weren't sure that we'd have time to see everything we would be paying for and still be able to see other sights in Williamsburg, so we decided to forego Colonial Williamsburg. We rode our bikes into town.

Before long, we found ourselves on Duke of Gloucester Street, the main street of Colonial Williamsburg. Where were the barriers to keep out the people who hadn't bought admission tickets? There were none! Instead, a small sign informed us that motorized vehicles were not allowed, and that, to enjoy fully our visit to Colonial Williamsburg, we could buy a ticket at several locations.

This sign was the only indication we had that there is no charge to wander around the streets of Colonial Williamsburg and look at the buildings. What the basic admission ticket provides is admission, for the date on the ticket, to the *exhibits* in the Historic Area. We didn't want to see any exhibits, so we just rode our bikes through the complex and saw the Governor's Palace, the Capitol, houses, shops, restaurants, horses and carriages, oxen and carts, and numerous people wearing colonial attire. And it cost us nothing.

Near the Historic Area is the Wren Building of William and Mary College. Designed by Christopher Wren, the famous English architect, the building is the centerpiece of the lovely campus. Classes are still held in the building, and a student, on duty to greet visitors, told us some of the rooms are open to the public.

We looked into one of the original classrooms, perhaps the same one used by three presidents of the United States—Jefferson, Monroe, and Tyler—when they attended classes at the College. We also visited the original refectory and chapel, both located in this building. Throughout the building are portraits of people who figure prominently in the history of the College.

John Blair house, Colonial Williamsburg

Outside, the campus was swarming with students, purposefully going from place to place. They had books underarm and serious demeanors on their faces. Most of the students were alone, but we saw some walking in pairs and others in small clusters having lively conversations. Some, mimicking Manhattan messengers, were zipping around on bicycles. The atmosphere reminded me of how great college life is and how it ends too quickly.

We had lunch at the College Deli. Joan liked the way the deli had named many of their sandwich offerings after individual States. Since the deli was across the street from the campus, students could readily go there and ease their homesickness with a sandwich. What I particularly appreciated about the place was its large cooler full of beer at the beginning of the order line. Sipping on an ice-cold beer, while waiting to give our order and get our sandwiches, made the wait seem shorter.

Wren Building, William and Mary College

Riding our bikes through various neighborhoods, we noticed that the town residents have parking stickers on their cars. Considering the thousands of cars bringing tourists to the town, we weren't surprised. Also, we noted, these residents take recycling seriously: colorful bins with separated trash were placed in front of each house.

The trip back on the Colonial Parkway seemed twice as long as the ride we had had in the morning. The rough pavement tired us physically, and the little markers on the side of the road that mark each kilometer took a mental toll.

After three trips across the Highway 17 bridge, we should have been hardened veterans, but we weren't. The fourth trip was as terrifying as the first trip.

It's a shame that road engineers don't consider the rights and needs of pedestrians and bicyclists when they design their projects. Could it be that the state troopers didn't arrest us for walking across the bridge because they know the bureaucrats' oversight is more criminal than our refusal to obey the law?

Surviving the bridge ordeal put us in high spirits. We went to the dockmaster's office at the marina, and I asked the woman working there how much we owed for tying our dinghy to their pier for two days.

"Why, you don't owe us anything!" she said, somewhat surprised at my question.

I went to a pay phone to call the Lowreys and let them know we would be at Salt Ponds, an anchorage down the block from their house, that Friday afternoon. Two weeks earlier we had sent them a postcard informing them of our approximate arrival date at Hampton.

Freed answered the phone.

"Ken! Where are you?"

"Freed, I was wondering that myself!"

There was a little chuckle at the other end of the line.

"We're anchored at Sarah Creek, just off the York River," I told him. "You know where it is?"

He told me he did. Then we discussed plans for meeting. He had made arrangements for us to use his neighbor's pier. We would meet there at five o'clock on Friday.

Joan and I returned to *Delphina*. After listening to the weather forecast and hearing that our perfect weather was turning to rain by Thursday afternoon, we decided to leave early the next morning and anchor that night at Salt Ponds. I hoped we would get there before the rain came. We spent the evening relaxing on deck and enjoying the idyllic weather while we had it.

CHAPTER TWENTY-FIVE

Salt Ponds

The clouds that had rolled in overnight gave the dawn a gloomy look. Rain was on the way. The ten-knot breeze cheered me, however, and as soon as we cleared the entrance light to Sarah Creek, we put up the sails and began sailing down the York River.

Oyster season had begun, and we watched Virginia watermen using patent tongs to get the oysters. The workboats we saw had a patent tong on each side. As each tong bit into the muck for a load of oysters, the boat tipped over precariously and looked as if it would capsize. But each time, the boat bounced back. The crews on the workboats were so absorbed in their work that they never looked up as we sailed past them.

The sail down the Bay to Salt Ponds was leisurely and easy. *Delphina*'s motion was gentle as she heeled to the easterly breeze. Navigation was a simple matter of following numbered, yellow buoys until we came to the entrance light for the channel leading to Salt Ponds.

Salt Ponds was an appropriate place for us to choose as our final anchorage before leaving the Bay. We'd be close to the Lowrey home, and we had read in an issue of *Chesapeake Bay Magazine* that development of the area had caused some controversy. I hoped I would have a

Patent tongers, Virginia

chance to talk to someone about this controversy before we left the Bay, since we had seen conflicts between development and conservation in other areas of the Bay during our travels that summer. Also, spending a few days at Salt Ponds would give us an opportunity to reflect on our journey.

The channel leading to the entrance of Salt Ponds was no problem for us, but the entrance itself was tight. Immediately after entering, we had to make a sharp turn to port before the channel straightened out. Then we motored slowly toward civilization.

Lining both sides of a marsh that lay before us were piers in various stages of completion. Beyond these piers were yet more piers, but boats were tied to some of them. To our right were expensive homes in a major subdivision. On our left were condominium buildings and a marina with a fuel dock. The effect was one of overwhelming encroachment on a defenseless bastion of nature.

The older guidebooks we had read indicated the area was a secure anchorage. But because of all the piers that had been constructed since those books had been written, the room for boats to anchor was severely limited.

After placing both anchors, I looked around to ensure we wouldn't be a hindrance to anyone. *Delphina* was the only boat anchored in Salt Ponds.

From where we had anchored, we could easily see the pier where we would leave *Flipper* the next evening and meet Freed. It wasn't raining yet, so we loaded our bikes onto *Flipper* and went to the fuel dock, on the other side of the marsh. The Salt Ponds Marina looked new, well built, and expensive. We tied up *Flipper* and went to find the dockmaster. He wasn't in his office, but he soon came up in a golf cart.

"Hi, there! What can I do for you folks?"

I asked him if we could leave our dinghy inside the

Salt Ponds, Virginia

fuel dock.

"Oh, sure you can! But I'm afraid the restrooms are out of order today. We're having a problem with a water pipe. It should be fixed by tomorrow, though. Say, is that your schooner anchored over there? Sure, it must be! She's beautiful!"

There was something about this man that we both liked immediately.

"She's a pinky, built of steel. Her name's *Delphina*," Joan told him.

"That's interesting," he said. "I'm looking at possibly buying a steel boat myself."

We talked about the advantages and disadvantages of steel boats. Then I asked him the question that was uppermost in my mind.

"Why are there so many empty slips here?"

"We don't have utilities to all the slips yet, but there's not much doubt the slips are needed," he answered. "The pressure to get more boating facilities in this area is tremendous, to say nothing of how much people want homes on the water. The developers are just responding to the demand. It's no different here from other places on the Bay."

"How do you personally feel about the development?" I asked him.

"Well, I'll tell you. I was born and raised in Hampton. I used to play in this area all the time when I was a kid. Back then, there wasn't a house here, nothing but the water, the marsh, and the forest. So I know what it was like. I won't say that I'm overjoyed with all of the building, but then, I'm a realist. Growth is going to happen, whether we accept it or not. What we have to ensure is that the growth is responsible—that we take the environmental impact into account. Here, for instance, the developer held a series of public meetings to see what the locals thought about the way the developer was planning to build up the area. The input from the public went into the final plans. Also, none of the marsh grass was removed or replaced by all the construction. I feel the developer did the best job he could. Some other developer could have easily messed up the Salt Ponds."

Although I was disappointed to see all the development around me, I felt good about meeting this person who so well articulated his perspective on what he saw happening around him. His approach was balanced, and he tried to weigh evenly both sides of the development issue. I was happy to know that he realized there are two sides; some people overlook that simple fact to everyone's detriment. But the issues that surface in decisions regarding growth are far too complex for amateurs to resolve in a dockmaster's office.

I reflected on my feelings about the condominium building on Deal Island. Had I been selfishly one-sided in my criticism of it? What motives were behind the building of that condominium? Was Deal Island really violated, or did the building represent a new economic opportunity for the island's residents who have been adversely affected by recent trends in the Bay's seafood harvests? I knew, for the time being, I would leave the questions unanswered and be thankful I had seen so much of Chesapeake country that hadn't been developed.

The skies were becoming more threatening. Nonetheless, we got on our bikes and went in search of a supermarket. We wanted to get some choice steaks to grill at the Lowreys' the next evening. Just thinking of beef, after eating chicken, crabs, and tuna fish all summer, made me ravenous.

On our way back to the marina, after getting the steaks, we were thoroughly soaked by heavy rain, but the rain was warm. After locking our bikes at the marina, we went to *Delphina*.

Just as the weekend of my family reunion had flown

by in a whirl, so too did that weekend with the Lowreys.

We met Freed on Friday as scheduled. He was surprised to hear that we had arrived on Thursday.

"Why didn't you come over then?" he asked.

"We didn't want to interfere with your family's routine during the school week," I told him.

He frowned at my answer.

Suzi had caught a cold, but that didn't dampen her spirit. The steak we had bought was plenty for everyone, including the boys. The steak, garden macaroni salad, and a cheesecake that Joan had made on the boat made a wonderful reunion dinner.

On Saturday morning, we were treated to watching the youngest Lowrey boy, Colin, terrorize his opponents on the soccer field. Suzi and Freed were more exhausted after the game than Colin was; even I was a little hoarse after all the yelling I had done.

The afternoon was filled with a visit to The Mariners' Museum in Newport News. Of the museums we visited in the Bay area, this one has the most comprehensive exhibit of life on and around Chesapeake Bay and covers every aspect from heavy industry to recreation. The walls, covered with magnificent black-and-white photographs enlarged to more than life-size, create a stunning effect. We found it rewarding to reflect on our journey as the various photographs and exhibits brought back memories of the places we had visited and the people we had met.

After a supper of grilled hamburgers at the Lowreys', we sat on the patio and talked about our trip. Too soon, it was time for us to leave, and our farewell was harder than the one in July. In the morning we were leaving Chesapeake Bay.

The air was much colder the next day. The north wind was brisk; the skies were clear. Autumn was coming to the Bay and would bring with it the seasonal changes that attract so many more thousands of visitors. We would miss those changes and miss them deeply.

After I raised the anchors, Joan steered *Delphina* to the fuel dock. For the first two hundred miles of our voyage home, we would be on the Intracoastal Waterway, and we wanted *Delphina*'s fuel tank full when we began our trip. And we had to get our bikes, which we had left on shore.

The dockmaster greeted us at the dock and helped with the lines. I was glad to see him there on that Sunday morning; he would be the last person we talked to on our Chesapeake Bay journey, and he is representative of the warm, friendly people we had been blessed with meeting throughout our cruise.

"Now you come back and see us next time you're up this way! And have a great trip!" he shouted as we slipped away.

As we sailed past Old Point Comfort and headed for Norfolk Harbor Reach, I felt the sadness of leaving giving way to the excitement of the voyage ahead of us. Once we got past the heavy traffic of the Norfolk-Portsmouth harbor area and the numerous drawbridges for the next ten miles, we would have smooth sailing all the way home. Or so I thought. But that's another story.

Chesapeake Bay lighthouses. Clockwise, from top left:
Concord Point, Thomas Point, Point No Point, Wolf Trap

APPENDIX

When we visited the National Aquarium in Baltimore, we viewed a video presentation of what can be done to clean up the Bay. As we left the presentation, we picked up a brochure entitled "10 Ways You Can Clean Up The Chesapeake Bay." It is reprinted here in its entirety.

Working closely with state and federal officials, Anheuser-Busch and its wholesalers in Maryland, Virginia and Pennsylvania recently launched a comprehensive public education campaign to protect and preserve the Chesapeake Bay.

The campaign includes television and radio commercials reminding Chesapeake Bay residents of the importance of protecting this priceless natural resource. At the same time, company wholesalers sponsored special educational material listing these 10 ways to help restore the Bay. This program has been recognized as a positive example of industry and government joining together to address a major environmental need.

1. GET INVOLVED

   Since each of us pollutes the Chesapeake, each of us can help save it. Our individual contributions may seem small, but joined with 13 million other citizens in the watershed, they can help make a difference.

2. SAVE WATER

   Saving water helps the Bay by reducing the volume of water going through sewage treatment plants. It also saves you money. In one day, a dripping faucet wastes 20 gallons of water and a leaking toilet 200 gallons. If your water meter dial moves when no water is running, you have a leak. Use water sparingly while brushing your teeth, washing dishes, or shaving. Install a water conservation shower head and take short showers instead of baths.

3. DISPOSE OF HOUSEHOLD PRODUCTS CAREFULLY
Many household products like paints, preservatives, brush cleaners and solvents can harm the Bay. So never pour them down the drain since sewers and septic tanks do not treat these materials. Buy the product with the least amount of toxic material. Used turpentine and brush cleaners can be filtered and reused. Stuff paint cans and other chemical containers with newspaper before discarding.

4. CARE FOR YOUR LAWN CAUTIOUSLY
Lawns with trees and shrubs prevent erosion, soak up nutrients before they run off into streams, and improve soil quality by adding organic material. Plant the right grass by testing soil annually. Use the proper fertilizer and do not over-fertilize. Water your yard only when it's dry by soaking the soil to a depth of four to six inches.

5. CONTROL PESTS SENSIBLY
A better way to eliminate harmful garden bugs is to encourage helpful bugs and animals. Firewood attracts termites. So make sure it's stored away from your home. Remove water from old tires to prevent mosquitos from breeding. Follow pesticide directions carefully and buy only what you need. Do not apply pesticides near water and do not apply if rain is forecast.

6. CONTROL RUN-OFF FROM YOUR YARD
Most of the rain that falls in Maryland, Virginia and Pennsylvania finds its way into the Bay. Rainwater can carry the fertilizer and toxic chemicals you use on your yard into the Bay. By keeping rainwater in your yard, you improve water quality, reduce erosion, replenish the groundwater supply, and reduce the need for fertilizers. Trees, shrubs and ground cover should be planted as a buffer around your yard and in bare areas to soak up nutrients and to reduce run-off.

7. CONTROL SOIL EROSION

When rain falls on hard surfaces such as walkways, patios and driveways, it can enter storm drains and find its way into the Bay. This water can't nourish the soil, and it deposits sediments and nutrients which overload the Bay. Slow down run-off by reducing the amount of hard surfaces around your home. Wood decks with space between the boards allow water to drain into the ground. Brick or interlocking stone walkways also permit water to seep into the soil. Diverting rain from paved surfaces and roofs onto grass reduces run-off into storm drains.

8. MAINTAIN YOUR SEPTIC SYSTEM

If a septic system fails, its untreated waste can seep into rivers, groundwater, and into the Bay. Your system is not working properly if drains and toilets drain slowly or if effluent seeps upward from the ground. Never use your toilet as a garbage can. Use your garbage disposal sparingly to reduce grease and solids in your septic system. Know the locations of your septic system, and keep heavy equipment off the drainage area.

9. USE CAR CARE PRODUCTS WISELY

Wash your car on grass so that water and detergent is filtered through the grass before entering the Bay. Motor oil, anti-freeze and battery acid harm the Bay if they flow into storm drains or off paved surfaces into a waterway. Contain these fluids when you change them. To dispose of these materials, contact your local service station or call:

VA 1-800-552-3831   PA 1-800-346-4242
DC 1-202-724-2100   MD 1-800-492-9188

10. CONTAIN CHEMICAL SPILLS

If pesticides, oil, gasoline, or similar products leak or spill onto the garage floor, driveway, or other hard surface, do not wash down the area. This will cause further contamination and may carry the material to storm drains or other water sources. Surround the contaminated area with dirt or sprinkle sawdust, kitty litter, or other absorbent material over the spills. Put the material into a strong plastic bag, and put the bag in the trash.

If you would like to know what more you can do to help clean up the Bay, please write to:

Governor's Chesapeake Bay Communications Office
c/o The State House
Annapolis, Maryland 21401
(301) 974-5300

BIBLIOGRAPHY

Chesapeake Bay Magazine, *Guide to Cruising the Chesapeake Bay* (Annapolis, Maryland: Chesapeake Bay Communications, Inc., 1989)

Laskin, David, *Eastern Islands: Accessible Islands of the East Coast* (New York, New York: Facts on File, Inc., 1990)

Niemeyer, Lucien – Photographs; Meyer, Eugene L. – Text, *Chesapeake Country* (New York, New York: Abbeville Press, 1990)

Stone, William T.; Blanchard, Fessenden S.; and Hays, Anne M., *A Cruising Guide to the Chesapeake* (New York, New York: G.P. Putnam's Sons, 1989)

Warner, William W., *Beautiful Swimmers: Watermen, Crabs, and the Chesapeake Bay* (New York, New York: Viking Penguin Inc., 1987)

Waterway Guide: Mid-Atlantic Edition (Atlanta, Georgia: Communication Channels, Inc., 1989)

INDEX